Ralph Storer is an experienced and well-respected climber, walker and mountain biker, who lives and works in Edinburgh. He currently lectures in computer studies at Napier Polytechnic and writes frequently for mountaineering and outdoor magazines. This is his third book, following the highly successful *100 Best Routes on Scottish Mountains*.

Also by Ralph Storer:

100 BEST ROUTES ON SCOTTISH MOUNTAINS
SKYE: WALKING, SCRAMBLING AND EXPLORING

EXPLORING SCOTTISH HILL TRACKS

Ralph Storer

WARNER BOOKS

A *Warner* Book

First published in Great Britain by David & Charles in 1991
This edition published by Warner Books in 1993

Copyright © Text & Illustrations by Ralph Storer 1991

The moral right of the author has been asserted.

A CIP catalogue record for this book
is available from the British Library.

ISBN 0 7515 1355 X

Typeset by Leaper & Gard Ltd, Bristol, England
Printed in England by Clays Ltd, St Ives plc

Warner Books
A Division of
Little, Brown and Company (UK) Limited
165 Great Dover Street
London SE1 4YA

To those who love the wild places

Not in vain the distance beckons.
Forward, forward let us range.

from 'Locksley Hall'
by Alfred, Lord Tennyson

CONTENTS

ACKNOWLEDGEMENTS

The considerable research required for a book of this nature would have been impossible without the generous help given to me by many people. In particular I would like to thank Robert Dickson of the Scottish Rights of Way Society and Richard Broadhurst of the Forestry Commission. I hope that the numerous landowners who have helped in the delineation of routes across their property will forgive me if I omit to mention them individually – on the whole I have received nothing but co-operation from them and the Scottish Landowners' Federation and thank them all. Grateful thanks also to all the mountain bike hirers in the Highlands who have unstintingly shared their valuable local knowledge with me.

There are others without whose specific help this book could not have reached fruition. In particular I am indebted to Cathy King once again for photographic processing beyond the call of duty and to Anne Porter for her meticulous map lettering.

Finally, and perhaps most importantly of all, I shall be forever grateful to Wendy and Simon, without whose company and support the long, painstaking and often frustrating process of research would have been less bearable.

INTRODUCTION

Travelling by road, in the words of a character in a Neil Munro novel, has only one advantage: 'that tame pleasure, comfort.' Travelling off-road under your own steam offers far greater pleasures: the sense of well-being that comes from physical exertion and fitness, the satisfying feeling of adventure that comes from exploring around the next corner or over the next horizon, and a physical closeness to the land and the elements that can become a spiritual experience. It is also more fun.

As the growth of roads has accelerated during the twentieth century so has the desire among increasing numbers of people to leave the tarmac behind and explore the wild places where the motor car cannot reach, and nowhere in Britain gives as much scope for such explorations as the Highlands of Scotland. The mountains of the Highlands are well known and well documented in numerous guidebooks, but the wealth of hill tracks and other cross-country routes that await the off-road explorer are less well known.

In England and Wales it has been necessary to manufacture a host of official long-distance footpaths in recent years in order to satisfy the growing demand for access to the countryside, but in Scotland there has existed for centuries a complex network of old drove roads, ancient military roads, Pictish roads, coffin roads, whisky roads, stalking paths etc, that covers vast tracts of wild land. Some of these ancient routes are now cart tracks, some are paths, others have disappeared from the map altogether and can be traced only by detective work on the ground (or by aerial reconnaissance). Their exploration offers the most adventurous cross-country walking in Britian, more wild, interesting and exciting than anything south of the border, and this book is for all walkers and mountain bikers who wish to explore this precious heritage.

ROUTE SELECTION
There are so many hill tracks in Scotland that in a single volume it would be impossible to describe them all in more than cursory detail. Route

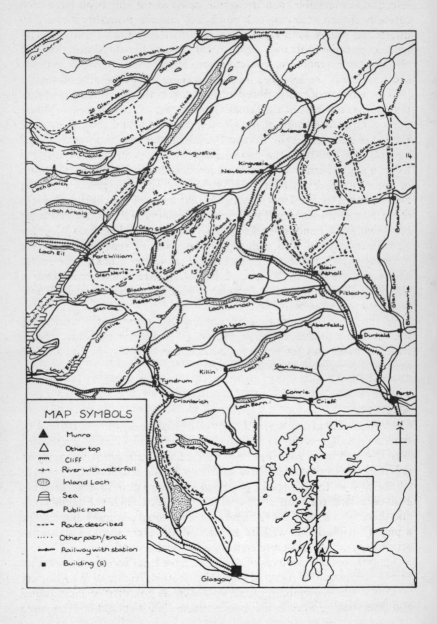

MAP SYMBOLS

▲ Munro
△ Other top
᠅ Cliff
⊬ River with waterfall
⬭ Inland Loch
⬚ Sea
〜 Public road
--- Route described
⋯ Other path/track
⊪⊪ Railway with station
■ Building (s)

selection is inevitable, and the routes selected for this book have been carefully chosen according to a number of criteria. Primarily they are all interesting routes, both scenically and historically. Each forms a worth-while expedition in its own right, usually one or two days' duration, but also links to neighbouring routes to form longer expeditions. In addition, shorter circuits are described for those seeking less demanding outings.

The network of routes thus described covers that great tract of mountainous country east of the Great Glen known as the Grampian Mountains, and includes most of the Central Highlands and the Cairngorms. From Loch Linnhe in the west to Deeside in the east, a distance of well over 60 miles (100km), this mountainous rib across the heart of Scotland forms a major barrier to communication between the north and the south of the country. Even today it is crossed by only one road (the A9 at Drumochter Pass) and it is no accident that many of the classic hill tracks of the Highlands are to be found here. Off-shoots to the north-west coast (via Glen Affric) and to the Lowlands (via the West Highland Way) are also described, but it is with regret that lack of space precludes the inclusion of other fine routes around the periphery, such as the routes across the Mounth in Angus and across the Great Wilderness east of Ullapool. These must await a second volume – apologies to those whose favourite route has been omitted.

In the route descriptions a track refers to a route that is sufficiently wide and well constructed to be used by a Land-Rover or a cart, while a path is suitable only for walkers and sometimes bicycles; the line between the two is sometimes blurred.

ACCESS

Unlike in England and Wales the law of trespass has not been defined by statute or by the courts in Scotland, and trespassers can be prosecuted only if it can be proven that they have caused damage or nuisance. In practice, such proof is difficult to obtain in the wild country through which most of the hill tracks described in this book pass, and there has evolved a long tradition of co-operation between Highland landowners and those who wish to use the land for recreational purposes. It would be a pity if inconsiderate walkers and mountain bikers were to abuse this privilege of access and cause an increase in access restrictions.

On private land members of the public have legal access only to routes legally recognised as rights of way. The Scottish Rights of Way Society (1 Lutton Place, Edinburgh EH8 9PD) acts as guardian of these routes and does sterling work in maintaining them, but it should be recognised that many rights of way are still disputed. The current legal position in Scotland relating to the use of pedal cycles on rights of way is confusing. According to the Roads (Scotland) Act (1984), it is an offence to cycle on a footpath without permission, but a 1930 legal ruling specifically states that a bicycle can be used on any pedestrian right of way because it 'merely facilitates the use of the individual's own muscle'. In open country, in practice, responsible cycling has traditionally been viewed with tolerance, but cyclists have a duty to those who follow it not to abuse this privilege (see Advice to Mountain Bikers, below). In the words of the Lord Advocate, 'consideration and common sense, mutual tolerance and good will can often be as effective in avoiding conflicts as the might and majesty of the law'.

Where a route is not a right of way, access may be permitted on tolerance of the landowner. Because of the law of trespass and the wild nature of much Highland terrain, most landowners accept responsible recreational usage of their land, but continued co-operation is vital. All routes described in this book are either rights of way or have been selected in consultation with the Scottish Rights of Way Society, the Forestry Commission and the Scottish Landowners' Federation and its members. For the sake of those who come after you, please follow the advice given in the text.

Finally, please heed any seasonal restrictions given in the text. Whatever one's view on deer stalking and grouse shooting, they are major sources of revenue to Highland estates and any interference in their pursuit is likely to lead to an increase in access restrictions. Consequently, walkers and mountain bikers are advised in general to avoid the hills and hill tracks, especially those that cross high moorland, during the most critical period from mid-August to mid-October; the West Highland Way (Route 1) is an exception. If in doubt contact the appropriate estate; addresses will be found in 'Heading for the Scottish Hills', compiled by the Mountaineering Council of Scotland and the Scottish Landowners' Federation, and published by the Scottish Mountaineering Trust.

Access during the lambing season, from about mid-April to the end of May, is also a concern for landowners; dogs should not be taken on the hills at this time, and should be kept under control at all other times. The Forestry Commission, whose land many of the tracks in this book cross, has an increasingly open access policy, but restrictions here may also be necessary during harvesting operations.

It should also be noted that under Scottish law it is an offence to camp or to light fires on private property without permission, but in practice camping in wild country is widely tolerated; it is again a question of common sense and co-operation.

ADVICE TO WALKERS

Many of the hill tracks in this book cross high, remote and inhospitable terrain, which even in the height of summer should be treated with as much respect as Scottish mountains. As this book is a guidebook rather than an instruction manual for hillwalkers, it is assumed that all parties attempting these routes will be kitted out with adequate clothing, good footwear, provisions, map, compass, torch and emergency equipment (first aid kit, whistle, survival bag and spare food), and be at all times prepared for inclement weather by carrying warm, windproof and water-proof clothing (including gloves and balaclava). Some of the routes require more than a day to complete them, in which case camping or bivouac gear will also be necessary. A booklet entitled *Safety on Mountains* is published by the British Mountaineering Council, Crawford House, Precinct Centre, Booth Street East, Manchester M13 9RZ.

Under snow hill tracks become much more serious propositions. Paths are obliterated, grassy hillsides become treacherous slopes, walking becomes more difficult and tiring, terrain becomes featureless, and white-outs and spindrift reduce visibility to zero. Winter conditions vary from British to Alpine to Arctic from November through to April, although sometimes occurring earlier and later and varying from locality to locality – it is possible to encounter hard snow and ice even in October and May. No one should venture into the Scottish mountains in winter without adequate clothing, an ice-axed and experience (or the company of an experienced person). In hard winter conditions crampons may also be required on some routes, while other routes may be avalanche prone. The increasing number of accidents, many of them fatal, which have occurred in Scotland over the last few winters should leave no one in doubt as to the need for caution. Many of the major Scottish hill tracks have an Alpine, sometimes Arctic, ambience in winter, and exploring them on foot or on skis can be immensely rewarding, but if you are in doubt stay off the hill.

At all times follow the Country Code (as approved by the Countryside Commission for Scotland).

The Country Code
1 Enjoy the countryside and respect its life and work.
2 Guard against all risks of fire.
3 Fasten all gates.
4 Keep your dogs under close control.
5 Keep to paths across cultivated farmland.
6 Use gates and stiles to cross fences, hedges and walls.

7 Leave livestock, crops and machinery alone.
8 Take your litter home.
9 Help to keep all water clean.
10 Protect wildlife, plants and trees.
11 Take special care on country roads.
12 Make no unnecessary noise.

Mountain weather forecasts:
  Western Highlands: 0898-500-441 and 0898-654-669
  Eastern Highlands: 0898-500-442 and 0898-654-668

THE MOUNTAIN BIKE

Is dona 'mharcadh nach fhearr na sior-choiseachd.
It's a bad mount that's not better than constant walking.

(Old Gaelic Proverb)

Over the past few years there has been a renaissance in the exploration of Scottish hill tracks owing to the advent of the mountain bike, a much sturdier machine than its on-road cousin and one whose construction and frame geometry enable it to go boldly where no bike has gone before. The term mountain bike (also all-terrain bike or ATB) is in practice a misnomer, for there are few types of terrain on which any bicycle can be ridden off-road, especially uphill, and on most hill tracks a mountain bike has to be pushed or carried for varying distances.

Nevertheless, the mountain bike has revolutionised access to remote Scottish mountains that otherwise require long walks-in along seemingly endless Land-Rover tracks, and it has helped to promote a rediscovery of the ancient routes across the mountains. It is fitting that this should be the case, for it was in Scotland in 1840 that the world's first pedal-driven bicycle was invented by Kirkpatrick Macmillan, and tracks such as the Lairig Ghru (Route 9) have a long cycling tradition.

Mountain biking is an exhausting but exhilarating activity that at its best combines the pleasures of the hill with the thrills and joys of a roller-coaster ride. Walkers who have not yet had the opportunity to try it out or to object to it on ethical grounds would do well to hire a bike for the day from one of the increasing number of hirers dotted around the Highlands; there are few who will not succumb to its delights. Many of the hill tracks of the Highlands are ideally suited to mountain biking, but prospective bikers would do well to heed the following advice.

Advice to Mountain Bikers

This guidebook is not the place to discuss technical data or riding techniques: if you are contemplating purchasing a mountain bike, get expert advice from a reputable dealer and invest in a manual that tells you how to ride it and look after it. If possible, hire one first; get to know your requirements.

In terms of fitness, equipment and clothing, mountain biking the hill tracks of Scotland should be considered an extension of hillwalking, and all the above advice to walkers applies equally to mountain bikers. The Scottish Highlands is no place for high-street cycling fashions that trade function for style, and neither is it the place for kamikaze riding techniques of the kind seen in mountain-biking competitions. It would be foolhardy not to treat Highland weather and terrain with respect; in general, mountain biking requires more fitness, alertness and technique than walking.

Short-sleeved tops and shorts are suitable only on the warmest days, and even then there can be an appreciable wind chill once you are out of the glens. On cloudless days sunburn at altitude can also be a problem, especially when there is snow on the ground. Consequently, long-sleeved tops and trousers are usually more suitable, especially as they would otherwise have to be carried. On-road cycling footwear is inadequate as the soles are unsuitable and potentially dangerous for the inevitable walking sections. Specialist mountain-biking boots are increasingly available at exorbitant prices, but they are rarely waterproof; having come close to frost-bite myself on a couple of occasions in late autumn, I now use lightweight walking boots with Goretex inners when I am on major routes. On low-level routes after rain wellingtons may sometimes be the best footwear. Gaiters or stop tous can also be useful for keeping mud, stones, heather and other parts of the landscape out of boots while you are walking.

Among clothing accessories, padded gloves will greatly reduce jarring on rough descents and if you wear glasses a sun visor will help to keep the rain off them. The wearing of a helmet is a personal choice, but it may save your life. On major routes it is important to carry foul-weather gear, as for hillwalking: sweater, anorak, overtrousers, mitts, balaclava, plus normal safety equipment such as compassi, bivi blanket, etc. Make sure that mitts fit over cycling gloves if you use them and that an anorak hood fits over a helmet if you wear one. If you use ordinary overtrousers remember to wear cycle clips to keep them away from the chain.

Useful cycle accessories include a rear rack, panniers that double as rucksacks, bar bags and saddle-bags (for storing odd items), toe-clips (on at least one pedal, for security under pressure), a shoulder holder (for carrying the bike), mudguards and flaps (essential after rain), a water-bottle holder, crossbar pads, a chain-wheel protector and a bell. Do not forget to carry a pump, a spare inner tube (the hill is no place to mend a puncture) and other spare parts, especially nuts and bolts, which can shake loose with alarming regularity. With some truth it is said that every mountain biker has a screw loose somewhere. Anyone who carries a camera on their bike is asking for it to be damaged; always carry it on your person. On one painful occasion even my seat bolt broke in two, an incident after which my bike, for reasons we need not go into, was nick-named The Nutcracker.

The following tips may also prove useful. Beware of fashionable accessories such as revolver wheel discs, unless you wish to become airborne in high winds. A short length of rope slung around the seat post and attached to a waist loop by a karabiner provides an energy-efficient means of pulling a bike uphill on a good path. When you decide on which direction to cycle a route, make wind direction a major factor. In damp warm weather in summer a speeding cyclist can soon become coated with midges, especially on forest tracks; vegetarians should keep their mouths shut. Fording rivers is easier with a mountain bike, but do not be seduced unheedingly into fast-flowing torrents. Keep the bike upstream of you to break the current and lean it into your body to form a tripod with your legs. Cross slowly, moving only one point of the tripod at a time while maintaining balance with the other two.

Finally, be aware that when on your bike you are an ambassador of a new sport that many landowners and hillwalkers see as an incursion into what until now they have viewed as their own territory. Garishly clad mountain bikers who show no concern for the erosive potential of wheels and speed past pedestrians and animals without warning should be banned from the hill, otherwise their behaviour may lead to a ban on all mountain bikers. In England restrictions on mountain biking in some areas have already had to be enforced, and it would be a pity if this were to spread to Scotland. Those who take their bikes to the hills have a responsibility to those who come after them not to give the sport a tarnished name. A number of cycling clubs are developing guidelines for mountain bikers, but in the absence of a code of conduct that is geared to the Highlands, the following is put forward as a suggestion:

Mountain biker's code of conduct
1   Ride only where you know you have approval or a legal right.

2   Stay on tracks. Don't cut corners. Don't ride beside the track. Don't damage fragile ecosystems.
3   Use tracks carefully. Don't ride muddy tracks. Don't skid or spin wheels. Don't ride in large groups.
4   Give way to others, be they other mountain bikers, walkers, horse riders or whoever. Stop and get out of the way if necessary. Let others overtake you if they are going faster than you.
5   Overtake carefully. Let others know you are there.
6   Ride defensively, not only for your own safety but also to avoid unseen hazards or other track users. Know your limits.

THE CONSERVATION ISSUE

Whenever man is allowed into an environment he leaves his imprint, and in a fragile environment like the Scottish Highlands he can eventually destroy the very things that attract him in the first place. Those who love the wild land of Scotland constantly have to balance a desire to maintain that wildness with the needs of industry, commerce, hydro-electric schemes, forestry operations, skiing developments and other tourist developments, and developers must also become aware that a balance must be struck if the Highlands as we know them are not to be irretrievably destroyed.

Let not walkers and mountain bikers add to to environmental problems. Leave only footprints and tyre tracks, take away only photographs and memories. Erosion on the more well-used tracks is a growing concern, and in places footpath management schemes of the kind prevalent in England and Wales have had to be instigated. In this context, it has to be said that bicycle tyres have greater potential than boots for erosion and disturbance to flora, if only because they remain in constant contact with the ground.

There is a long tradition of cycling on Scottish hill tracks; the Lairig Ghru (Route 9), for instance, has long been a challenge for the adventurous, while Comyn's Road (Route 3) was indeed built for wheeled transport. It would be a shame, therefore, if indiscriminate mountain biking in sensitive areas were to lead to bans on what is otherwise an environmentally friendly mode of exploring the Highlands. Estate owners are becoming increasingly worried about irresponsible cycling and it is imperative that mountain bikers should heed the Country Code and the above advice.

The worst erosion is caused by all-terrain motorised vehicles that are used for stalking and fishing; to see the damage that such vehicles do to fragile peaty land is distressing. Pony trekking also causes much damage, so does skiing on inadequate snow cover as well as mass-participation walking and cycling events. If the erosion problem is not solved there could well come a day when access to the Highlands will be restricted. That day can be postponed only if every person who uses the Highlands for recreational purposes is aware of his or her responsibilities to the land upon which they have the privilege to venture. The future is in your hands (see also Modern Hill Tracks, p30).

LOGISTICS

Most of the hill tracks described in this book evolved from cross-country routes that were developed over centuries as a means of communication between one place and another, and hence few of them return you to your starting point. Suggested off-road return itineraries are given in the text where possible, sometimes via another route in the book, and these can enable attractive multi-day trips to be devised. Suggestions are also given for linking two or more routes into longer expeditions, for those who wish to make the most of the fact that the routes are described from an extensive off-road network.

Those not wishing to return across country to their starting point have an equally interesting logistical problem to solve in planning to meet public or private transport at the end of the route. Nearly all the start and end points of the routes described are served by buses, and many of them by trains. Trains are of especial interest to mountain bikers as buses cannot be guaranteed to carry bicycles (consult bus companies for up-to-date information). At the time of writing, British Rail's policy on the transportation of bicycles is in a state of flux, partly because of the increasing popularity of mountain biking (consult British Rail for up-to-date information). Bus and rail addresses, timetables, etc are listed in *Getting Around the Highlands and Islands*, published annually by Farm Holiday Guides Ltd in association with the Highlands and Islands Development Board (available from Bookshops or Farm Holiday Guides Ltd, Abbey Mill Centre, Seedhill, Paisley PA1 1JN).

The availability of accommodation and provisions is indicated in the text for each route, but outside of the major centres it would be unwise to depend on a single village shop for provisions or a remote bothy for accommodation, especially during the summer months. Some hotels close during the winter and youth hostels also may not be open all year round (verify opening times with the Scottish Youth Hostels Association, 7 Glebe Crescent, Stirling FK8 2JA). The following useful books, *Scot-*

land: Hotels and Guest Houses, Scotland: Self-catering, Scotland: Bed and Breakfast and *Scotland: Camping and Caravan Parks* are available from bookshops or the Scottish Tourist Board, PO Box 705, Edinburgh EH4 3EU.

SKETCH MAPS
Each route description is accompanied by one or more sketch maps that highlight its major features, but to fulfil this function they are necessarily lacking in cartographic detail and are not intended to replace official maps in practice. They are hand-drawn to a scale of 1:100,000, the scale traditionally used by cyclists for road touring, but for off-road travel this is inadequate in practice, and 1:50,000 OS maps are recommended for more precise delineation of tracks. The OS 1:25,000 Outdoor Leisure map of the High Tops of the Cairngorms is recommended for this more complex area.

The route summary map on p2 gives an explanation of detailed sketch map symbols. The classification of mountains as Munros or Tops is based on the 1984 edition of Munro's Tables, incorporating Brown and Donaldson's revisions. Briefly, a Munro is a separate mountain over 914m (3,000ft) and a Top is a subsidiary summit over 914m (3,000ft).

CONTOUR PLANS
In addition to sketch maps, each major route is accompanied by one or more contour plans that act as visual aids to route appreciation and planning. Each plan has a horizontal scale of 1:100,000 (ie, the same scale as sketch maps) marked in miles, and a vertical scale of 2cm per 150m (¾in per 500ft).

MEASUREMENTS
Route distances are specified in both miles (to the nearest half-mile) and kilometres (to the nearest kilometre); short distances in the text are specified in metres (an approximate imperial measurement in yards). Heights are specified in metres and feet. Metric heights have been obtained from OS 2nd Series 1:50,000 maps. Equivalent heights in feet have been obtained by multiplying the height in metres by 3.28 (rounded down); these may not tally with heights on old OS one-inch-to-the-mile maps, which were obtained from an earlier survey. The approximate total amount of ascent for the whole route is specified to the nearest 10m (50ft).

Route times (normally to the nearest half-hour) are based on the time it should take a person of reasonable fitness to complete the route in good summer conditions, excluding halts. They take into account length of route, amount of ascent and type of terrain, but do not make allowances for stoppages and adverse weather. Time taken for halts varies from person to person, and to enable more realistic timings it is left to each individual to add an appropriate allowance to the times given to obtain an overall time. The times are based more or less on the author's experience and are necessarily subjective, but they are roughly standard between routes for comparison purposes and can be adjusted where necessary by a factor appropriate to the individual.

In winter and foul weather routes will normally take much longer, depending on conditions, and some indeed become major expeditions in terms of technical difficulty, route-finding and survival skills (see Advice to Walkers, p5).

HIGHLAND NAMES

A guideline to the pronunciation and meaning of Gaelic names is given where space allows. The production of such guidelines is made difficult by OS misspellings, misunderstanding, misuses and misplacements, and in addition some names have become anglicised to such an extent that it would be pedantic to enforce a purist pronunciation on a non-Gaelic speaker. Despite these problems the phonetic guidelines given in this book should enable a good attempt at a pronunciation that would be intelligible to a Gaelic speaker.

In connection with the guide the following points should be noted:

Y   before a vowel pronounced as in 'you'
OW   pronounced as in 'town'
CH   pronounced as in Scottish 'loch' or German *noch*
TCH   pronounced as 'ch' in 'church'
OE   pronounced as in French *oeuf* or the 'u' in 'turn'

Toponomy (the study of place-name meanings) is complicated by OS misspellings, changes in spelling and word usage over the centuries, words with more than one meaning and unknown origin of names (Gaelic, Norse, Irish, etc). Meanings given in the text are the most commonly accepted, even if disputed; some names are too obscure to be given any meaning.

TRACKS IN TIME

Most visitors to the Highlands of Scotland are attracted by the breath-taking scenery to be found there, and most of those who leave the road-side to climb the mountains or explore the glens and mountain passes do so for recreational reasons – for the views, for the pure mountain air, for the exercise or the challenge, or for the thrill of being in wild places. A network of roads and railways facilitates access, and once the walker is away from these modern lines of communication an even larger network of old hill tracks leads deep into the hills, far from the madding crowd.

The originators of these tracks would no doubt view their modern recreational use with astonishment and irony, for they were not developed to showcase the beauty of the Highland landscape. On the contrary, they came into existence out of economic and social necessity, when they were the sole means of communication between one community and another. Despite their age a surprising number of them still exist, relatively undisturbed by modern developments in communications, and the invitation to explore them is difficult to ignore. Even a passing acquaintance with their origin and history will greatly enhance such explorations, and the following is an introduction to their fascinating story.

EARLY PATHS AND TRACKS

Travel in the Scottish Highlands has never been easy, nor was ease of communication always desirable, for in less civilised times inaccessibility meant safety. The rugged Highlanders of old were quite content to live in isolated communities, eking out a meagre living in remote glens, separated from other communities by untracked mountains. They bore allegiance to local clan chiefs rather than to Scottish or English kings or parliaments and were wary of other clans from beyond the mountains. Anyone encroaching into clan territory was as likely as not to be a raider, and so difficulty of travel across Highland terrain was viewed as a useful security. Inaccessability had the additional benefit of keeping Lowland influence at bay. Highlanders distrusted Lowlanders, with whom they shared neither culture nor language, and any improvement in communication was seen as a threat to the isolated Highland way of life and the clan system.

The earliest paths in the Highlands were local ones, beaten out over the years by people walking from one public place to another, linking such places as farms, mills, churches, schools, wells and peat bogs (for fuel). Walking was much more an accepted part of life than it is today. Even as late as the nineteenth century people would walk up to 10 miles (16km) to church each week, as in the parish of Rogart, Sutherland, and children might have to walk barefoot for 3 or 4 miles (5–7km) to school each day, as in the north of Raasay. Rivers were a hazard on such walks and various means were employed to negotiate them, such as fords, stepping-stones, ferries and bridges; in places like Dollar people became expert at using stilts. In dry weather, on the other hand, river beds sometimes provided the best routes.

Travelling further afield was possible only outside the winter months. Walking 40 miles (65km) in a day was not considered unreasonable for a younger person on good terrain, but no one travelled further than necessary because of the danger of being attacked by thieves. Bands of cattle thieves were perhaps the earliest long-distance travellers, ranging the length and breadth of the country on their raids. Other travellers included pedlars and ministers, who journeyed considerable distances to visit their parishioners.

Horses were used by those who could afford them, especially as beasts of burden. On suitable terrain they might be required to pull sledges, which later developed into two-wheeled tumbrils and four-wheeled carts. In those male-dominated days women were also used as load carriers; it was often more economical for a crofter to marry than to buy a horse, for a woman was cheaper to feed and could carry loads and knit at the same time.

Over the course of time long-distance paths developed to link one community with another. According to a thirteenth-century map the Highlands at that time were 'marshy and impassable, fit for cattle and shepherds', but some long-distance paths, such as the ridgeway paths of the Southern Uplands and the Mounth paths between Deeside and Tayside, were probably already in existence by then. Certainly routes such as Comyn's Road (Route 3), the Minigaig Route (Route 4) and Drumochter were in use by the fourteenth century and the Shinagag Road (Route 6) by the sixteenth. Many of the other routes described in this book may be at least aso old, but we shall probably never know.

Among the longest paths that developed were Coffin Roads. It was the custom for Highlanders to be buried in their birthplace alongside their forefathers, and this sometimes required the transportation of coffins across country for great distances. When Lady Mackenzie died in Gairloch in 1830, for instance, five hundred men took turns in carrying her coffin the 60 miles (100km) to Beauly. When bearers paused for a break, often at the top of a rise, they built cairns on which to rest the coffins. Many of these cairns still exist, repaired by generations of passers-by. There is an ancient Gaelic curse on those who pass a cairn without adding a stone to commemorate the dead.

Many paths, tracks and 'roads' thus came into existence over the centuries, but the building of roads in the modern sense of the word lagged far behind the rest of Britain. Unlike elsewhere the Romans did not penetrate the Highlands with their roads (although they did cross the Mounth and reach the Moray Firth), and no planned and maintained system of communication was attempted in the Highlands until Wade's network of military roads was built in the eighteenth century. A catalogue of obstacles awaited the prospective road builder. Rocks had to be moved out of the way or, if they were too large, undermined and sunk (Wade resorted to gunpowder). Bogs had to be crossed by causeways, which would sink over time. Bridges would be washed away by winter storms. Fords, carefully floored with small stones during the summer, would be destroyed during the winter. Roads needed constant maintenance.

A first attempt to legislate for an improved road system was made in 1617, when the Scottish parliament placed the upkeep of roads, bridges and ferries in the hands of the Justices of the Peace. A further act of 1669 obliged tenants to provide a horse and cart, labour and tools for road maintenance for six days each year on pain of confiscation of goods. Succeeding acts varied the amount of statute labour required, but it made little difference as enforcement proved impracticable.

Sometimes it fell to the schoolmaster to keep the statute labour records, and unless he was prepared to fix the books he could well find himself ostracised from the community. In some areas it became the practice to give money in lieu of labour, which did little for road improvement. Of those who did work on the roads, John Knox describes one such party on Skye, completely unskilled, with few useful tools, travelling 8 miles (13km) from home, having nowhere to stay, and accompanied by a bagpiper.

It is no surprise, therefore, that even in the eighteenth century roads were still in a parlous state. Wade considered that military communication was virtually impracticable, and according to Edmund Burt, an official who worked for Wade, 'The old ways (for roads I shall not call them) consisted chiefly of stony moors, bogs, rugged, rapid fords, declivities of hills, entangling woods and giddy precipices'. Telford considered the roads before Wade to be 'merely the tracks of black cattle and horses, intersected by numerous rapid streams, which being frequently swollen into torrents by heavy rains, rendered them dangerous or impassable'. It was not until military concerns became important at the time of Jacobite unrest that the situation was to improve and the Highlands receive its first concerted road-building programme.

DROVE ROADS

Thanks to the cinema, droving is more likely to conjure up images of Wild West cowboys than of Scottish Highlanders, but for centuries the movement of cattle across country was a mainstay of the Scottish economy, and the great droves of the nineteenth century saw herds up to several miles long traversing the mountain passes. The origins of the Scottish cattle trade are lost in the mists of time, but certainly in medieval times dairy produce was the main source of food and wealth was measured in cattle.

The earliest drovers were undoubtedly bands of cattle thieves who roamed far and wide in their activities. In clan times cattle raiding was an accepted part of life; some used it as a proof of manhood, while others such as Rob Roy ran blackmail rackets and demanded protection money from passing drovers. The word 'blackmail' derives from this time, the black mail, or tribute, being the black cattle extorted. The Gaelic word *spreidh*, meaning cattle, originally described a cattle raid, and it is from the sportive, high-spirited nature of the activity that the English word 'spree' is derived.

Some raids resulted in full-scale clan battles; the last battle ever fought on Skye soil, in Coire na Creiche in the Cuillin in 1601, followed a MacDonald cattle raid into MacLeod country, and in 1603 a similar battle in Glenfruin between Clan MacGregor and Colquhoun of Luss resulted in the loss of eighty men. Some of the longest raids were undertaken by the clans of Lochaber, who crossed Rannoch Moor and passed by Loch Erichtside to Speyside in order to plunder the fertile plains of Moray (Routes 11, 15 and 16). Thieving remained rife until the arrival of military patrols following the Jacobite uprising of 1745.

The droving of cattle from Scotland to England can be traced back at least as far as the fourteenth century, and records show its growing importance over the centuries as more settled times reached the Highlands and political and economic barriers with England were removed. In the eighteenth and nineteenth centuries the demand for beef to feed the

16

expanding British fleet and the growing cities and industrial areas of England and the Scottish lowlands saw the trade reach a peak in the 1830s.

Drovers and dealers met at cattle markets or trysts. By the end of the seventeenth century the autumn tryst at Crieff, on the edge of the Highlands, had become the focal point for Highland drovers to meet and sell to dealers from the south Falkirk Tryst took over this function in the mid-eighteenth century and remained an important and lively gathering until the 1860s. A total of 130,000 cattle were sold at Falkirk in 1827 amidst scenes more like a circus than a market, with all sorts of pedlars, gamblers, singers, jugglers and the like plying their trade. Dozens of temporary tents were erected to serve as makeshift drinking dens.

Drovers converged on Falkirk and Crieff from all over the Highlands and Islands, making their way southwards at the rate of 10 miles (16km) a day, overnighting at 'stances' where the herds could graze. From the far north they came via the northern glens of the eastern seaboard to the local tryst at Muir of Ord. From the west they reached Muir of Ord via Gleann Lichd and Glen Affric (Route 20); from the northwest they came via Glen Achall, Strath Cuileannach and Strathcarron. For these northern drovers Muir of Ord was the gateway to the south. From here they could follow either of two routes to Dalwhinnie and then cross the Grampians by Drumochter Pass. One route followed the line of the modern A9 via Aviemore and Kingussie, but many drovers preferred the better grazing to be found on the less populous route that went along Strath Glass, across the hills to Glen Moriston and Fort Augustus (Route 19) and then across the Corrieyairack Pass to Dalwhinnie (Route 17).

In those days Dalwhinnie was an important stance on the droving route south and in autumn it must have presented an altogether more animated scene than that which greets motorists scurrying along the busy A9 bypass today. It is recorded that at Dalwhinnie on 31 August 1723 there were no less than eight droves on their way southwards to Crieff, with others further south already on their way over Drumochter. Once over Drumochter the drovers left the present A9 at Dalnacardoch and passed by Trinafour, Coshieville and Aberfeldy to reach Crieff via the Sma' Glen.

From Skye and the Outer Hebrides the cattle were roped nose to tail and made to swim across the dangerous waters of Kyle Rhea to reach the mainland at Glenelg. From here some herds went over the Mam Ratagan pass to Glen Shiel, Glen Moriston and Fort Augustus to join the traffic from the north over the Corrieyairack. Others turned south at Cluanie,

17

or went south from Glenelg via Kinlochhourn, to reach Glen Garry and Spean Bridge. From here some went by the Lairig Leacach and Rannoch Moor to Glen Lyon and Killin, then through Glen Lednock to Crieff. But the majority went either by Loch Linnhe and Glencoe village or by the Lairig Mor and the Devil's Staircase (Route 1) to congregate at the Kingshouse stance at the head of Glen Coe. From the Kingshouse they crossed to Inveroran and Bridge of Orchy, from where they headed eastwards either to join the Killin herds or to follow the line of today's roads to Crieff and Falkirk.

From Aberdeen and the north-east the main barriers to the drovers were the Cairngorms and the Braes of Angus, to the north and south of Deeside respectively. Some drovers skirted the high Cairngorms to the east, using routes such as that over the Bealach Dearg (Route 13). Further west some took short cuts from Speyside to Atholl via Drumochter or the Minigaig (Route 4), or from Speyside to Deeside via Lairig Ghru (Route 9) or Lairig an Laoigh (Route 10). The Lairig an Laoigh (Pass of the Calves) was easier than the higher Lairig Ghru and was used by the less hardy cattle, hence its Gaelic name.

From Deeside the obvious route south via narrow Glen Tilt (Route 5) was usually avoided in favour of Gleann Fearnach (Route 6) or Glen Shee, which now carries the main A93 road. Further east drovers made use of the numerous ancient routes that crossed the Braes of Angus. Most of these Deeside routes converged on Kirmichael in Strathardle, where one of the most important trysts outside Crieff and Falkirk was held. From here the drovers headed west across the hills to Balinluig and Dunkeld, then down the Sma' Glen to Crieff.

From the west also, from the hills and glens of Argyll and the Inner Hebrides, drovers crossed the breadth of the country to converge on the north end of Loch Lomond. When Crieff was the main tryst they headed north from here to join the drove route from the north-west at Crianlarich. When Crieff declined in importance they crossed to Loch Katrine or followed the shore of Loch Lomond southwards to Balloch to reach Falkirk.

From Crieff and Falkirk the journey south to England was easy, and drove roads funnelled out all over the Southern Uplands and the Cheviots. From Dumfries and Galloway further routes converged on Carlisle to take a more westerly route. Dumfries Tryst itself was the most important south of the Highlands.

After its peak in the 1830s droving went into a steep decline and disappeared altogether in the last years of the century. Many factors contributed to its downfall. The routes open to the drovers and the amount of wayside grazing available to the herds was reduced by the enclosing of land for farming and the growing use of land for grouse shooting and deer stalking. Many rights-of-way cases appeared in the courts, and the cross-country traveller of today owes a great debt to the drovers who fought them.

Some landowners began to demand payment for grazing at overnight stances, and toll houses on the growing network of roads further increased the cost of the drove. The new roads made droving easier, but many drovers hated the gravel surfaces, which prompted many to shoe their cattle before venturing upon them. Steamships and railways offered better alternative methods of transport for the fatter, less hardy cattle of the late nineteenth century, and yet another result of improving nationwide communications was that English dealers could go north of the Crieff and Falkirk trysts and buy direct.

All these factors contributed to the decline of droving, but above all there were the hardy Cheviot sheep, which replaced not only the cattle but the people too. All over the Highlands and Islands people were systematically and callously evicted from the land to make way for the more profitable sheep. Other factors besides greedy landlords played a part, including the potato famine, overpopulation in some areas and tenants who could not afford to pay their rents, but such was the appalling violence and disregard for human life with which the evictions were carried out that the whole sorry episode in Scottish history, known as the 'clearances', still arouses passion to this day.

The clearances resulted in the Highlands as we know them today, a land relatively empty of people and cattle, a land given over to sheep. Gone for ever are the days of the great cattle droves and trysts. Many of the droving routes through the hills have been lost to memory, while others carry modern trunk roads, but fortunately there are still others that have been handed down to us as wild and remote as ever. Many of these make magnificent cross-country expeditions for those who wish to leave their cares behind and face the same challenges as the drovers of yesteryear, whose hillcraft was as highly tuned as any mountaineer's. As Sir Walter Scott wrote of the drovers: 'They are required to know perfectly the drove roads which lie over the wildest tracts of the country, and to avoid as much as possible ... the turnpikes which annoy (their) spirit.'

Let the knowledge and spirit of the drovers live on in all who venture into the wild places of the Highlands today.

WADE ROADS

The first attempt to build a road system in the Highlands was made in the eighteenth century by an English army of occupation commanded by an Irishman, over 1,700 years after a Roman army of occupation had done the same thing in England. The Highlands at that time were experiencing a period of such great economic, social and political upheaval that the English stationed troops north of the border to quell any unrest. Whether this amounted to a policy of pacification or repression depends upon your point of view, but the presence of English soldiers in the glens certainly did not bring peace; guerrilla warfare and full-scale military campaigns followed, leading to the last battles ever fought on British soil. To facilitate troop movement the English built a road network whose remnants, ironically, survive as peaceful off-road tracks for cross-country travellers of today.

To understand how the military roads came to be built it is necessary to understand the uneasy relationship that existed between England and Scotland at the time. When Elizabeth 1 died childless in 1603 and James VI of Scotland became James I of England, the way was opened for a closer union between the two countries. It was to be a further century, however, before the 1707 Act of Union dissolved the Edinburgh parliament in favour of rule from Westminster, and meanwhile, in 1688, William and Mary ousted James VII/II from the throne.

James was forced into exile in France, but there were many who remained loyl to him, especially in the Highlands of Scotland, and in the half-century following 1688 many plots were hatched by his supporters (named Jacobites after Jacobus, the Latin for James). In 1689 a Jacobite army under Viscount Dundee defeated William's army at Killiecrankie but was then itself defeated in the streets of Dunkeld and annihilated the following year at the Haughs of Cromdale. In 1715 the largest rebellion of all culminated in an indecisive battle at Sherrifmuir; James's son James ('The Old Pretender') landed in Scotland and set up court at Perth, but eventually had to retreat back to France. In 1719 a Jacobite army supported by a small Spanish expedition was defeated at Glen Shiel.

In 1745 The Old Pretender's son Charles (Bonnie Prince Charlie, 'The Young Pretender') landed in Scotland and marched his army as far south as Derby before retreating and being routed at Culloden. The three months he spent on the run in the Highlands and Islands following this defeat have left an indelible mark on the country's folklore, and although the '15 had the greater chance of success, it is the '45 that is most popularly remembered.

To combat rebellion English troops were stationed in Scotland from 1689 onwards. In 1724 George Wade, a major-general in the army and MP for Bath, was sent north to report on the continuing Highland unrest, and as a result of his investigation he was appointed commander-in-chief, North Britain, with a brief of bringing peace to the Highlands.

One of Wade's priorities was to strengthen and link the forts that housed his troops. A number of such forts were scattered around the Highlands, notably along the Great Glen at Fort William (named after William of Orange), Killichuimen (Fort Augustus) and Inverness. Wade strengthened Fort William and built new forts at Fort Augustus and Inverness (on the site of the present castle). Both new forts were later destroyed by the Jacobites in 1746, but Fort William held out against a siege; later it was sold to the West Highland Railway Company and the site on which it stood is now a humble car park.

A fourth fort, Ruthven Barracks near Kingussie, was enlarged with stables to accommodate a regiment of dragoons; it was burnt by the Jacobites in 1746 but its gaunt ruins remain a conspicuous sight on Spey-side and are worth a visit. There were also two other barracks, at Bernera (Glenelg) at the ferry point to Skye and at Inversnaid on Loch Lomond, but Wade considered these to be poorly sited and of little importance.

Having decided upon his four military bases Wade next looked at the logistics of moving troops between them. He stationed a galley on Loch Ness to secure communication between Inverness and Fort Augustus and then turned to the problems of land travel, which was 'impracticable from the want of roads and bridges'. In an effort to overcome these problems he became an enthusiastic construction engineer, and in a great burst of activity between 1725 and 1732 he built four major roads and a link road, totalling almost 250 miles (400km). To find the best routes many hundreds of miles were surveyed, and the link between military and road surveying was eventually acknowledged when the Ordnance Survey was founded in 1791 (the ordnance being the department of the army that deals with supplies).

During the summer months Wade had up to 500 soldiers in 100 strong parties working on the roads. Poorly equipped and housed, beset by hostile terrain, weather, locals and midges, these 'highwaymen', as Wade affectionately called them, found solace in drink whenever they could. Camps were established about every 10 miles (16km), and many of these developed into inns or 'kingshouses', so-called because they were on the king's highway. The kingshouses in Glencoe and Strathyre still retain this name.

The roads were made 16ft (5m) wide and straight whenever possible, surfaced with gravel and flanked by a drainage ditch and banks. On steep ground terraces (zigzags) were constructed, of which the best surviving examples are those on the Corrieyairack Pass. On marshy terrain the road was floated on rafts of brushwood or timber. Streams were crossed by fords whenever possible, as these were easily constructed with small stones, but as they needed to be remade every spring after winter storms, Wade found himself building an increasing number of bridges.

Wade believed his road system would make a valuable contribution to peace and stability in the Highlands, but needless to say it was not viewed in this way by the Highlanders themselves. From their point of view the new roads brought English soldiers into the glens, reduced the security of their mountain fastness and made guerrilla warfare tactics less effective. Many drovers hated the gravel surfaces. Horses had to be shod. It was even claimed that bridges made people weak and less able to ford rivers! There is no doubt, however, that Charlie and his army were grateful for the roads in 1745.

As commander of an army of occupation Wade had no need to listen to local complaints. His first road, linking the three forts of the Great Glen, was begun in 1725 and was more or less completed in 1727. The original route from Inverness went through Essich and down the east side of Loch Ness along the line of the present B862 to Fort Augustus, but in 1732–3 a lower road was built along the shores of Loch Ness (B862, B852) to rejoin the original road just before Whitebridge. Good examples of Wade bridges can still be seen upstream of the present bridges at Whitebridge and Inverfarigaig. Numerous lochs and waterfalls, such as the spectacular Falls of Foyers, make the area well worth exploring.

South of Fort Augustus Wade's road followed the eastern shores of Loch Oich and Loch Lochy to Spean Bridge and Fort William, mostly along the line of the A82. The 4 mile (7km) section beside Loch Oich is still extant and can be used as part of a fine off-road route between Fort Augustus and Spean Bridge (Route 18). Spean Bridge itself did not exist in Wade's day; he crossed the Spean at High Bridge (GR 201821), a spectacular 280ft (85m) long three-arched bridge whose remains are still a startling sight and well worth a visit if you are in the vicinity. Approach it from the north side via the old Fort William–Fort Augustus railway line (see p195) or from the south side via a minor road south of Spean Bridge (leave the roadside on the corner beside the house at GR 199820 and follow a track down across the moor).

Wade's second road was built in 1727–30 to link Dunkeld, where the road from Edinburgh then ended, with Ruthven Barracks and Inverness. Its route followed more or less the line of the present A9 over Drumochter Pass to Speyside and then through the Slochd Mor to Inverness. Most of the road has been lost to later reconstructions but two sections several miles in length survive: Etteridge (GR 686925) to near Ruthven (GR 751991) (6 miles/10km) and just north of Aviemore (GR 905170) to the Slochd Mor (GR 839252) (8½ miles/14km). The former is a fine off-road alternative to the A9 for people travelling north of Dalwhinnie (see p106), while the latter makes a rewarding excursion in the vicinity of Aviemore (see p104).

Shorter versions of Wade road survive throughout the length of the A9 (check the OS map). In particular a 3 mile (5km) stretch survives north of Bruar Falls, with a fine bridge (the Drochaid na h-Uinneige (*Droch*itch na *Hoon*yika, the Eye of the Window bridge)), restored in 1985 by the Association for the Preservation of Rural Scotland. Other Wade bridges can be seen at the Dalwinnie turn-off (GR 639828) and at Crubenbeg (GR 680923).

One mile north of Dalnacardoch, on the east side of the road at GR 693718, stands the 2½m high Wade Stone, one of many that originally marked the line of the route. The stone was carefully repositioned here from its original site during the latest road reconstruction. For his own amusement Wade is reputed to have placed a guinea on top of the stone and returned the following year to recover it untouched.

When Wade arrived at Scotland in 1724 there was already a road from Stirling to Crieff, and his third enterprise extended this road to Dalnacardoch to connect Glasgow and the west of Scotland with the Highlands. The road was built in 1730 and more of it survives today than any other Wade road, especially between Crieff and Tummel Bridge, but as it is much broken by the present road and lies outside the area covered by this book it is not described here in detail. The OS map marks several sections of it and it contains several interesting bridges, notably old Tummel Bridge and the ornamental Aberfeldy Bridge, which still carries traffic and for which Wade is probably most remembered.

To complete his road network and to link Ruthven Barracks with Fort Augustus Wade built a road over the Corrieyairack Pass in 1731. From Dalwhinnie the route followed the line of the A889 to near Laggan Bridge in Strath Mashie before striking west and then north, zigzagging up to 775m (2,543ft) at the summit of the pass. The section beyond Laggan Bridge was abandoned in the early nineteenth century and the last 12 miles (19km) of this now form the longest stretch of original Wade road that still survives. It makes a magnificent cross-country route and is described in the text as Route 17.

Wade was promoted to general in 1739 and left Scotland in 1740. As field-marshal at the age of 72 in 1745 he marched against the Jacobite army, but his military mind was not what it once was and he was twice outmanoeuvred by the enemy. He died in 1748.

CAULFEILD AND LATER MILITARY ROADS

Wade's work on the military roads was taken over by another Irishman, Major William Caulfeild, who so greatly admired Wade that he named his son after him and reputedly penned the lines:

Had you seen these roads before they were made
You would lift up your hands and bless General Wade.

Caulfeild's interest in construction work appears to have extended far beyond roads, for his house Cradlehall was said to have been named after a device that hoisted guests up to their rooms after an evening drinking the local firewater.

Caulfeild was appointed inspector of roads by Wade in 1732 and held the position for the next thirty-five years, until his death in 1767. During these three and a half decades a succession of commanders-in-chief relied totally on his knowledge and advice concerning road construction. Initial road works were interrupted by the Jacobite rebellion of 1745, during which Caulfeild acted as quartermaster to Sir John Cope, but following the final defeat of Charlie's army on Culloden Moor road building continued apace.

A draconian Disarming Act was passed, banning not only weapons but also kilts and bagpipes in an attempt to eradicate Highland culture from the face of the earth. Military patrols swept through the Highlands butchering Jacobite sympathisers mercilessly and committing untold atrocities in the name of pacification. Caulfeild found himself in charge of a vastly expanded military road-building programme that was aimed at facilitating movement of the 15,000 government troops stationed in the Highlands at that time. In 1749 no less than 1,350 soldiers worked on the roads.

Altogether Caulfeild built 750 miles (1,200km) of roads, which, when added to Wade's 250 miles (400km), gave a 1,000 mile (1,600km) military road network. Among the roads for which Caulfeild was responsible were: Stirling to Fort William via Lochearnhead, Crianlarich, Tyndrum, the Devil's Staircase and the Lairig Mor; the Loch Lomond and Inveraray Roads; perhaps Contin to Poolewe; and Coupar Angus to Fort

George near Inverness via Glen Shee, Braemar and the Lecht. Work was also begun on a road from Fort Augustus to Bernera Barracks.

Like Wade's roads most of Caulfeild's roads have become modern thoroughfares, but many sections have been abandoned by later construction engineers and await rediscovery. Two sections in particular make classic off-road routes; the 40 miles (64km) from Tyndrum to Fort William via the Devil's Staircase and the Lairig Mor (Route 1) and the first part of the Fort Augustus–Bernera road (Route 19). Also in the area covered by this book is an interesting 3 mile (5km) stretch of the Lecht road (see p153). Like Wade's roads many of Caulfeild's roads are marked on OS maps, but unlike Wade's they are for some reason not attributed to their maker, being described simply as 'old military roads'.

By the time of Caulfeild's death the Jacobite threat had passed into memory and the government found itself faced with increasing road maintenance costs. A few roads continued to be built, including the Fort William–Glen Coe road via Ballachulish Ferry, but the great period of military road-building was over. By 1784 there were about 1,100 miles (1,800km) of military roads in existence, many of them in a bad state of repair and becoming increasingly derelict as the troops who worked on them were withdrawn from Scotlands. After 1790 soldiers stopped working on the roads altogether and maintenance was carried out by civilian contractors, although there were still those who thought it best to keep soldiers 'employed on the public roads rather than to have them lounging half-idle in towns and cities, debauching the inhabitants and being debauched by them'.

To ease the maintenance burden the government began to hand over the roads to the counties, who could call on statute labour to maintain them. Only roads that passed through the wilder and less populated parts of the Highlands continued to be maintained by central public funds as their upkeep was judged to be essential to the Highland economy. Such maintenance grants were continued with increasing reluctance throughout the first half of the nineteenth century, with the government abandoning some roads and fighting a constant battle with the counties over who should pay.

In 1814 responsibility for the upkeep of the 255 miles (410km) of military roads that were still in the hands of the government was transferred to the Commission for Highland Roads and Bridges (see below), and by the time the commission ended in 1862 there was in practice no longer any distinction between military and parliamentary roads.

In retrospect the building of the military road network was a mixed blessing for the Highlands. It opened up the Highlands to modern influences, but the influx of military and civilian personnel and the new ideas that followed led to the destruction of the ancient Gaelic culture. Change and even assimilation was perhaps inevitable, but those who tread the abandoned military roads today would understand and appreciate the Highlands and Highlanders better if they paused to consider the turbulent times in which the roads were spawned.

TELFORD AND LATER PARLIAMENTARY ROADS

In the second half of the eighteenth century economic and social conditions in the Highlands changed rapidly. The people became less rebellious and increasingly apathetic in the face of growing economic problems that were already leading to clearance and emigration. To solve the economic problems better roads than the decaying military roads were needed – for farmers, for drovers, for fishermen, for industry, for improved social welfare and for growing integration with the English economy and political system.

In response to this need parliament in 1803 appointed a Commission for Highland Roads and Bridges, and from that time onwards the story of roads in the Highlands becomes of more interest to transport historians than to walkers and mountain bikers. Nevertheless, the story is not without relevance and a brief overview will bring the history of Highland tracks and roads up to date.

The Commissioners appointed an enthusiastic Thomas Telford as their engineer, and with the aid of his able chief inspectors, John Mitchell and his son Joseph, Telford supervised the building of much of the road network that survives. The task was a daunting one. Wade's and Caulfeild's efforts had been directed towards the movement of military personnel who were expected to endure any hardship. It became common practice, for instance, for soldiers to fortify themselves with liquor at Garvamore King's House before tackling the Corrieyairack Pass. Telford's opinion of the military roads pulled no punches: 'The Military Roads, having been laid out with other views than promoting Commerce and Industry, are generally in such directions and so inconveniently steep as to be nearly unfit for the purposes of Civil Life.'

Outside of the military road network road conditions were even worse, and travellers were certainly not reticent about airing their views on them, often in print. After a tour of the Highlanders Alexander Irvine wrote in 1803: 'It is hardly agreed upon by travellers which is the line, everyone making one for himself. The paths, such as they are, take such oblique and whimsical directions that they seem hardly to have been drawn by rational beings. Our sheep follow better lines.' Further north,

Thomas Pennant did not see a single road in Caithness in 1769, and in the 1790s there was only one bridge in the whole of Sutherland. Perhaps the best judgement on travel in the Highlands in those days was made by the traveller whose assertion that 'Nothing tamer than undeniable necessity would commit one to it' can still strike a resonant chord two centuries later when the weather is driech and curtains of rain sweep horizontally down the glens.

The Commission's response to the state of the roads was a great burst of road construction between 1803 and 1821, when nearly 3,000 men were employed annually in building roads. In those 18 years 920 miles (1,480km) of road and 1,117 bridges were built, including the 'Road to the Isles' between Fort William and Arisaig, the Loch Laggan road (linking Lochaber and Speyside), Dingwall to Lochcarron via Achnasheen (linking east and west coasts) and many of the major roads in Skye. Many fine bridges were built, including those over the Tay at Dunkeld and over the Spey at Craigellachie, which still stand as memorials to Telford.

The Caledonian Canal survives as further testament to Telford's engineering skills. The idea of a navigable waterway linking east and west coasts caught the public's imagination, especially at a time when ships on the high seas were subject to attack by Napoleon's privateers, but the construction of the canal took much longer and cost much more than anticipated. Nineteen years in the building, the canal was finally opened in 1822 and was commemorated in a poem by Robert Southey, whose exhortation to travellers to 'Contemplate now what days and nights of thought, what years of toil, what inexhaustive springs of public wealth the vast design required' paid tribute to a magnificent feat of engineering.

Unfortunately, the canal was never a great commercial success. It was not deep enough to attract the sailing ships that plied the Atlantic Ocean and the Baltic Sea, the rise of the steamship made safer the alternative Northern Passage through the Pentland Firth and the growing road and rail network took further potential custom away. Even nature seemed to conspire against the canal, with winds that made navigation difficult and great floods that caused widespread damage in 1834 and 1849. It is nothing short of a miracle that the canal still remains open today, and walkers and mountain bikers should be doubly grateful for this, for two sections of the canal towpath provide lovely off-road routes along the Great Glen (Route 18).

For the four decades after 1821 the Commission for Highland Roads and Bridges concentrated almost entirely on the maintenance of its now extensive road network. For most of this period Joseph Mitchell was chief inspector, and his many Highland adventures were later to be recorded in a classic volume of memoirs.

In the wake of the new roads came an increase in long-distance stage-coaches, some time after they were commonplace further south, but the heyday of Highland coaching was short owing to the coming of the railways. Most people welcomed the roads, but there were exceptions. Their gravelly surfaces were hated by drovers and others, such as the inhabitants of certain parts of Skye, who refused to walk on the roads for some years after their construction.

Additional funds for road maintenance were raised by levying tolls on users of certain roads, known as 'turnpike roads' after the counterbalanced bars that were erected on them at toll collection points. Tolls were legalised in Scotland in 1669 and first collected in 1750, but it was not until the commission's great road-building programme that turnpikes came into their own. The Edendon toll house at Dalnacardoch on the Drumochter road, for instance, came into existence in 1821.

The right to collect tolls was let to toll-keepers who could make extra money for themselves by selling alcohol or, at Gretna Green and other places near the English border, by conducting marriages, taking advantage of the more lenient Scottish marriage laws. In general, however, toll-keepers and turnpikes were understandably unpopular with travellers, some of whom attempted to avoid paying the toll by jumping the toll-gate on horseback. Drovers used the Minigaig Pass rather than Drumochter to avoid the Edendon toll. Tolls were eventually abolished in 1878, when at midday on the day the toll houses closed the keepers fired a commemoratory shot into the air.

Meanwhile, in 1846, the failure of the potato crop brought widespread suffering to the Highlands. A Central Relief Committee was formed in Edinburgh and Glasgow and funds were raised to provide meals in return for community work. In this way some roads were made outside the auspices of the Commission, and they acquired the unfortunate name of Destitution Roads. Examples include the Braemore–Dundonnell road (now the A832) and the road through Strathmore from Altnaharra to the north coast, whose foundations were laid with stones from houses left empty by the brutal Sutherland clearances, so that the land no longer 'showed the devastation where people had lived'. Those were hard times.

In 1862 Parliament voted to end the Commission and to give total responsibility for the upkeep of roads to the counties. Road-building did not end there, of course, but modern motorways and dual carriageways spluttering with exhaust fumes are no place for those who seek the peace and quiet of the hills.

RAILWAYS

For a time in the nineteenth century it looked as though the road system constructed by the Commission for Highland Roads and Bridges would become of only secondary importance, for during Mitchell's time as chief inspector railway mania reached the Highlands. Lines from the south reached Perth in 1848 and Aberdeen in 1850, and a spate of railways followed in the north-east.

Mitchell's engineering skills were much sought after during this period of railway expansion and he became an ardent supporter of the iron way. His masterpiece, much maligned by conservationists of the time, was the line over Drumochter Pass linking Perth and Inverness. He first proposed this route as early as 1845, but it was then ahead of its time and was rejected. 'Ascending such a summit as 1,480ft is very unprecedented, and Mr Mitchell is the greatest mountain climber I have ever heard of,' commented one opponent. The line was eventually opened in 1863 and it became the backbone of the Highland Railway, which moved on to Thurso and Wick in 1874 and Kyle of Lochalsh in 1897. In 1898 the section between Aviemore and Inverness was opened to replace the original Aviemore–Forres route and so complete the line as we know it today.

One of the foremost objectors to the Highland Railway was the academic and poet Principal Shairp, who wrote of the trains:

Nay! whate'er of good they herald,
Whereso' comes that hideous roar,
The old charm is disenchanted,
The old Highlands are no more.

Further west, the West Highland Railway from Glasgow to Fort William was opened in 1894 and extended to Mallaig in 1901 and Fort Augustus in 1903. In the Central Highlands lines from Stirling and Crieff joined at Balquhidder junction and went on to Killin and Crianlarich to join the West Highland line. Westwards the railway reached Oban and even Ballachulish at the gateway to Glen Coe. Grandiose schemes were proposed to build lines all over the Highlands and Islands: from Ballachulish to Fort William, from Fort William along the Great Glen to Inverness, from the East coast to Poolewe, Ullapool and Lochinver on the north-west coast, on the isles of Skye and Lewis, and even through Glen Coe and to the summit of Ben Nevis.

Since those heady days the arrival of the motor car has enabled the road system to regain the upper hand, and many of the railways that were built have since been closed. Those that remain open are a boon for walkers and mountain bikers reliant on public transport, while those that have closed now provide a network of abandoned tracks that provide pleasant walking and cycling routes. Some have been reopened as officially recognised walking and cycling routes, such as the Spey Way between Dufftown and Grantown and the old line along the west side of Loch Lubnaig, north of Callander.

Such railway routes cannot be classed as hill tracks and are therefore not considered in detail in this book, but they provide pleasant excursions and can be useful for approaching, returning from or linking hill tracks. Of particular interest in the area covered by this book are the abandoned Fort William–Fort Augustus line (see p193), abandoned lines between Glasgow and Loch Lomond (Route 1) and the spectacular, remote and still used West Highland Line, beside which Route 16 runs for some distance.

The story of the railways would be incomplete without mention of the Lochaber Narrow Gauge Railway, built in 1925 to link Fort William with Loch Treig and facilitate construction of the Lochaber hydro-electric power scheme. The railway was abandoned in 1977 and its 19 mile (30km) route high on the south side of Glen Spean, reaching a height of 340m (1,120ft), now makes a tough but fascinating hill route (see p184).

MODERN HILL TRACKS

The making of hill paths and tracks is a continuing process; not all paths date from olden days. In particular a great number of paths have been constructed in the last century or so to aid deer stalking. Some of these stalkers' paths are beautifully engineered and provide fine routes onto the hills; examples include the paths up Gleouraich from Loch Quoich and up Meall Gorm from Loch Fannich. Other new paths have been built to replace the older paths that have been inundated by hydro-electric schemes, such as the paths along Loch Ericht and Loch Monar. Other paths have been rebuilt because of erosion, such as that up Ben Nevis from Fort William and many sections of the West Highland Way.

More controversially, a few official long-distance footpaths have appeared in Scotland in recent years, and many people have voiced concern at the trend. Objections to such paths are rooted in a number of different issues: the different law of trespass north of the border and the fear that official path designation will bring with it restriction of freedom to roam off-path, the danger of attracting walkers unfit for the rigours of Scottish walking, a desire not to diminish the wilderness quality of Scottish hillwalking, an antipathy towards commercialisation and the problems arising from erosion caused by the channelling of walkers across boggy Scottish terrain.

Afficionados of the fine old hill tracks described in this book may find official, manufactured paths at best an addition to and at worst a destructive imposition on an already splendid off-road network, but there is no doubt that they have facilitated access in certain areas and given many a satisfying introduction to the pleasures of Scottish hillwalking and mountain biking. The debate is still open.

At the time of writing the popular West Highland Way between Glasgow and Fort William is currently the only long-distance footpath in the area covered by this book, and it is described as Route 1. In the near future the Countryside Commission for Scotland also intend to link many of the paths described in Route 18 to form the Great Glen Way.

The construction of vehicular tracks is also a continuing process. Since the days of Telford and Mitchell the coming of motorised transport has resulted in the continued expansion of the public road system and alongside it the growth of a private system of farm and estate tracks serving isolated farmhouses and shooting lodges. For many years these private tracks kept to low ground below the tree line, but in the latter half of the twentieth century modern construction machinery and improved cross-country vehicles have enabled tracks to be built at a much higher level across inhospitable terrain. Their tendrils now reach out towards the very tops of the mountains themselves.

The result is a vast network of upland vehicular tracks, both tarmaced and untarmaced, built to aid forestry extraction, to service radio masts, to power transmission lines, to enable the construction of upland reservoirs and downhill ski developments, and to provide access to high ground for the shooting of grouse and deer. The continuing proliferation of such tracks is cause for ever-increasing conservational concern because their construction, their presence and their erosion over time can all cause considerable ecological damage, disturbing drainage patterns and the habitat of upland flora and fauna. Moreover, from an environmental point of view there is a limit to the number of tracks that can be built in upland areas without reducing the amount, quality and variety of wild land left in Britain.

It is a contentious issue, for many of the tracks serve a useful purpose and not all of them have a negative impact on the environment. Some tracks that were built to serve grouse- and deer-shooting interests might have to be replaced by great swathes of forestry were the estates to lose this sporting revenue. Some tracks serve a dual purpose, having a secondary use – for example, in transporting winter feed to livestock. Some, like more ancient tracks, become (or will become) assimilated into their surroundings; new forestry tracks may eventually become beautiful arboreal avenues. Forestry tracks for the most part are built to a high specification; they are well drained and well surfaced, with gentle curves and easy gradients that are ideal for cross-country walkers and especially for mountain bikers.

The issue of upland vehicular tracks is an emotive one that cannot be divorced from equally emotive issues involving the pros and cons of afforestation, hydro-electric schemes and blood sports. It raises questions of the need for wild land in an industrialised society, of conservational versus economic priorities, of public versus private access to land, and political questions of land ownership and the rights and responsibilities of landowners. Walkers and mountain bikers who object to upland vehicular tracks are faced with a particularly difficult ethical dilemma, for they facilitate access and are difficult to ignore. Few people would avoid using a track as an access route even if they objected to it; if it already exists it might as well be used, 'because it is there' – witness the erosion on the Cairngorm plateau caused by easy summer access for walkers via Coire Cas access road and chairlift.

The problem is especially acute in the Cairngorms whose convex hill-sides and plateau summits are conductive to road building. In 1978 a Countryside Commission for Scotland report estimated that there were about 120 miles (200km) of upland vehicular tracks within a 6 mile (10km) radius of Braemar alone. Of these, 75 per cent served forestry, 10 per cent farms and 15 per cent 'sporting' activities. It is currently estimated that less than 13 per cent of the Cairngorms is more than 2 miles (3km) from a road, vehicular track or ski lift, and this in what for many is Britain's premier wilderness area.

One track rises to nearly 1,100m (3,600ft) on Beinn a' Bhuird, another to nearly 900m (3,000ft) on Broad Cairn, another to nearly 1,000m (3,300ft) above Glen Feshie. It is difficult not to think of these tracks as an environmental violation, and to make matters worse, four-wheel-drive vehicles and motor cycles go beyond the track-ends. The impact upon land, flora and fauna is almost completely destructive.

Some kind of balance is required, but one of the problems we have in Britain is that there is currently no overall government policy for the management of wild land and the control of its development. There are innumerable landscape designations – National Scenic Area (NSA), National Nature Reserve (NNR), Site of Special Scientific Interest (SSSI), Environmentally Sensitive Area (ESA), Forest Nature Reserve (FNR) and Area of Great Landscape Value (AGLV), to name but a few, but they do not provide sufficient defence. In the 1980s a ski tow was built within an SSSI on Glas Maol, vehicular tracks were built in an NSA in Glen Feshie, hillsides within NNRs all over the north-east were ploughed and replanted with exotic conifers. The list goes on and on.

Scottish National Parks are being mooted as one answer. A park along the lines of the English Lake District, with all the problems its overdevelopment has generated, would be counterproductive in the Highlands, but perhaps something closer to the American concept of national park wilderness areas, as inspired by that émigré Scotsman John Muir, would be worth consideration. Certainly something needs to be done before it is too late.

Meanwhile, the case for wild land is fought by an uneven alliance of government bodies, organisations, societies and charities, and it is up to each individual to decide for himself or herself where his or her sympathies and responsibilities lie (See also The Conservation Issue, p9).

1
THE WEST HIGHLAND WAY

TRACK RECORD

After ten years of surveying and access battles the West Highland Way was opened as Scotland's first official long-distance footpath in 1980, and since then it has attracted both more praise and more criticism than any of its founders could have anticipated. With an estimated 60,000 people a year currently tackling the Way there can be no doubting its popularity, but there are many others, some of them well-intentioned and well-respected figures in the walking world, who question the very existence of the route.

Does the Way provide a good introduction to Highland walking or is it too commercialised to provide an authentic Highland walking experience? Is it an interestingly intricate route or a mere man-made contrivance? Does it represent the state of the art in path making or is it a manufactured excrescence? Is it too close to roads in places to give rewarding walking? Has it provided a solution to access problems or has its existence entrenched restrictions elsewhere?

Perhaps in a country the size of Scotland there is a place for the Way. It provides a route into the Highlands from Scotland's largest city and gives an introduction to Highland walking to those who might otherwise not come or otherwise get into difficulties. There are those who would turn back such people at the border, but the opening up of the Highlands is important both economically and culturally. If those who walk the Way become more cognisant of and appreciative of their environment, the Way serves a useful purpose. But let it also be said that a plethora of such routes on an English-like basis would destroy the existing network of old Highland hill tracks, as exemplified by the other routes in this book, and diminish the traditional attractions of Scottish hillwalking.

Given these reservations, the Way provides a lengthy, rewarding, often exciting cross-country route for long-distance walkers and back-

ROUTEPLANNER

OS map: 64/57/56/50/41
Start point: Milngavie railway station (GR 555744)
End point: Fort William railway station (GR 105742)
Total distance: 95 miles (152km)
Total ascent: c2,830m (c9,300ft)

	Distance (miles)	Ascent (metres)	Accommodation	Youth Hostel	Campsite	Provisions	Station
Milngavie	0	–	●			●	●
Drymen	12	180	●		●	●	
Balmaha	6	350	●			●	
Rowardennan	7	170	●	●			
(Inverarnan)	15	340	●				
(Crianlarich)	6	140	●	●		●	●
Tyndrum	6	210	●		●	●	●
Bridge of Orchy	7	100	●				●
Inveroran	3	170	●				
Kingshouse Hotel	10	280	●				
Kinlochleven	8	360	●		●	●	
Glen Nevis	13	530		●	●	●	
Fort William	2	–	●			●	●

NB The undulating nature of the Way makes estimates of ascent approximate only.

packers, with several sections that are idea for mountain bikers and bike-packers.

There are also hotels at Inversnaid and Ardlui, campsites at Milarrochy and Cashel, north of Balmaha, and additional facilities at other places near the Way. Up-to-date information can be obtained from the Countryside Commission for Scotland, Batterby, Redgorton, Perth, PH1 3EW.

Bothies en route: Rowchoish (GR 336044) and Doune (GR 332144) on Loch Lomondside. Wild camping is permitted along the way except on Forestry Commission ground (unless there are notices to the contrary), Conic Hill, between Inversnaid and Crianlarich, and between Tyndrum and Bridge of Orchy.

The West Highland Way is an official recognised long-distance foot-path, established under the provisions of the Countryside (Scotland) Act (1967), and is administered by the Countryside Commission for Scotland.

The Way begins at the railway station in Milngavie, 7 miles (11km) from the centre of Glasgow. Trains run frequently (excluding Sunday) from Glasgow Central. The West Highland Railway and the A82 from Glasgow to Fort William cross the Way at several points, making explorations of individual sections of the Way using train or bus practicable. Mention should also be made of the Loch Lomond ferries, which can be used to shorten the long and tiring tramp along the east side of Loch Lomond:

1   Balloch–Balmaha–Luss–Rowardennan–Tarbet–Inversnaid   (Maid of the Loch Ltd, Balloch Pier, Balloch; tel: 0389-52044)
2   Rowardennan–Inverbeg (Rowardennan Hotel; tel: 036-087-273)
3   Inversnaid–Inveruglas (Inversnaid Hotel; tel: 087-786-223)
4   Ardleish–Ardlui (Cuillins Boat Hire, Ardlui, near Arrochar; tel: 03014-244)

The ferries normally operate only during spring and summer; you should verify details before travelling.

The Way is best tackled from south to north, giving an easier start and leaving the best scenery until last. From Fort William public transport will return you to your starting point, while those still full of energy can continue their explorations of Highland hill tracks along the Great Glen or Glen Spean (Route 18). Many sections of the route were not built to take the traffic that now uses them and at one time became badly

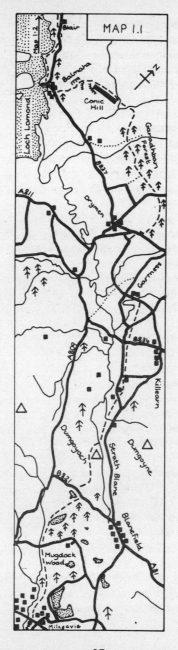

MAP 1.1

eroded; most of these sections have been improved by path renovation schemes but some still become quagmires after rain and at such times are best avoided, especially by mountain bikers (see below).

Fellrunners have completed the Way in 15 hours, but most people divide it into seven or eight single-day stages, making it an ideal expedition for a week's holiday.

ROUTE DESCRIPTION
Milngavie to Drymen
The first 12 mile (19km) section of the Way from Milngavie to Drymen is relatively flat. Excellent paths take you along the Allander Water and through the beautiful parkland and woodland of Mugdock Country Park, and then an old coach road continues past Craigallian and Carbeth Lochs to reach more open country at the B821, 4 miles (6km) out of Milngavie. There are good views from here across Strath Blane to the Campsie Fells, with shapely Dumgoyne (427m/1,402ft) prominent. Farm paths skirt the tree-clad lump of Dumgoyach Hill into green and gentle Strath Blane, where the Way takes to the disused line of the old Blane Valley Railway. The line is muddy in places but continues to provide easy going for the next 4 miles (6km) to Gartness, and then a further 2 miles (3km) of back roads bring you to the lovely village of Drymen.

Drymen to Balmaha
From Drymen the next 6 mile (10km) section of the Way leads to the shores of Loch Lomond at Balmaha. The route climbs through Garadhban Forest on good forest tracks to reach a crossroads where there are two alternative ways forward. The normal route goes straight on over multi-topped Conic Hill (358m/1,175ft) to give a first taste of real Highland country. The well-made path climbs around the north side of the hill and gives wonderful views in all directions, especially of that most beautiful of lochs, Loch Lomond, whose many islands are spread before you. These hump-backed islands represent a continuation of Conic Hill and mark the line of the Highland Boundary Fault, which separates the Highlands from the Lowlands.

The ascent and descent of Conic Hill are steep, and some walkers may prefer to make the easier but less interesting alternative route that goes left at the crossroads in Garadhban Forest to join the B837 to Balmaha. Note that for a period of four weeks during lambing in April/May the Conic Hill path is closed (look for notices) and the B837 must be taken.

MAP 1.2

N

BEN VORLICH

Ardlui

Doune

Map 1.3

Inveruglas

Inversnaid

Loch Lomond

Tarbet

Rowchoish

BEN LOMOND

Inverbeg

YH

Rowardennan

Map 1.1

Sallochy

Luss

Blair

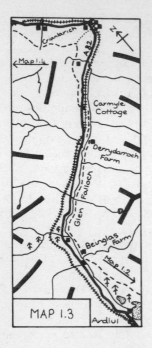

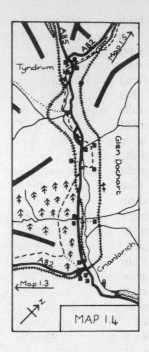

Balmaba to Rowardennan

The 7 mile (11km) section above Balmaha follows the eastern shore of Loch Lomond to the road-end at Rowardennan. The Way avoids the road for the most part by taking to the woods and shoreline on its left. Although never very far from the road, the path passes through some beautiful scenery, whether penetrating dense woodland, running beside the lapping waters of the loch or climbing over waterside crags. Above Rowardennan towers the popular summit of Ben Lomond (974m/3,195ft).

Rowardennan to Tyndrum

The next 14½ mile (23km) section from Rowardennan along the east side of Loch Lomond into Glen Falloch is generally recognised as having the toughest terrain of the whole route. The path hugs the lochside but is rarely level as it negotiates a variety of obstacles such as lochside crags, tree stumps and roots, boulders and streams; at one point there is even a chain handrail for security. It is extremely rough, boggy and tiring. After rain it is awash with ankle-grabbing mud. On the plus side there are some

40

fine lochside spots and some interesting crag and oak woodland scenery, but the tiresome going can detract from all of this unless you are mentally prepared for it.

The worst sections are from Ptarmigan Lodge to Rowchoish Bothy (3 miles/5km) and from Inversnaid to Doune Bothy (4 miles/6km). The first of these sections can be avoided by an excellent forest track that runs parallel to the Way higher up the hillside; by taking this track the only item of real interest that you would miss is Rob Roy's Prison, a lochside crag on whose ledges Rob is said to have kept his prisoners. From Rowchoish Bothy it is a further 3 miles (5km) to Inversnaid, where there is an hotel and a fine waterfall, and then the second very rough section begins. Near the start of this section the Way passes an impressive rock face and negotiates a massive rockfall at its foot, where Rob Roy's cave lies among the fallen boulders. Keep a lookout also for the wild goats that frequent this part of the route.

Beyond Doune bothy the going eases as the path climbs away from the loch and descends to Beinglas Farm in Glen Falloch. There is then a mile of good track before the Way again becomes rough and often muddy as it runs beside the banks of the River Falloch to Derrygarroch Farm. Pleasant woodland and river scenery, including the Falls of Falloch, ease the going. At Derrygarroch Farm the Way crosses the river and continues as a renovated path directly below the A82 to reach Carmyle Cottage, 2½ miles (4km) from Crianlarich.

At Carmyle Cottage the path crosses the A82 and climbs to join a track that once formed part of Caulfeild's military road from Glasgow to Fort William. The track rises gently across the hillside and when it ends an excellent path continues to a junction from where a branch path descends to Crianlarich. The main path goes left at the junction and crosses into Glen Dochart, bypassing Crianlarich. For the first time since Conic Hill it becomes a true hill path, climbing to a high point of nearly 300m (1,000ft) on the shoulder of Kirk Craig. This point is almost exactly half-way along the Way and is a major turning point, for the great north–south trench of Loch Lomond and Glen Falloch that has brought you this far is now left behind for wider and more mountainous country. The path descends through trees into Glen Dochart and crosses the A82 to join a tarmaced road leading to the ruins of St Fillan's Chapel. A farm track leads onwards to recross the A82 further along and become a narrow, often muddy riverside path to Tyndrum, 8 miles (13km) from Carmyle Cottage.

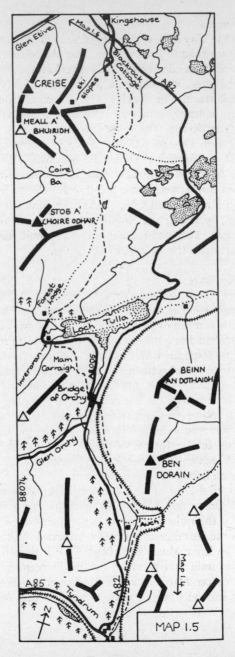

MAP 1.5

Tyndrum to Inveroran

After Tyndrum the Way follows the old public road to Glen Coe and then Caulfeild's military road to Fort William. The old public road was closed in 1931; a surface of rounded cobbles, compacted through years or usage and now grassed over, still exists in places, but mostly the road has reverted to rough track. The 7 miles (11km) section from Tyndrum to Bridge of Orchy is mostly intact apart from a collapsed bridge, which necessitates a short detour. The route crosses a low pass and skirts the foot of shapely Ben Dorain 1,074m (3,523ft) whose conical summit towers overhead. At Bridge of Orchy the old road is abandoned for a couple of miles to follow Calfeild's route across the shoulder of Mam Carraigh to Inveroran Hotel. Some Wayfarers prefer to avoid the 170m (560ft) climb up Mam Carraigh, especially after rain when the path can get very muddy, by taking the A8005 around the hill from Bridge of Orchy to Inveroran. The road route is only half a mile further and gives pleasant walking beside the shores of Loch Tulla.

Inveroran to Kingshouse

The next 10 mile (16km) section skirts the attractive Blackmount Range to the Kingshouse Hotel at the entrance to Glen Coe. The Way follows the A8005 from Inveroran to its end less than a mile away at Forest Edge and then goes straight along the old public road again. In some places the line of the road corresponds with Caulfeild's military road, but for much of the way Caulfeild's road runs higher up the hillside, much overgrown. Keeping to the old public road, the Way climbs gently to the brow of a hill and then descends past reedy Lochan Mhic Pheadair Ruaidh to Ba Bridge at the entrance to Coire Ba. Coire Ba is an enormous bowl surrounded by fine mountains and is reputed to be the largest corrie in the Highlands; on the north side of the corrie the pointed shoulder of Clach Leathad (Clachlet) looks particularly impressive. The old bridge is a fine spot to pause beside the cascading river.

Climbing out of the far side of the corrie, the Way reaches a high point where the Orchy and Blackmount mountains are left behind for new horizons. To the right now is the vast expanse of Rannoch Moor, while ahead lies the entrance to Glen Coe, guarded by Buachaille Etive Mor (Boo-a*chil*-ya Etive Moar, Big Shepherd of Etive; 1023m/3,352ft) the great rock pyramid that is one of Scotland's premier rock-climbing sites. The track descends to Blackrock Cottage at the foot of the White Corries chairlift and ski slopes, and then the ski access road is followed across the A82 to the Kingshouse Hotel.

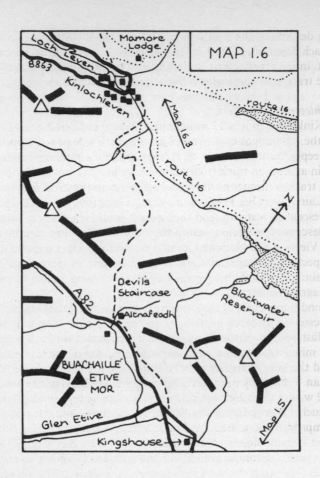

MAP 1.6

Kingshouse to Kinlochleven

From the Kingshouse Hotel it is 8 miles (13km) to the next staging post of Kinlochleven. West of the hotel the Way keeps close to the main road as far as the houses at Altnafeadh, and then it leaves Glen Coe to zigzag up one of the most famous sections of the whole route – the Devil's Staircase. This rough 260m (850ft) ascent was once the steepest section of Caulfeild's road, but it is not as difficult a climb as its name implies and the summit, the highest point on the Way, is soon gained. The view from the summit is fittingly perhaps the best of the whole route, for to the north is spread before you the whole Mamore Range and, if the weather is fine, Ben Nevis itself, the roof of Britain.

The descent of the northern side of the Devil's Staircase takes you right back down to sea level at Kinlochleven. It is a long, steep and tiring descent, into a grassy corrie at first, then contouring across the hillside to join the track that comes down from the Blackwater Reservoir.

Kinlochleven to Glen Nevis

From Kinlochleven it is 12 rough miles (19km) to Glen Nevis. The path leaves the road opposite the school on the north side of town and climbs very steeply through woods to rejoin Caulfeild's military road, which comes in as a rough track from Mamore Lodge.

The track continues north-westwards through the great grassy trough of the Lairig Mor (Big Pass) on the south side of the Mamores. There is a short descent to a stream and then a long gentle rise leading to another short descent to a stream before the final climb to the summit of the Lairig. Views of the Mamore tops and connecting ridges become increasingly spectacular, especially the backward view of Stob Ban (White Mountain; 999m/3,080ft) whose sparkling, gleaming quartz summit is a truly magnificent mountain prospect.

Beyond the summit of the pass one last rise around the shoulder of the most westerley Mamore heralds the end of the Lairig Mor and the start of the last section of the Way. The track descends through a wood to reach a minor road to Fort William, and at the top of the last rise before the road the Way branches right into the wooded valley of the Allt nan Gleannan, eventually to cross the low ridge at the head of the valley that bars the way to Glen Nevis. This section used to be very muddy but it has been much improved and now carries an excellent well-drained path, a great improvement underfoot after the rough military road. Soon the immense convex slopes of the south face of Ben Nevis dominate the horizon, with the tourist path to the summit clearly visible as it zigzags skywards.

Once the ridge at the head of the valley of the Allt nan Gleannan is cleared all that remains of the Way is a final descent through woods to Glen Nevis. The descent begins as a staircase-like path over tree roots, but soon a forest track is reached and the remainder of the route is straightforward. At a junction of tracks go right and then left to reach the glen near the campsite and youth hostel, or go left to reach the road-side nearer Fort William.

MOUNTAIN BIKING THE WEST HIGHLAND WAY

The Way is an obvious mountain-biking challenge and much of it gives excellent sport on sturdy surfaces. There are some sections, however, that are best avoided in order to prevent both erosion and frustration. Many of these sections occur on the southern half of the route, and the Countryside Commission for Scotland advises against cycling here.

The start of the Way at Milngavie presents an immediate problem as cycling is not permitted on the Allander Walkway. A good alternative route can be found by taking the road to Mugdock Reservoir north out of town, just before the last houses turn left along Craigallian Avenue and at its end continue along a path to join the Way. The tracks through Mugdock Country Park and past Craigallian and Carbeth lochs to the B821 provide good cycling, but the remainder of the route up Strath Blane to Gartness is rough in places and often muddy; the A81 is an obvious and easier alternative.

An attractive alternative route to Loch Lomond for cyclists avoids the Way altogether. This is the Glasgow–Loch Lomond Cycleway, a 21 mile (34km) route along disused railway lines and waterside paths all the way from Glasgow city centre to Balloch. This fine route, opened in the late 1980s, was designed by SUSTRANS Ltd and a route map is available from their office at 53 Cochrane Street, Glasgow G1 1HL.

Beyond Drymen the Way improves again to provide excellent cycling through Garadhban Forest, but few will opt to take the Conic Hill variation to Balmaha. The path over the hill is a push nearly all the way on account of its steepness and the great number of steps that in places turn it into a staircase. From Balmaha to Rowardennan the Way adopts a circuitous route to avoid the road and few cyclists will have the motivation or patience to stick to its contortions. It is often rough and

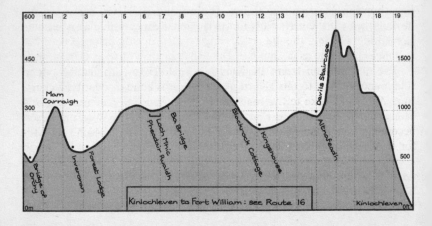

46

awkward, with substantial ascents. The climbs out of Balmaha, Sallochy and through Ross Wood are particularly steep and awkward, with many steps. Again, the whole section should be avoided when muddy.

Beyond Rowardennan things get even worse; the whole eastern side of Loch Lomond is a nightmare with a bicycle, requiring extreme care and patience. The alternative forest track noted above provides a good route for the first few miles to Rowchoish Bothy, but beyond here is for masochists only. Many cyclists will opt to take one of the ferries across Loch Lomond to join the A82 into Glen Falloch (verify in advance that bicycles are carried). Much of the Glen Falloch section of the Way is also unridable, with some wooded sections that are particularly awkward, and cyclists will find any attempt to avoid the nearby road merely frustrating.

The next section from Carmyle Cottage in Glen Falloch to the A82 in Glen Dochart requires a good push onto the shoulder of Kirk Craig, but otherwise the route provides excellent mountain biking, with an exciting descent into Glen Dochart. The alternative road route via Crianlarich is, of course, much easier. After reaching the road in Glen Dochart the Way takes an often unridable route to Tyndrum, and the proximity of the road again makes tarmac tempting.

It is beyond Tyndrum, with 40 miles (60km) still to go to Fort William, that the Way really comes into its own as a mountain-biking route and many cyclists choose to begin their trip here. The section along the old public road to Bridge of Orchy is an excellent ride, involving only one short push around the collapsed bridge mentioned above. The steep push over Mam Carraigh from Bridge of Orchy to Inveroran should be avoided as it is often muddy and prone to erosion; the short ride along the A8005 makes a more pleasant alternative. From Inveroran to the Kingshouse is a particularly fine section along the old public road, passing through the sort of country that would convert anyone to mountain biking. Cycling the old road, which is now mostly a rough track, is not always as tame as it sounds.

The next section from the Kingshouse Hotel to Altnafeadh is very rough and so close to the A82 in places that it is almost pedantic to keep to it. Many will take to the road in their impatience to reach the Devil's Staircase, which is the most exciting section of the whole Way and is fast becoming a mountain-biking test piece, with a descent of 540m (1,770ft) for a climb of only 260m (850ft). On ascent some push their bikes around the zigzags while others carry them up a steeper line; there seems little to choose between the two approaches, the ascent taking about an hour in each case. The descent of the northern side is ridable most of the way but there are some very rough sections to trap the unwary. It begins

47

steeply and ends with a fast descent of the Blackwater Reservoir track. Nerves, muscles and brakes will all be on fire by the time you roll into the back streets of Kinlochleven.

The rough climb out of town to join the Lairig Mor track is a nightmare with a bike, but fortunately there is a good alternative route that is ridable if you still have the energy. This is the roughly tarmaced road that leaves the main road about 800m beyond the Way and climbs to Mamore Lodge where refreshments are available. The lodge stands on Caulfeild's old military road, which is followed left to rejoin the Way.

The Lairig Mor track has no major ascents throughout its undulating length, but it is a long rough ride and many will be unconvinced that some of the ascents are indeed minor. The last section of the Way along the valley of the Allt nan Gleannan to Glen Nevis is best avoided; there are some extremely awkward sections where a bike would have to be carried, including maze-like tree roots, lots of steps and even a steep wooden staircase. Instead, take the road that continues to Fort William from the end of the Lairig Mor track. Even this is no easy finish to the Way. There are still many counter-climbs to come, including three very steep hills that are killers at the end of a long day. When the rooftops of Fort William finally come into view, it will not be before time.

2

THE GAICK

TRACK RECORD

The lonely Gaick (*Gaa*-ick, Cleft), a mere 5 miles (8km) east of Drumochter Pass on the busy A9 and only 30m (100ft) higher, is one of the lowest and most obvious passes between Atholl and Speyside, but surprisingly it has never been used as a major through-route. In the eighteenth century General Wade chose to route his road through Drumochter rather than the Gaick and in the nineteenth century drovers preferred the Minigaig route to both Drumochter and the Gaick in order to avoid the toll house at Dalnacardoch.

There were other compelling reasons to avoid the Gaick, for it has the most evil reputation of any place in the Highlands, a reputation given substance by the number of fatalities that have occurred there over the centuries. 'Black Gaick of the wind-whistling, crooked glens, ever enticing her admirers to their destruction' was how it was described by one eighteenth-century Gaelic bard.

The most infamous incident, known to history as the Loss of Gaick, occurred in the first week of January 1800, when Captain John MacPherson and four companions were killed by an avalanche while on a shooting expedition. MacPherson, known as the 'Black Officer', was for many years the local army recruitment officer and was notorious for his devious recruiting methods. The avalanche, which demolished the bothy in which his party was staying and carried part of the roof for nearly a mile, was seen as a judgement. The incident became the subject of a famous elegy written by the Gaelic bard Duncan Mackay, and a memorial stone now marks the site of the bothy.

Gaick avalanches are legion. Snow from the flat windswept plateaux above accumulates on the steep, uniform, grassy hillsides of the defile and awaits the effect of gravity. Some avalanches are triggered by passing deer. The largest seem to occur in the vicinity of Gaick Lodge

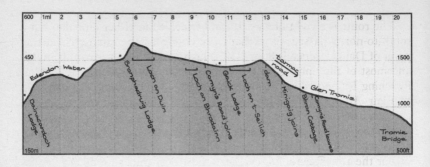

and those on the scale of the one that killed the Black Officer in 1800 are reputed to occur about once a century. Another occurred in 1911, when enormous blocks of snow and ice missed the lodge by metres. The next avalanche should be due within the next decade or two!

As a summer route the Gaick continues to be as enticing as ever as it twists its way through lonely country that has an almost Tibetan quality. The trough that it cuts through the mountains is so deep that the highest point reached en route is only 180m (600ft) above the starting point at Dalnacardoch. Steep frowning hillsides line each side of the defile, drawing the traveller ever onwards into the interior. At every turn there is some new surprise, including no less than three lochs hidden in the heart of the mountains. Land-Rover tracks for most of the way make progress easy. The only problem under normal conditions is the fording of the Allt Loch an Duin, but this is more of a nuisance than a difficulty unless the river is in spate. In all the Gaick is by far the easiest cross-country passage between Atholl and Speyside and has much to offer the discerning off-road adventurer.

ROUTEPLANNER

OS map: 42/35

Start point: Dalnacardoch Lodge (GR 723703)

End point: Tromie Bridge (GR 790995)

Total distance: 21 miles (34km) + Tromie Bridge to Kingussie: 2½ miles (4km)

Total ascent: 240m (800ft); in reverse: 230m (1,050ft)

Total time: 8hr (mb:5hr + halts)

Dalnacardoch: nearest accommodation/provisions/station: Blair Atholl (10 miles/16km); Dalwhinnie (13 miles/21km). Hotel also at Struan (6½ miles/11km). Campsite at Blair Atholl.

Kingussie: hotels, provisions, station, youth hostel, campsite.

The route is a right of way. It can be tackled in either direction but a south-to-north passage is perhaps preferable as the southern starting point of Dalnacardoch is 80m (250ft) higher than Kingussie in the north and most of the uphill is over and done with within the first few miles. Reaching Dalnacardoch by public transport can be awkward: trains stop at Blair Atholl and Dalwhinnie and some buses may stop at Dalnacardoch itself (check with bus companies).

On foot the Gaick is a lengthy single-day walk or a pleasant two-day backpack, with an overnight camp or bivi in the wilds recommended to savour the atmosphere. For cyclists Land-Rover tracks for all but 2 miles (3km) of the route make it a good introduction to mountain biking in the Highlands. Walkers can avoid the tarmaced section of Glen Tromie by using Comyn's Road as a short cut to Kingussie (see p64).

The rail link between Kingussie and Blair Atholl provides a means of returning south and also makes a weekend trip through the Gaick from central Scotland possible for both walkers and mountain bikers. It is possible to take the train to Blair Atholl or Dalwhinnie on Saturday morning, walk or cycle to Dalnacardoch and into the jaws of the Gaick for an overnight camp, then on Sunday continue through to Kingussie and catch the evening train back south.

From Dalwhinnie to Dalnacardoch the A9 provides a fast, mostly downhill run for cyclists, but it can hardly be recommended for safety reasons. Blair Atholl is 3 miles (5km) nearer Dalnacardoch and provides a route that avoids the A9 completely. Two miles (3km) west of Blair Atholl a footbridge over the Garry (GR 871649) gives access to a track that becomes a lovely riverside road to Struan and Calvine, from where the deserted old A9 (now a no-through-road to cars) continues all the way to Dalnacardoch. Note also that at the back of Blair Atholl another footbridge over the Garry gives access to a minor road that continues eastwards beside the river to provide a pleasant route to Killiecrankie and Pitlochry.

If an off-road return route southwards from Kingussie is required, Comyn's Road (route 3) or the Minigaig (Route 4) can be used to complete an excellent circuit. Mountain bikers returning from Kingussie via the A9 can avoid the section between Kingussie and Dalwhinnie by taking the interesting and excellent 6 mile (10km) stretch of Wade road from Ruthven to Etteridge (see p102) and then following a minor road (also Wade's route) to Dalwhinnie.

Those seeking to extend the Gaick into a more extensive off-road expedition can head south-westwards from Dalwhinnie along Loch Ericht (Route 15), north-westwards from Laggan Bridge over the

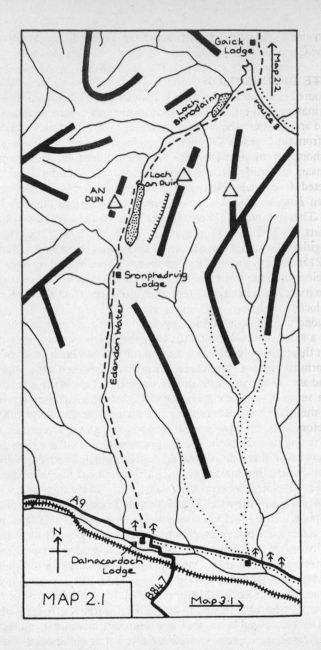

Gaick
Lodge

Map 2.2

route 3

Loch
Bhrodainn

Loch
an Duin

AN
DUN

Sronphadruig
Lodge

Ederdon Water

A9

N

Dalnacardoch
Lodge

B847

Map 3.1 →

MAP 2.1

Corrieyairack (Route 17) or eastwards from Tromie Bridge to Glen Feshie and the Cairngorms (Route 7).

ROUTE DESCRIPTION

The route begins on the A9 near Dalnacardoch Lodge, directly opposite the Trinafour turn-off. A good Land-Rover track climbs steadily through a wood and out onto the bleak moors above the Edendon Water, a world away from the bustling A9.

A short descent takes the track across the Edendon (bridge) and along a pleasant riverside section between glacial moraines, and then a concreted ford leads back across the river to Sronphadruig Lodge (Strawn *Fat*rick, Patrick's Promontory; 5 miles/8km; 2hr/mb:1¼hr + halts). This impressive old building is situated in a small pinewood on the flats at the foot of An Dun (825m/2,707ft), the truncated, rectangular-shaped hill directly ahead. The steep slopes of An Dun rise at least 215m (700ft) above the moor on all sides and it does indeed resemble a dun (an old Celtic fort). Its situation beside Loch an Duin adds to its attractiveness, and it is easily ascended from the southern end of the loch.

Beyond the lodge the track veers left to ford the river once again and end at a small dam. The path through the Gaick appears to go straight on, but this leads only into peat bogs at the head of Loch an Duin. These bogs form the almost imperceptible watershed between Atholl and Speyside and are the highest point of the route; those who stray into them will need a sense of humour to negotiate them with equanimity. Instead, follow the main Land-Rover track across the river for about 200m and then reford the river (which is easily done), looking for cairns on the far bank that indicate the path, which climbs high to avoid the bogs.

Sandwiched in the deep trough between An Dun and Craig an Loch, Loch an Duin is the most dramatic of the Gaick lochs, especially when the wind, funnelled between the peaks, whips the waters into a frenzy. 'High, high, high's the wind, High's the wind upon the Dune' runs an old Gaick poem. Bare islets and underwater rock shelves testify to ancient glacial action. The path is good but it crosses the steep hillside well above the lochside and care is needed: on a bicycle it is quite exposed and only short stretches are ridable. One can well imagine the smooth hillside's avalanche potential under snow.

At the mouth of Loch an Duin the Allt Loch an Duin must be forded. It is normally possible to find a wide shallow stretch of river and sometimes it is even possible to cross dry-shod, but more often than not the ford will result in wet feet. On the far side a new bulldozed Land-Rover

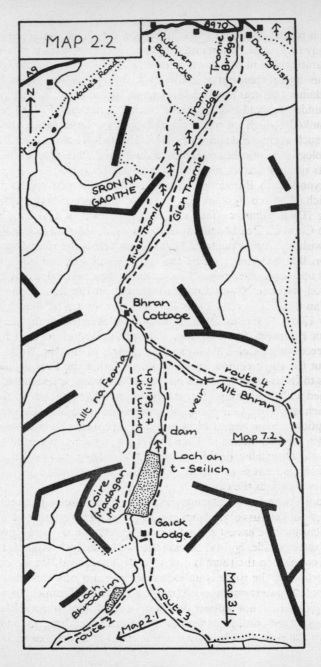

MAP 2.2

A9

Wade's Road

N

Ruthven Barracks

B970

Tromie Bridge

Tromie Lodge

Drumguish

SRON NA GAOITHE

River Tromie

Glen Tromie

Bhran Cottage

Allt na Fearna

Drum an t-Seilich

route 4

Allt Bhran

weir

dam

Map 7.2

Loch an t-Seilich

Coire Madagan Mor

Gaick Lodge

Map 3.2

Loch Bhrodainn

route 3

route 2

Map 2.1

track is picked up almost immediately and the remainder of the route, all the way to Tromie Bridge and Kingussie, is easy. Cyclcists will find it an exhilarating and mostly downhill ride.

The unsurfaced but smooth track sweeps down to lovely Loch Bhrodainn (Vrottan), which is cupped in a twist in the glen and surrounded by bold hills and deep corries. Wade and Telford can never be thanked enough for routing their roads over Drumochter and leaving glens such as this wild and traffic-free. The loch is named after Brodan, a mythological Celtic hound which chased the White Stag of Ben Alder into its swirling waters, where both were lost for ever.

Beyond Loch Bhrodainn another twist in the glen reveals Loch an t-Seilich (*Chell*ich, Willow) ahead, and soon afterwards the Allt Gharbh Ghaig (Owlt *Gharrav Ghaa*-ick, Rough Stream of Gaick) is crossed, where Comyn's Road comes in from the right. Intrepid mountain bikers may wish to keep to the track as it swoops across the river, but, like the author, less ambitious cyclists and walkers will seek out easier crossing places upstream (the bridge 100m upstream was taken down in 1989).

Soon well-kept Gaick Lodge is reached on the flats at the head of Loch an t-Seilich – yet another fine spot surrounded by steep hills ($10\frac{1}{2}$ miles/17km; $4\frac{1}{4}$hr/mb:$3\frac{1}{2}$hr + halts). On the right is the sharp ridge of Sgor Bhothain (Skorr *Vo*-han, Peak of the Bothy), on the left are the deep recesses of Coire Madagan Mor (Corrie of the Big Wolf). Keep a lookout for the memorial stone commemorating the Loss of Gaick – it stands to the right of the track just before the lodge, immediately beyond a ruined walled enclosure. It was erected in 1902 on the site of the bothy in which the Black Officer and his companions perished. The weathered inscription is now almost illegible but is repeated on a metal plaque; it includes the last stanza of Duncan Mackay's Gaelic poem on the incident, which includes the fine couplet: *O duisgibh-se mu'm fas sibh liath, 'S dluithibh bhur cas ris an t-sliabh* (Oh waken before you go grey, Quicken your foot towards the moor).

From Gaick Lodge adventurous walkers may prefer to complete the journey to Kingussie via Comyn's Road on the west side of Loch an t-Seilich, but the easiest route follows the continuing Land-Rover track along the east side. Not far beyond the end of the loch a dam is reached, and from hereon the route is a private tarmaced road. On a bicycle this last section of the route is an extremely pleasant downhill jaunt beside the rippling waters and wooded banks of the River Tromie, but note that Glen Tromie is not known as 'The Glen of the Stormy Blasts' for nothing. At the confluence with the Allt Bhran the Minigaig route comes in from the right. Further down, a fine stand of dwarf juniper is passed, and then the lower glen opens out through woods to reach Tromie Bridge.

Kingussie is only another 2½ miles (4km) away along the B970. En route, atop a roadside knoll, stand the ruins of Ruthven Barracks, which are well worth a look. The English garrison that was stationed here during the Jacobite rebellions succumbed to an assault by Bonnie Prince Charlie in 1746, and the building was burned.

3
COMYN'S ROAD

TRACK RECORD
Comyn's Road is a route of great antiquity, which is now so overgrown in parts that in some places it can only be distinguished by aerial reconnaisance as it crosses the high moorland plateau between the Gaick (Route 2) and the Minigaig (Route 4). Given that you have only a pair of boots or a mountain bike rather than a light aircraft with which to explore it, be assured that it is one of the toughest routes in this book, requiring navigational skill and, especially with a bike, fitness and determination.

Like its close neighbour the Minigaig, which it pre-dates by a considerable time, Comyn's Road was built to link Atholl with Speyside. Its origin can be dated quite specifically to the end of the thirteenth century, when it was built by one of the Comyns of Ruthven, earls of Atholl and Badenoch, to link his castles at Ruthven and Blair. According to tradition the earl was so taken with some ale he had tasted at an inn near Blair that he built a road specifically for the transportation of the brew across the trackless wastes to Ruthven, surely the most capricious and hedonistic reason for building a road.

At this late date it is impossible to know how much Comyn's Road was used for the transportation of ale or other goods, but certainly it and the Minigaig have been well used over the centuries by military expeditions, including Edward I's invasion of Scotland in 1295, Edward III's march from Perth to Speyside to raise the siege of the Castle of Lochindorb in 1336 and the Marquis of Montrose's expeditions in 1644. In 1500 a contract was drawn up between local landowners allowing 'freedom for all and sundry' to come and go as they wished between Atholl and Speyside, proving that there is nothing new about right-of-way issues in the Highlands.

Mountain bikers looking for an historical precedent for taking their bikes onto the old hill tracks need look no further than Comyn's Road,

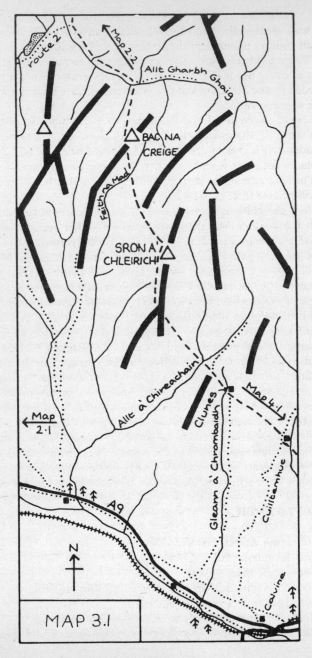

MAP 3.1

for it was specifically built for wheeled transport. There is even a sixteenth-century manuscript that refers to it as the Rad na Pheny (Way of the Waggon Wheels), after the carts that used to pass along it. Today, it is not so easily negotiable, even by the seventeenth century it had been superseded by the Minigaig and the intervening years have not improved its state of preservation.

The 'road' today has Land-Rover tracks at its Blair Atholl end and along a stretch it shares with the Gaick, but elsewhere it is an adventure. The moors that it crosses are remote, uncairned and achingly lonely. In some places the route is no more than an overgrown terrace on the hillside, in other places it has been completely lost and only an expert navigator will be able to keep to its line.

On foot the going is mostly good on short moorland turf and paths through the heather, but there are several rougher sections and some appreciable ascents, including a 380m (1,250ft) climb up to the high point of the route close to the summit of Sron a' Chleirich (Strawn a' Chleerich, Nose of the Priest; 816m/2,677ft). Mountain bikers will find the route one of the toughest in the Highlands. There are several long unridable sections where wheel-grabbing heather makes pushing strenuous, while struggling uphill through the heather with a bike on your shoulder is no easy alternative. Only fit and capable mountain bikers should aspire to tackling the ancient Way of the Waggon Wheels.

In adverse weather Comyn's Road is an extraordinarily bleak and demanding route that requires accurate compass work on the featureless moors, and in such conditions or after rain, when some sections can get quite boggy, it is best avoided altogether, especially by mountain bikers. At such times the moors are no place for humans. Comyn's Road should be saved for a good day, when it is a haunting route that has a wonderful air of spaciousness and the feel of the Middle Ages about it. It may not be in as pristine a state as it once was, but this fine old road deserves to be more widely known before it disappears from the landscape for ever.

ROUTEPLANNER
OS map: 43/42/35
Start point: Blair Atholl (GR 877655)
End point: Kingussie (GR 756766)
Total distance: 27 miles (43km)
Total ascent: 1,150m (3,770ft); in reverse: 1,230m (4,030ft)
Total time: 14hr (mb: 13½hr) + halts
Blair Atholl: accommodation/provisions/station/campsite.
Kingussie: accommodation/provisions/station/youth hostel/campsite.

The route is not a right of way and crosses high moors that are used extensively for deer stalking and grouse shooting. Atholl Estates have no objection to the use of the road outside the critical period of the stalking season (mid-August to mid-October), but visitors are asked to behave responsibly and, if in doubt about access, to contact the estate office at Blair Atholl (tel: 079-681-355).

Bothies en route: Clunes (GR 800726). There is little to choose between a south-to-north and north-to-south crossing of Comyn's Road as the highest points of the route are roughly equidistant from each end and the gradients on either side are comparable. A Blair Atholl start has the disadvantage of being 100m lower than Kingussie, but the Land-Rover track up Glen Banvie compensates for this, at least for mountain bikers.

Whether on foot or mountain bike only the superfit should contemplate tackling Comyn's Road as a single-day expedition. An over-night camp makes it less strenuous, but it remains a tough route and the featureless moors are no place for inexperienced walkers or mountain bikers to venture. Mountain bikers especially will not find the route a rewarding experience unless they are extremely fit and skilled.

Considerations of return routes between Kingussie and Blair Atholl and extensions to the route to link it into a longer expedition are as for the Gaick (see p51).

ROUTE DESCRIPTION

To avoid Blair Castle and its grounds, which obscure the original beginning of Comyn's Road, take the minor road from Blair Atholl to Old Blair, following the river Tilt to Old Bridge of Tilt and then turning left to reach a crossroads (GR 868667), where tarmaced roads go left and right and an unsurfaced track continues straight on. Turn left, then keep right past St Bride's church, passing under a dry arch that spans the road and crossing the bridge over the Banvie Burn.

About 50m beyond the bridge take the Land-Rover track on the right that climbs steadily through the trees high above the west bank of the Banvie Burn. The river lies hidden deep within its wooded gorge but comes into view as the track levels off to meet it at Rumbling Bridge, an old (1762) bridge beneath which are some interesting rock pools and cascades. Across the bridge on the far bank of the Banvie Burn is the Minigaig track, but Comyn's Road stays on the west bank. Continuing beside the river it reaches the edge of the woods, where a right fork descends to another old bridge across the Banvie Burn. This is the Quarry Bridge, built in 1770 with stones from an old quarry a short distance upstream. The Minigaig is still in view on the far bank of the river but is about to branch away to pursue its own route to Ruthven.

Keeping to the west bank of the river, the track becomes rougher as it leaves the wood behind and climbs gently across the moor to the watershed between Glen Banvie and Glen Bruar. After passing the confluence with the Allt na Moine Baine, look for the old path that zigzags up the hillside across the river. The hill is called Tom nan Cruach (Hill of the Peat Stacks) and the path was formerly used to collect peat for the fires of Blair Castle. Looking back, there is a fine view over the trees to Ben Vrackie. Further up the Banvie, again across the river, can be seen the extensive dykes, ruins and green fields of Chapeltown. At one time several families lived here, but now only the simple word 'shieling' on the OS map betrays the presence of this once large settlement.

At the watershed the track enters another wood; leave it here to take a bumpy right branch that crosses the moor and descends past the dilapidated cottage at Ruichlachrie into Glen Bruar. The Bruar Water is surprisingly easily crossed, normally dry-shod, owing to hydro-electric works upstream, and on the far bank you reach the boarded-up cottage of Cuilltemhuc and the track up Glen Bruar from Calvine to Bruar Lodge (6 miles/10km; 2½hr/mb: 1½hr + halts).

An old tale tells of the laughing man of Cuilltemhuc, who was one day found drunk in a water trough, laughing at some private joke that he never ever divulged. Perhaps he had some premonition of the adventures that await those seeking a continuation of Comyn's Road, for ahead now rises a low heather ridge that has no trace of a path. The route goes straight over the ridge to Clunes Bothy in Gleann a' Chrombaidh (Chromby), but navigation is complicated by the fact that Clunes is on the next OS map. A compass bearing of 315° will find the most direct line.

At Clunes you join the Land-Rover track from the A9 up Gleann a' Chrombaidh. It swings left to follow the line of Comyn's Road over another low ridge into the glen of the Allt a' Chireachain, in whose steep-sided gorge can be seen the numerous ruins of the Kirrichan Shielings. The short stretch of track between the two glens is a welcome respite before the climb ahead, for beyond the Allt a' Chireachain rises the great moorland dome of Sron a' Chleirich, towards whose summit Comyn's Road makes a bee-line.

To negotiate the gorge of the Allt a' Chireachain walkers can leave the Land-Rover track when it bears right up the glen and descend steep heather to cross the river near the ruined shielings. Mountain bikers should stay on the track until a rough side track cuts back left down to

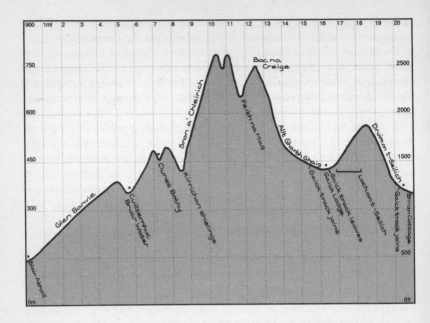

the river just above the shielings. It is normally possible to cross the river dry-shod. The sheer number of ruined dwellings in so remote a spot comes as a surprise, and once can only wonder at what life here must have been like when they were inhabited (8 miles/13km; 3¾hr/mb: 2¾ + halts).

From the Kirrichans walkers can ascend Sron a' Chleirich directly. No trace of the road remains on this side of the Sron and so it is a case of picking your own way up the Nose. With a bike it is best to aim further left to avoid the steepest section, seeking grassy stream banks among the heather in order to make pushing easier. Once onto the south-west ridge of the Sron the going is good on short turf, but there is no avoiding the peat bogs at the foot of the ridge. Mountain bikers may well resort to carrying their bikes some of the way; it is the toughest section of the route.

Nearing the summit plateau of Sron a' Chleirich look for the overgrown terrace on the left that marks the continuation of the ancient road across the hillside west of the summit. The high point of the whole route is reached soon afterwards, less than five minutes' walk from the summit trig point. The view from the summit must be one of the most spacious in the Highlands, with a wonderful panorama north-eastwards to the High Cairngorms and southwards and westwards across the Central Highlands to the distant peaks of Glen Coe. It is a surprisingly fine vista for such a small peak, one that it owes to its prime position on the edge of the Grampians. The immediate vicinity, on the other hand, is relentlessly bleak – a hauntingly remote spot surrounded by seemingly endless moorland.

From its high point Comyn's Road descends diagonally across a very steep hillside to cross the Allt a' Mhuilinn (Voolin, Mill). There is a very narrow and exposed path along the terrace; great care is needed if you are attempting to cycle it, especially near the stream crossing itself, where landslides have carried the terrace away. One wonders what it must have been like for fourteenth-century carts in this wonderfully wild country.

On the far side of the stream the road climbs left and then right again across the brow of the next moorland top before descending steeply to cross the Feith na Mad (Fee na Maad, possibly Stream of the Dog). On this section the path becomes increasingly difficult to follow and eventually disappears altogether, but you should keep going in a straight line towards the grassy terrace that can be seen climbing Bac na Creige (Bachk na Craiga, Bank of the Crag) on the far side of the Feith na Mad. the going is mainly good except in the vicinity of Feith na Mad itself, where the tussocky heather is especially frustrating with a bike.

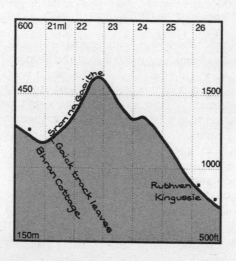

One last steep climb up the grassy terrace puts you on the flat summit ridge of Bac na Creige, where the path reappears to guide you through the heather. Keep a lookout for the place where it bears left to take a diagonal line down off the moors into the glen of the Allt Gharbh Ghaig (Owlt *Gharrav Ghaa*-ick, Rough Stream of Gaick). The path disappears on the grassy hillside but the terrace teasingly reappears to stretch your trail-finding abilities. As for its riding potential, it is so bumpy that any attempt to cycle it while remaining in the saddle could ruin any parental aspirations. It was around here that Walter Comyn met his end when he became unseated from his horse and was dragged along until his leg was severed from his body. The incident was seen as just retribution for his decree that all women between the ages of 12 and 30 should work naked in the fields.

The steep final descent to the Allt Gharbh Ghaig needs care as landslides have again taken their toll on the road over the centuries, but a new path has been cut into the hillside to ease the going. The river is crossed by a bridge and suddenly you find yourself on flat ground deep in the glen. From the right a path comes in from the direction of the Minigaig (see p72), but the route onwards to Kingussie goes left downstream. The path is now good to walk but it remains obstinately awkward to ride for about a mile, until the glen widens and a Land-Rover track is reached.

A further mile and two stream crossings later you reach the Gaick Land-Rover track and, about one mile further along, Gaick Lodge (16 miles/26km; 8hr/mb:7½hr + halts). Both walkers and mountain bikers may have had enough of the moors by now and may find it difficult to ignore the continuing Gaick track which leads out of the wilderness all the way to Tromie Bridge and Kingussie, but, true to form, Comyn's Road takes an altogether more direct route to Kingussie and eventually heads for the hills again. This final section of the route involves two more ascents and much pathless wandering across the moors. The going underfoot remains relatively good and there are fine views to be had, but trail-finding abilities will be exercised like never before. Unless they have masochistic tendencies, mountain bikers should stick to the Gaick track.

At Gaick Lodge Comyn's Road leaves the Gaick track and crosses the Allt Loch an Duin to reach the west side of Loch an t-Seilich. The exact route is no longer known, but follow the perimeter fence around the lodge to avoid the private grounds and cross the modern bridge over the Allt Loch an Duin. Continue across the grassy flats at the head of the loch to the stream that comes down from Coire Madagan Mor and then take a sheep path that climbs steadily away from the loch, taking a diagonal line up onto the flat moor of Maol an t-Seilich (Moel an Chellich, Hill of the Willow).

Infrequent cairns and the finely graded ascent indicate that you are on Comyn's Road once more, even if it is difficult to imagine this narrow, rocky path through the heather ever carrying cartloads of ale with any success. In a heatwave such as that which prevailed when I last explored the route, with the loch surface reflecting like a mirror and the hillsides shimmering with haze, little of the beverage would have been left by the time Ruthven was reached. The view back over the loch to the jaws of the Gaick is magnificent.

The path eventually climbs more steeply to its high point, marked by a prominent cairn, and then takes a level course right of the crest of Maol an t-Seilich. After a while it crosses to the left of the crest and descends the broad ridge of Druim an t-Seilich (Drum, Ridge) to regain the Gaick track, now a tarmaced road, at Bhran Cottage in Glen Tromie (20 miles/33km; 10½hr/mb: 10½hr + halts). The line of the route becomes so indistinct that it is best seen from the air; if (or perhaps when) you lose it descend further left to follow an earthy Land-Rover track that runs beside the Allt na Fearna to Bhran Cottage. The River Tromie is crossed by a bridge just south of the cottage to reach the Gaick road on its east bank. The whole section of Comyn's Road between Gaick Lodge and Bhran Cottage can be bypassed by using the Gaick road.

The original line of Comyn's Road did not cross the Tromie at Bhran Cottage, it stayed instead on the west bank of the river, where it is still possible to follow sheep paths. Only purists will do so, however, when there is a tarmaced road on the other side and another bridge one mile along that enables you to regain the west side. At this next bridge Comyn's Road leaves the Gaick road for good to cross the low hills that separate Glen Tromie from Speyside. It climbs diagonally up the hillside past Carn Pheigith (Peggy's Cairn), said to commemorate a fourteenth-century suicide, and across the saddle north of Sron na Gaoithe (Strawn na Goo-y, Nose of the Wind). You will be unlikely to spot either Peggy's Cairn or the road, which is an overgrown, barely discernible terrace through the heather that only a diligent search will reveal.

On the saddle near Sron na Gaoithe a path that comes from the now non-existent bridge over the Tromie at GR 763936 joins Comyn's Road to make the route discernible again. It still requires route-finding ability in places, but with your hard-won experience of the alignments of Comyn's Road it should be possible to follow its line all the way. It descends round Beinn Bhuidhe (*Voo*-ya, Yellow), where it resumes its terrace-like appearance, and is mostly a fast tramp.

Soon Kingussie is in sight at last. The path joins another path that comes over the hill from Glentromie Lodge and makes a bee-line for Ruthven. Beyond the Burn of Ruthven, Comyn's Road at last becomes the cart track it originally was for its last short descent to the roadside just east of Ruthven Barracks (26 miles/42km; 13½hr/mb:13½hr + halts), and from here it is a short walk along the B970 into Kingussie.

4
THE MINIGAIG

TRACK RECORD

The Minigaig is the most easterly of the three routes that cross the moors
east of Drumochter Pass, and like its close neighbour, Comyn's Road, it
is an altogether more strenuous and exciting affair than the Gaick. The
name Minigaig (Meeny *Gaa*-ick) is a puzzle. *Gaick* derives from the
Gaelic *gag* (cleft), but *mini* is open to several possible interpretations. It
may derive from *moine* (moss), *mion* (small) or *min* (level), but there are
no clefts on the Minigaig and there is nothing that is small or level about
it.

Minigaig is the highest route in this book, reaching a height of 836m
(2,745ft) on the desolate plateau between Glen Bruar and Glen Tromie,
where the wonderfully wild moorland is perhaps the bleakest and most
featureless terrain crossed by any major Scottish hill track. The path
bypasses the very highest points on the moor to seek shelter from the
elements, giving some sections of the route a peculiarly closed-in aspect
that adds to one's feeling of being a mere speck of humanity, in the vast
uncaring wilderness.

Before Wade built his road over Drumochter Pass in the 1720s the
Minigaig was the main route between Atholl and Speyside, replacing its
forerunner, Comyn's Road, some time before the end of the sixteenth
century. As a route between Blair and Kingussie it is some 15 miles
(24km) shorter than Drumochter, 9 miles (15km) shorter than the Gaick
and even slightly shorter than Comyn's Road. It climbs much higher
than Drumochter, but to the hardy Highlanders of old, directness was far
more important than the amount of ascent involved. The fact that its
highest reaches were blocked in winter was also of little consequence as
there was little winter communication between settlements.

After the building of the Drumochter road the Minigaig fell into dis-
repair, although troops continued to use it as a shortcut until after the

1745 Jacobite rising. It was almost reprieved as the premier Grampian crossing in the early nineteenth century when Telford considered building a modern road over it as a shorter alternative to Drumochter, but its height militated against it and the Drumochter road was improved instead. As a result of the Drumochter improvements a roadside toll house was established at Dalnacardoch in 1821, and this prompted cattle drovers to use the Minigaig instead in order to avoid paying.

The Minigaig had other attractions for drovers, including its directness, its lack of tarmac and lush grazings at places such as Coire Bhran, and even after the Dalnacardoch toll house closed in 1878 they continued to use the route until the end of the droving trade at the beginning of the twentieth century. This caused much consternation for Atholl Estate, which vainly attempted to stop the drovers or else to charge them for use of the land, but the drovers insisted on their right of way and continued their trade undaunted.

Today, the Minigaig still carries a good path for most of its length and remains in a good state for walkers. The path and the more gentle ascents make it a slightly easier route than Comyn's Road, but it remains a major expedition, especially with a mountain bike, which must be pushed for most of the central section.

As on Comyn's Road the featureless moors are no place to be caught out in adverse weather, and only fit, experienced and capable navigators should contemplate tackling it. Even in high summer, conditions on the moors can deteriorate rapidly and it is worth remembering that many have died here. Perhaps the worst tragedy, according to folklore, was the loss of a company of soldiers during the manoeuvres of 1745. Needless to say, the Minigaig is best avoided when the weather is foul or there is snow on the ground (even a light dusting can obliterate the path).

On a personal note, I have had my fair share of close encounters with intransigent Minigaig weather. On one particularly wet, chilly autumn day a companion and I spent an uncomfortable and dispiriting hour in the Allt Schiecheachan Bothy desperatelytrying to coax a few flickering flames from some damp twigs of heather. After failing to generate any semblance of heat we set off again to get our circulation moving, only to be immediately faced with the Allt Schiecheachan in spate. The crossing of this stream is a normally simple manoeuvre that for some reason I have yet to accomplish with dignity and dry feet, and on this particular day no amount of stepping-stone construction could avoid a further wetting. We eventually succumbed to a bedraggled bivi in Glen Bruar and awoke the following morning to see new snow on the hills and horizontal sleet driving down the glen. We were ignominiously driven back down the glen to Blair Atholl, glad to have survived the capricious Minigaig.

ROUTEPLANNER
OS map: 43/42/35
Start point: Blair Atholl (GR 877655)
End point: Kingussie (GR 756766)
Total distance: 26 miles (42km)
Total ascent: 1,020m (3,350ft); in reverse: 1,120m (3,675ft)
Total time: 12½hr (mb:11½hr) + halts
Blair Atholl: accommodation/provisions/station/campsite.
Kingussie: accommodation/provisions/station/youth hostel/campsite.

Bothies en route: Allt Schiecheachan (GR 835737). The route is a right of way but like Comyn's Road it crosses high ground that is extensively used for deer stalking and should be avoided from mid-August to mid-October. If you are in doubt about access, contact Atholl Estates Office at Blair Atholl (tel: 079-681-355).

As with Comyn's Road there is little to choose between a south-to-north and a north-to-south crossing. Blair Atholl in the south is 100m (330ft) lower than Kingussie in the north, but excellent Land-Rover tracks and paths on the south side of the central moorland section make ascent easier, especially with a mountain bike. A south-to-north crossing also gives you the option of opting out of the last section from Glen Tromie to Kingussie by taking the private tarmaced road along Glen Tromie.

Again, like Comyn's Road, only the fittest should contemplate tackling the Minigaig as a single-day expedition, and even a two-day backpack/bikepack still requires fitness and hillcraft. The inexperienced should not venture onto the moors, and only the fittest and most skilled of mountain bikers will find it a rewarding endeavour.

Considerations of return routes between Kingussie and Blair Atholl and extensions to the route to link it into a longer expedition are as for the Gaick (see p51).

ROUTE DESCRIPTION
From Blair Atholl take the minor road to Old Blair and across the Old Bridge of Tilt to the crossroads at GR 868667, as for Comyn's Road. Go straight on at the crossroads along an unsurfaced track that climbs through mixed woodland and rhododendron bushes beside the Banvie Burn. On reaching a higher track the old Minigaig route branches right

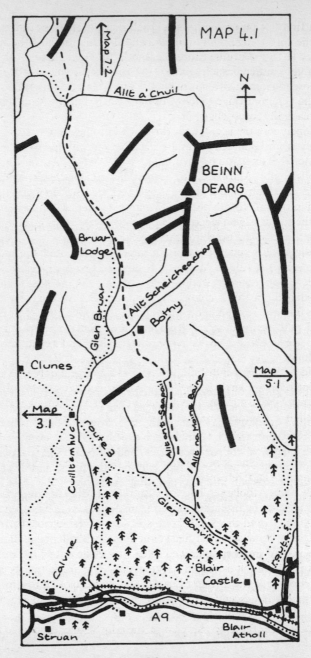

MAP 4.1

N

Allt a'Chuil

BEINN
DEARG

Bruar
Lodge

Glen Bruar

Allt Scheicheachan

Bothy

Map 7·2

Map
5·1

Clunes

Map
3·1

Cuilltemhuc

route 3

Allt an t-Seapoil

Allt na Meine Baine

Glen Banvie

Calvine

Blair
Castle

route 5

A9

Struan

Blair
Atholl

70

and then first left on an overgrown track that degenerates into a boggy path at the forest edge. Only purists will take this route as the modern track goes left to continue more pleasantly up Glen Banvie. At a fork beyond a gate either branch will do, the left taking you past Rumbling Bridge close to Comyn's Road (see p60). The next left branch crosses the river at the Quarry Bridge to join Comyn's Road, but the Minigaig keeps right to reach the forest edge.

Once open country is reached, the track becomes rougher as it bears right away from Glen Banvie and rises more steeply up the glen of the Allt na Moine Baine (Moan-ya Ban-ya, White Moss). At the top of the rise stands Lady March Cairn, a prominent landmark that commemorates nothing more than a spot where the eponymous lady picnicked in the nineteenth century. Mountain bikers will find the earthy track to the forest edge a steady and pleasant ascent, but the climb up to Lady March Cairn is a much tougher proposition.

Immediately beyond the cairn the modern track and the old path reunite to cross the Allt na Moine Baine and make a long leisurely climb across the moor into the shallow glen of the Allt an t-Seapail (pronounced chapel, meaning: chapel). Keep a look-out for the old trackside milestone that marks the 3 mile (5km) point from Old Blair. Just beyond it the old path again diverges from the new track to cross the upper slopes of Meall Dubh (Myowl Doo, Black Hill) and rejoin the track further along.

The old path is very indistinct and will again appeal only to Minigaig purists, but note the large cairn that it passes as it crosses Meall Dubh. This is Carn Mhic Shimidh, which commemorates a battle between the men of Atholl and some Fraser raiders. The Frasers were returning home from a successful raid when they heard a cock crow. As they had sworn to leave no living things, a few men were sent to dispatch the bird. During this foray some Atholl men attacked and overcame them, dressed in their clothes and returned to the unsuspecting main Fraser party. Meanwhile other Atholl men had arrived from the direction of Bruar and the Frasers found themselves attacked from both sides. Few survived.

Some 40m beyond the 3 milestone and 15m to the left of the track is hidden another stone slab that marks the Fuaran Bhadenoch (Badenoch Well), a beautiful small circular well filled with clear water; the well may be hard to find but it is worth seeking out. The track makes a long sweeping run beside the Allt an t-Seapail and then crosses it to climb over the watershed and descend to the Allt Scheicheachan and its welcoming bothy, which has stood on this spot since 1881.

The track veers right up the glen of the Allt Scheicheachan to climb onto the moors south of Beinn Dearg (*Jerr*ak, Red), the remote Munro on the west side of Glen Bruar whose stony summit plateau often takes on the colour that gives it its Gaelic name. The Minigaig leaves the track at this point to cross the stream and pursue a course northwards into Glen Bruar, beginning as a narrow path that climbs through the heather onto an outlying spur of Beinn Dearg. About 100m beyond the bothy stands yet another large ramshackle pathside cairn that is said to commemorate a shepherd who was murdered here over three hundred years ago.

The crest of the spur is a fine vantage point with good views both up and down Glen Bruar, a great trench of a glen that sweeps past Bruar Lodge to push deep into the barrier of hills that bars the way to Speyside. The path descends into the glen and crosses riverside flats to reach the Land-Rover track up the glen at Bruar Lodge, a still inhabited building that was built in 1789 to replace a smaller lodge further up the glen. Avoid the private grounds of the lodge by keeping left around the perimeter fence to rejoin the track on the far side.

NB   The Glen Bruar track offers an alternative start to the Minigaig (see p75).

The whole of this first section of the Minigaig from Blair Atholl to Glen Bruar gives excellent mountain biking, with varied terrain and ascents and descents of all gradients. As far as Allt Schiecheachan Bothy it is possible to stay in the saddle nearly all the way, and some of it is very pleasant riding indeed. The climb out from the bothy involves a short push, but the descent into Glen Bruar is mostly ridable and is a good test of skill.

From Bruar Lodge the Land-Rover track continues up Glen Bruar between steepening hillsides, passing Loch Bruar, an artificial lake that was formed in 1912 for trout fishing, and rounding craggy Creag na h-Iolair Mhor (Hillyer Voar, Big Eagle) to reach the hidden upper glen. The track has quite a good surface but is very rutted, channelling so much water after heavy rain that sub-aqua gear may be necessary; mountain bikers need to be watchful of pedal clearance. At the end of the glen an impasse is reached beneath the steep heathery slopes of Uchd a' Chlarsair (*Ooch*ka *Chlaar*sir, Brow of the Harper), which rises ahead to block the way forward. The Bruar Water divides into two streams, the Feith Ghorm Ailleag and the Allt a' Chuil, which rise on the moors west and east of Uchd a' Chlarsair respectively. The track crosses the Allt a' Chuil (bridge) and comes to an abrupt half (11 miles/17km; 5hr/mb:3½hr + halts).

A path continues, taking the Minigaig high onto the moors to find a direct route to Glen Tromie many miles distant. The initial climb is steep and rough; bikes will probably have to be carried. Ignore the indistinct cairned path that branches right along the Allt a' Chuil after a short distance (this leads only to an old shieling upstream); instead continue straight ahead to a major Y-shaped fork higher up. The left branch here crosses a low watershed to join Comyn's Road (only 3 miles (5km) away) at the Allt Gharbh Ghaig not far from Gaick Lodge. There is a 1 mile pathless section at the watershed but it is nevertheless a useful escape route for those who, through a change of mind or weather, prefer not to tackle the next and hardest section of the Minigaig.

The Minigaig path goes right at the fork, leaving behind the shelter and safety of the glens to climb onto the high, desolate, empty, wind-swept moors. Pause for one last look at Glen Bruar, at the waterfall on the Allt a' Chuil and at the extensive summit plateau of Beinn Dearg before you knuckle down to the ascent. From the end of Glen Bruar to the first high point of the route near the summit of Uchd a' Chlarsair is a climb of 240m (790ft). The path is rough at first, but once the first steepening is passed it improves beyond all imagining to become a lovely route across short springy heather.

From Uchd a' Chlarsair the path descends to the Caochan Lub (*Kai*ochan Loob, Meandering Streamlet) and begins to deteriorate; from hereon it becomes increasingly overgrown as it plies its lonely moorland way to Glen Tromie and the true magnitude of the adventure you have undertaken becomes increasingly apparent. The shallow glen of the Caochan Lub is unusually well formed and grassy considering its situation high on the moor, and as the path proceeds along it the extensive views that one might expect at this height are cut off by rising ground all around. It is a peculiarly confined and claustrophobic section of the route compared to the vast open spaces of nearby Comyn's Road, but the shelter it affords is often welcome and may well have been a factor in the growth of the Minigaig as an alternative to Comyn's Road. It is easy to lose the path in some parts; if you do so remember that it stays well above the stream.

The path follows the Caochan Lub for some distance before crossing it and rising across the moor to the highest point of the route. This last uphill section is very indistinct and would be difficult to follow were it not cairned. The high point itself is a disappointingly featureless spot on the south shoulder of Leathad an Taobhain (*Lay*-at an *Tai*vin, Slope of the Rafter; 902m/2,960ft) its only redeeming feature being the northern vista that opens up over the descent route to Glen Tromie.

Note that from here there is a way down into Glen Feshie that for

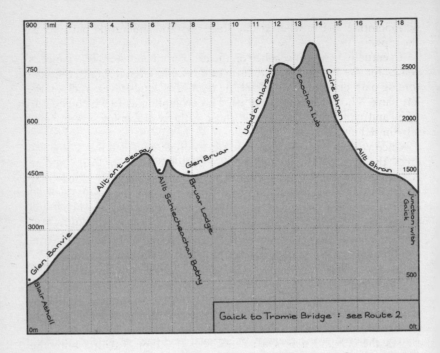

Gaick to Tromie Bridge : see Route 2

mountain bikers is much easier than the continuing Minigaig path. By climbing over the summit of Leathad an Taobhain to the next summit (912m/2,993ft; unnamed on the 1:50,000 map), a path will be found that heads across the plateau to the summit of Meall an Uillt Chreagaich (847m/2,779ft). From here a Land-Rover track descends all the way into Glen Feshie. It is a tempting alternative, for although the Minigaig path looks easier on the map, and indeed is so for walkers, it becomes a very narrow route through the entangling heather and is very awkward to negotiate if you are encumbered with a bike.

From its high point the Minigaig begins its descent into Glen Tromie by descending diagonally across the steep north-western slopes of Leathad an Taobhain beside the deep recess of Coire Bhran (Vran, Raven). It was here that drovers used to congregate before tackling the moors on their way southwards. The path eventually reaches the Allt Bhran, which drains the corrie, and runs beside it through a great open heather-clad valley all the way to Glen Tromie. It becomes just one more sheep path through the heather, not even cairned any longer, and is a

74

disappointing end to what at one stage was an exhilarating path across the tops.

Eventually, a weir is reached on the Allt Bhran and there is a choice of routes for the last mile to the tarmaced road in Glen Tromie: the continuing path on the right bank of the river or a Land-Rover track on the left bank. Those with bikes will need no prompting as to which route to take, and neither, I suspect, will those without (19 miles/30km; 9hr/mb:8hr + halts).

Once you are into Glen Tromie the Minigaig joins Comyn's Road to cross the River Tromie and head across the hills to Ruthven and Kingussie (see p65). It will be difficult to motivate yourself to leave the tarmaced road and climb up onto the pathless moors once again, but this is the historic line for those intent on finishing the Minigaig as it was meant to be finished. The alternative is a 5½ mile (9km) walk out to Tromie Bridge and Kingussie along the pleasant Glen Tromie road, and mountain bikers especially will find this an infinitely easier route.

Alternative Route into Glen Bruar

The Glen Bruar Land-Rover track begins at Calvine 4 miles (7km) west of Blair Atholl; it is a right of way and is worth noting as an alternative start to the Minigaig or an emergency escape route. From Calvine it crosses the A9 and makes a steep climb of 320m (1,050ft) onto the shoulder of Creag Bhagailteach, from where there is a fine view along Glen Bruar to the rolling plateau summit of Beinn Dearg. A descent of 100m (330ft) follows to Cuilltemhuc cottage, where Comyn's Road crosses the track, and then the track keeps close beside the river as it snakes its way up the glen to Bruar Lodge and beyond.

The track provides drier and easier going than the Blair Atholl approach described above, but the crossing of Creag Bhagailteach is steep and rough and much unnecessary height is gained and lost. The Blair Atholl approach is also more interesting historically and scenically. In general the Calvine approach has little to recommend it except perhaps as an interesting circuit for mountain bikers in combination with the Blair Atholl approach. Note also that above Calvine is a 3 mile (5km) section of Wade road that includes the Drochaid na h-Uinneige (see p23).

5
GLEN TILT

TRACK RECORD
The great trench formed by the River Tilt as it carves its way through the southern Grampians has been a major line of communication between Atholl and Deeside for centuries. It is easy to follow, contains no steep climbs and at its high point is only 510m (1,675ft) above sea level. At one time part of the route was even maintained as a road by statute labour.

Perhaps no other hill track except the Corrieyairack is as well documented by travellers of old, and opinions on its merits appear to have been mixed. That redoubtable traveller Sarah Murray found it 'beautiful' when she visited the glen in 1796, and Queen Victoria thought her journey through it from Blair to Balmoral in 1848, 'the pleasantest and most enjoyable expedition I have *ever* made.' 'Oh! what can equal the beauties of nature!' she enthused in her journal. Thomas Pennant, on the other hand, the thought the glen a 'wild, black, moory, melancholy tract' and described his 1769 journey through it as 'the most dangerous and horrible' he had ever done.

Since those days the internal combustion engine has transformed communication in the Highlands and Glen Tilt has been bypassed by the motor car, for which all lovers of hill tracks should be eternally thankful. Since 1853 it has been legally recognised as a right of way after a famous court case in which the newly formed Scottish Rights of Way Society brought a successful action against the 6th Duke of Atholl for refusing passage to Professor Balfour of Edinburgh and his party of botany students. The case was the making of the society, whose work remains as important today as ever.

The modern route through Glen Tilt is one of the most straight-forward long-distance hill tracks in the Highlands, and mountain bikers will find the Land-Rover tracks at each end especially inviting. Note that the complete journey between Braemar and Blair Atholl is a lengthy 28 miles (45km), however, and involves at least one major river crossing.

ROUTEPLANNER

OS map: 43
Start point: Linn of Dee (GR 062897)
End point: Blair Atholl (GR 877655)
Total distance: 22 miles (35km) + Braemar to Linn of Dee: 6 miles
   (10km)
Total ascent: 200m (650ft); in reverse: 430m (1,400ft)
Total time: 9hr (mb:5hr) + halts + Braemar to Linn of Dee: 2hr
   (mb:1hr)
Braemar: accommodation/provisions/youth hostel/campsite.
Blair Atholl: accommodation/provisions/station/campsite.
There is also a youth hostel at Inverey near Linn of Dee.

The route is a right of way. Between Blair Atholl and Marble Lodge the
right of way follows the path from Fenderbridge along the east side of the
glen, but Atholl Estates have no objection to the use of the Land-Rover
track that begins on the west side near Old Bridge of Tilt (GR 874663).
Permission to take a car along the track can be obtained from Atholl
Estates Office at Blair Atholl (tel: 079-681-355).

There is a Land-Rover track for all but the central 3 mile (5km)
section across the watershed, making the route a straightforward proposition in either direction. Only at the watershed are there likely to be any
route-finding problems in mist. The whole route stays surprisingly dry
even after heavy rain, but the Geldie Burn, which must be forded, can be
very awkward when it is swollen.

Linn of Dee is 230m (750ft) higher than Blair Atholl and the climb
from there to the high point of the route is only 140m (460ft); the route
is therefore described in a north-to-south direction in order to minimise
ascent. Mountain bikers will find a north-to-south crossing especially
attractive, not only because of the height differential but also because the
path on the north side of the watershed is good enough to be ridden
uphill most of the way. The path on the south side is more awkward to
ride, especially the very narrow and exposed section through the
Garrabuie, which needs great care.

The complete journey from Braemar to Blair Atholl is a tough single-
day expedition on account of its length, but private transport at either
end reduces the distance considerably and puts it within reach of reasonably fit walkers. By mountain bike it is an easy and exhilarating single-
day run.

There are no easy off-road return routes from one end of the route to
the other, and indeed no short return road routes either.

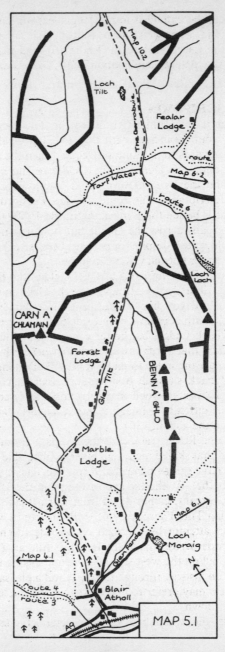

Loch Tilt

Map 10.2

Fealar Lodge

route 6

The Tarrabuie

Map 6.2

Tarf Water

route 6

Loch Loch

CARN A' CHLAMAIN

Forest Lodge

Glen Tilt

BEINN A' GHLO

Marble Lodge

Map 6.1

Glen Fender

Loch Moraig

Map 4.1

N

route 4

route 3

Blair Atholl

A9

MAP 5.1

Glen Tilt can be extended into a longer expedition by combining it with one of the trans-Cairngorm routes such as the Lairig Ghru (Route 9) or the Lairig an Laoigh (Route 10), and it also makes a fine circuit from the A9 in combination with Glen Feshie/Glen Geldie (Route 7).

ROUTE DESCRIPTION

From Braemar it is 13 miles (21km) to the Tilt watershed. The first section of the route coincides with that to Glen Geldie, following the public road westwards to the Linn of Dee and then the continuing Land-Rover track beside the Dee and the Geldie to the confluence of the Geldie Burn and the Bynack Burn about 1 mile beyond White Bridge (see p96 for description). The route to Glen Tilt fords the Geldie and heads southwards beside the Bynack. Until the 1970s there used to be a bridge of four spans across the Geldie but now it is necessary to wade through the cold water; despite (or perhaps because of) its width the ford is not difficult under normal water conditions.

On leaving the bleak horizons of Glen Geldie, the Bynack Burn and its meandering tributary the Allt an t-Seilich (Owlt an Chellich, Stream of the Willow) lead you into a landscape of rolling hills of grass and heather. The old path goes up the west side of the river and crosses to the east side at Bynack Lodge, but better going will be found on the newer Land-Rover track that fords the Bynack just before it joins the Geldie and continues past the lodge to end 2 miles (3km) along the glen at GR 998838. The Bynack is usually easier to ford than the Geldie. The ruined lodge and the devastated wood that surrounds it present such a forlorn picture that it is difficult to imagine Queen Victoria taking tea here on her way through the glen in 1861.

When the Land-Rover track ends the old path continues, narrow but so well surfaced that skilled mountain bikers will be able to ride it most of the way to the large grassy plain that forms the Tilt watershed (7 miles/ 11km; 3hr/mb:2hr). At the far end of the plain the Dubh Alltan (Doo *Owlt*an, Black Stream) comes down from Carn Bhac to begin the long descent into Glen Tilt. There was once a fight here in which the men of Atholl foiled an attempt by the men of Deeside to channel the Dubh Alltan northwards across the plain into the Allt an t-Seilich. Hidden behind the low hill on the west side of the watershed is Loch Tilt, where Pennant dined on his way through the glen, and a pleasant spot it is on a fine day. Walkers may prefer to make a detour via the loch and to rejoin the path further down.

Once across the watershed the character of the route changes

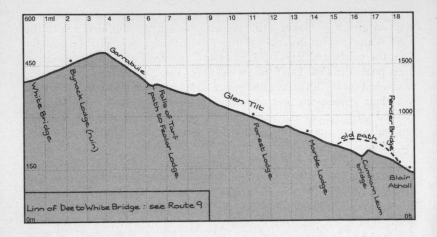

Linn of Dee to White Bridge : see Route 9

completely as you enter the Garrabuie, a 1½ mile (2km) defile that cuts a dead straight line between steep broken hillsides, 'like a gigantic canal-cutting' as one nineteenth century guidebook described it. The tumbling river after which it is named (Allt Garbh Buidhe: Owlt *Garra Boo*-y, Rough Yellow Stream) forms some fine pools and waterfalls, and there is just enough room beside it for some idyllic campsites. Massive Beinn a' Ghlo (Mountain of the Veil or Mist; 1,129m/3,740ft) now dominates the landscape, as it will for many miles.

The Garrabuie path clings to the hillside well above the river and is so narrow that Pennant complained 'our horses often were obliged to cross their legs to pick a secure place for their feet'. Mountain bikers will find that this part of the route demands skill, nerve and an impeccable sense of balance if a disastrous plunge to the riverbed is to be avoided. Queen Victoria's remark in her journal that the path is 'almost precipitous, and indeed made riding very unpleasant' has turned out to be curiously prophetic a century later. Even she had to dismount from her pony and walk at one point.

At the foot of the Garrabuie is a grassy promontory where the Allt a' Ghlinne Mhoir comes in from the left, and in the next mile or so the Tarf Water and An Lochain also join to form the River Tilt. This is perhaps the most scenic section of the glen, as it begins to take shape as a great trench through the hills to distant Blair Atholl. Beside the gorge of the Allt a' Ghlinne Mhoir the old path to Fealar can be seen climbing the hillside (see p91).

The promontory is surrounded by steep hillsides that give it the air of a secret grotto. It makes a fine picnic spot, but the confluence with the Tarf Water a short distance further down is even more picturesque, for here the celebrated Falls of Tarf cascade through a rocky gorge into a deep pool (the Poll Tarf). In former days the crossing of the Tarf was renowned for its difficulty. The water could be waist deep, and travellers lost their possessions and sometimes their lives here. Queen Victoria crossed on her pony preceded by two pipers whose job was to provide musical accompaniment to the royal progress, even when they were up to their waists in water.

A single-arched stone bridge was built across the pool in 1770 but it was taken down by the 6th Duke of Atholl in 1819 to hinder the use of the right of way. The current bridge was erected, appropriately enough, by the Scottish Rights of Way Society in 1886, to commemorate the death of the 18 year old English student Francis Bedford, who was drowned here in August 1879.

A few hundred metres beyond the Tarf you reach the start of the Land-Rover track that accompanies the Tilt for the rest of the way to Blair Atholl. From hereon the glen exhibits a classic simplicity of line as it cleaves a V-shaped trench through the hills, straight as a die for mile after mile; in places it seems barely wide enough to carry both river and track. Mountain bikers will find it an excellent run – a bit bumpy in parts and with a few counter-climbs, but mostly fast and exhilarating. In several places the old path diverges from the new track, but few seek it out these days. Picturesque river scenery compensates for lack of views, with numerous waterfalls on the Tilt and its feeder streams.

Passing the entrance to Glen Loch (see p88), you soon reach forestry plantations and sheep-farming country, with Forest Lodge the first of many inhabitants in the fertile lower glen. Just before Forest Lodge is a particularly fine waterfall and pool where there are the remains of a bridge (GR 938747). There is another dilapidated bridge at GR 918727, but the only usable bridge in this part of the glen is at GR 956763. Further down the glen, just before Marble Lodge, is an old single-arched stone bridge known as Gow's Bridge (GR 901718), built in 1759 and named after the owner of a local inn. Marble Lodge is named after a nearby marble quarry that was worked in the early nineteenth century. The track crosses Gow's Bridge and continues past Auchgobhal to Gilbert's Bridge (GR 881701), named after another local inhabitant who fought in the '45.

The lone building at Auchgobhal (Auchgowl) gives some indication of how the glen has changed in recent historical times, for in 1781 there were a number of houses here and a school that had fifty-six pupils. Life was hard then and the people eventually suffered the same fate as others all over the Highlands when they were cleared from the glen to make way for sheep and deer. Collectors of fascinating facts may wish to note that it was on a grassy plain hidden up the hillside above Auchgobhal that the first powered aeroplane was tested in 1907.

At Gilbert's Bridge the route along Glen Tilt recrosses the river and climbs across the hillside to Old Blair. The main route today goes straight on, along a track called the Drive that was built in 1805. The Drive runs through mixed woodland well above the river crosses the Tilt further fown at the Cumhann Leum Bridge (*Coo*-an L-yaim, Narrow Leap; GR 881685). Once across the river it climbs into the forest before making its final descent to the roadside near Old Bridge of Tilt, from which point Blair Atholl is less than a mile away.

The old right of way that pre-dated the Drive keeps to the east side of the glen. It is now a path that leaves the riverside just north of Auchgobhal and contours across the hillside high above the river to reach the roadside at Fenderbridge.

6

EAST OF TILT

To the south-east of Glen Tilt, beyond Beinn a' Ghlo, is an empty, lonely land whose bleak moors and long, mostly nondescript glens will not suit all tastes. The sights and sounds of settlements and summer shielings that once enlivened the glens and hillsides are lost to memory; the land is now given over the sheep and deer, and few walkers come this way. There is some pleasant river and glen scenery, but the area lacks the grandeur and picturesqueness of the nearby Cairngorms and is unlikely ever to become a popular hillwalking destination. Those who are attracted by wild places, however, will find here a true taste of Highland wilderness at the very edge of the Grampian Mountains.

As elsewhere in the Highlands the clearances are to blame for the depopulation of the land, but unlike elsewhere the history of many of the former settlements has been recorded, owing to the many disputes about land ownership and grazing rights that occurred. Perhaps the most famous case was the Seven Shielings dispute, a centuries-old disagreement over grazing and hunting rights in the Shinagag and Glen Loch areas that came to court in the seventeenth, eighteenth and nineteenth centuries. Now only ruins remain as testimony to what was once so important.

The area is delimited by Glen Tilt to the north and roads on the other three sides: the A9 through Blair Atholl to the west, the A93 along Glen Shee to the east and the A924 moorland road from Pitlochry to Strathardle to the south. Within these boundaries several old tracks, the roads of their day, fan out from Blair Atholl around the flanks of Beinn a' Ghlo, and ancient paths criss-cross the moors from glen to glen, linking former settlements and climbing to the shielings higher up.

From Blair Atholl the Brakoch Road climbed north-eastwards up Glen Fender, past the thirteenth-century church at Kirkton of Lude, to the Brakoch shielings in the upper glen. The Shinagag Road (still a right of way) climbed east of Blair Atholl to Loch Moraig, crossed the moor to Tomnabroilach and Shinagag, then headed south-east to Glen Brerechan and Strathardle. This road was travelled by Mary Queen of Scots on her way to Blair Castle for the great Glen Loch deer hunt of 1564 (see below), but it has long since fallen into disuse and is no longer marked on the OS map.

Another road ran south of the Shinagag Road, past Strathgroy, Lycondlich and Reinakyllich to join te Shinagag Road at the ford of Ath nam Breac (GR 979651); this route is still marked on the OS map as a path as far as Reinakyllich. Another climbed Glen Girnaig to Loinmarstaig to join this road near Reinakyllich (see p88). Some of these ruined settlements are still marked on the OS map, but one wonders for how much longer.

In the vicinity of Blair Atholl these old 'roads' are in a good state of preservation and can be linked to form short walking or mountain-biking tours. Further east towards Strathardle they are generally less distinct and no longer appear on the OS map, but they have not disappeared from the landscape altogether and in places are clearly visible on the ground if you know where to look. Those interested should consult old OS maps or John Kerr's fascinating booklet *Old Roads to Strathardle* (see Bibliography).

All these 'roads' skirt Beinn a' Ghlo to the south, taking the shortest line between Atholl and Strathardle, but there are others that skirt Beinn a' Ghlo's western flanks, penetrating the heart of the wilderness and providing perhaps the best cross-country routes in the area today. Note, however, that the interior is used extensively for deerstalking and should be avoided from mid-August to mid-October. The key through-route goes eastwards from Blair Atholl to Shinagag, turns north-eastwards into the area of the Seven Shielings, climbs over the watershed south of Beinn a' Ghlo and then veers south-eastwards via Glen Loch and Gleann Fearnach to reach the roadside in Strathardle near Straloch. It is described below as the Seven Shielings route.

The upper reaches of Glen Loch and Gleann Fearnach push northwards from the Seven Shielings route around the western flanks of Beinn a' Ghlo to provide connections to Glen Tilt. Glen Loch reaches Glen Tilt just below the Falls of Tarf, while the old right of way along Gleann Fearnach takes a much longer route across the moors to reach Glen Tilt just above the Falls of Tarf. Both of these routes are also described below. In combination with the Seven Shielings route and Glen Tilt they provide some adventurous walking and mountain-biking expeditions.

THE SEVEN SHIELINGS ROUTE

ROUTEPLANNER
OS map: 43
Start point: Blair Atholl (GR 877655)
End point: Strathardle (GR 051639)
Total distance: 17½ miles (28km)
Total ascent: 580m (1,900ft); in reverse: 700m (2,300ft)
Total time: 8hr (mb:5hr) + halts

Bothies en route: Ruidh Chuilein (GR 994718). The route is a right of way from Blair Atholl to Shinagag and again in its later stages along Gleann Fearnach, but there is doubt about the section in between, which hugs the flanks of Beinn a' Ghlo. It crosses pleasant and undeniably remote country where you will be unlikely to meet any fellow travellers. Land-Rover tracks at each end, a good path in the middle and a main ascent of only 220m (720ft) from Shinagag to the watershed make it of especial interest to mountain bikers.

From Blair Atholl the route follows the minor road up the south side of the Fender to Loch Moraig. It is a stiff start to the day, the road climbing 200m (650ft) in about 1½ miles (2km) and steepening to 1 in 5 in places. As an excuse for a break, pause half-way up at Fenderbridge to attempt to view the Falls of Fender, hidden in the trees just below the bridge.

The gradient eases off across the open farmland of upper Glen Fender and the road ends at the picturesque moorland loch of Loch Moraig, a paradise for birds, which in high summer emit the most piercing cacophony. The loch surprisingly drains not into Glen Fender but south-wards into Glen Garry, affording a route to Killiecrankie that was used by Viscount Dundee to gain an advantageous position before the Battle of Killiecrankie in 1689. Cars can be driven as far as the loch.

Beyond Loch Moraig the road bears left to Monzie farm while the Land-Rover track to Shinagag goes straight on. After about 400m the old Shinagag Road mentioned above can be seen branching right across the fields to Tomnabroilach. The modern track climbs to two locked huts, from where path branches left to climb the south-west shoulder of Carn Liath (975m/3,198ft, Carn *Lee*-a, Grey Cairn), the most southerly of Beinn a' Ghlo's three Munros, which towers overhead like a giant pyramid.

The track splashes across a stream, rises across the southern flanks of Carn Liath and bears right to descend to Shinagag farm, a lovely spot surrounded by sycamore trees (6 miles/10km; 3hr/mb: 1½hr + halts). The track ends here and the route onwards up the glen of the Allt Coire Lagain (Laakin, Hollow) is initially indistinct. It goes left up a grassy track 30m before the farm gate, passes through a gate higher up, leaves the track after a further 25m to branch left along a path and then crosses the hillside to the Allt Loch Valigan (bridge), deteriorating as it progresses. On the far side of the Allt Loch Valigan can be seen the ruins of one of the seven shielings.

The path continues up the glen of the Allt Coire Lagain to the watershed. At first it is difficult to distinguish among sheep paths, but as it contours around the steep upper slopes of quaintly named Sron na h-Innearach (Strawn na *Hinny*erach, Nose of the Field of Cattle Dung) it becomes an obvious terrace on the hillside, of ancient construction and reminiscent of Comyn's Road. The terrace is overgrown but a good narrow path runs along it. Across the river the great ridges and corries of Beinn a' Ghlo come into view one by one.

NB There is a new track that cuts out the long dog-leg around Shinagag. This useful, ridable track leaves the main track at the sharp right-hand bend at the start of the descent to Shinagag (GR 940683) and goes straight on across the hillside to end at the Allt Coire Lagain. It is then necessary to ford the stream (which is normally easy to do) and climb up the hillside to regain the path, but even so there is a considerable saving in time and effort over the old route.

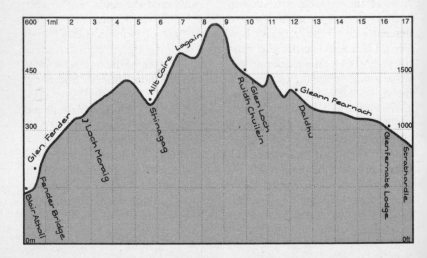

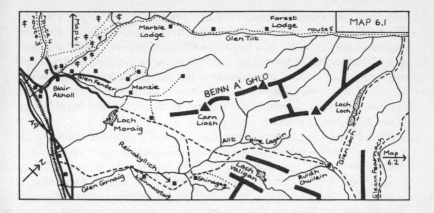

As the path rounds Sron na h-Innearach nd approaches the bealach (pass) at the watershed it again becomes difficult to follow among a myriad of sheep paths. It keeps well to the right of the bealach itself to avoid peat bogs and follows a wide terrace beneath the upper slopes of Stac nam Bodach (Stachk nam Bottach, Stack of the Old Man). Mountain bikers will find most of the path between Shinagag and the bealach unridable on ascent, but the terraced section is fun, requiring precision steering on the narrow path.

If you manage to keep to the path all the way to its high point on the right of the bealach, a track will be found that descends the far side, eventually leading all the way to Strathardle. It begins with a steep descent into the large grassy bowl at the foot of Beinn a' Ghlo, where Glen Loch cuts across the route from left to right. The descent is testingly rough on a mountain bike. At the bottom of the descent a small wooden hut beside the track marks the site of Ruidh Chuilein, another of the seven shielings (10 miles/16km; 5hr/mb: 3½hr + halts). It is a fine spot, with a small waterfall nearby and Beinn a' Ghlo towering above; the hut makes a useful shelter. The slopes of Ben Vuirich on the right give a magnificent view of Glen Loch and Loch Loch.

A few hundred metres beyond the hut a cart track cuts back left up Glen Loch, but the main track to Strathardle, still very rough, bears right down Glen Loch. It climbs high along the side of the broad featureless glen before descending to Daldhu to join the private tarmaced road that runs for the last 5 miles (8km) down Gleann Fearnach to the main road (see below).

Day Mountain-biking Circuits Using the Seven Shielings Route

From Blair Atholl the Seven Shielings route can be combined with the A924 and A9 to make a circuit of about 8 hours. Alternatively, the Blair Atholl and Strathardle ends of the route can be linked independently with parts of other routes to form shorter circuits. From Strathardle the section to Ruidh Chuilein can be combined with a loop around Gleann Fearnach and Glen Loch to form a tough expedition for the experienced. From Blair Atholl a return can be made from Ruidh Chuilein via Glen Loch and Glen Tilt, or more easily from Shinagag via Glen Girnaig. NB The Glen Loch route is partly pathless and involves the fording of the Tilt (see below).

The Glen Girnaig route is a right of way and is mostly ridable. It begins as a faint grassy track that leaves the Shinagag track shortly after crossing the Allt Girnaig (GR 951673). It loops left to cross a tributary by an old rickety bridge and then climbs across the hillside to the substantial ruins of Reinakyllich. On the far bank of the Girnaig note the dilapidated ruins of Little Shinagag, once the largest settlement in the area with well over thirty buildings, including an inn.

At Reinakyllich the path seems to go right, but ignore it and keep left of all the buildings to descend to a gate in a wall. On the far side of the wall pick up an old grassy track that goes right across the hillside to the ruined cottage of Coinmarstag. When the cottage comes into view branch right through a gate to descend past the cottage and cross the Girnaig (bridge). On the far side of the river the path soon becomes a lovely track that climbs through mixed woodland to reach a tarmaced road. The route ends with a fast descent of this beautifully engineered road, which goes under the new A9 to join the old road at GR 902636 a few miles from Blair Atholl.

GLEN LOCH

Sandwiched between the steep hillsides of Beinn a' Ghlo and Craig an Loch and far from the nearest road, Glen Loch has a lonely, timeless quality almost without equal among Highland glens. Few people pass this way these days and it is hard to believe that dozens of shielings once dotted the green riverbanks and hillsides, that drovers came here with their herds en route from the north to Kirmichael Tryst and that once upon a time not one but two monarchs stayed in the glen. In the mid-nineteenth century the 6th Duke of Atholl, in a misguided attempt to divert the Glen Tilt right of way, even planned to bridge the Tilt and to build a road through the glen. Thankfully, Glen Loch remains inviolate.

The glen is a right of way but should be avoided from mid-August to

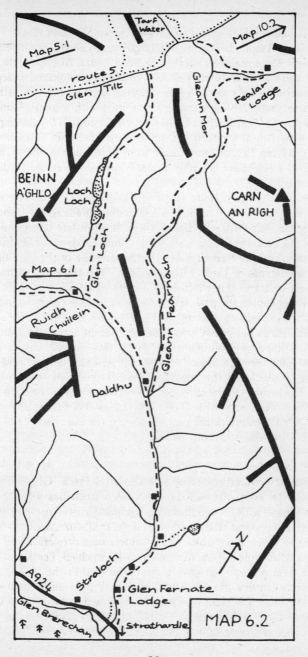

MAP 6.2

mid-October. Its usefulness as a through-route depends on the volume of water in the Tilt, which blocks the way at the northern end. The ford here was much used when Glen Loch was a droving route but is not to be treated so lightly these days; the Tilt is a major river and is deeper than it looks. Unfortunately, if the river cannot be forded to reach the Land-Rover track on its far side there is no practicable way up or down Glen Tilt owing to the steepness of the hillsides on the Glen Loch side of the river. The ford needs great care and should be attempted only by the experienced when the water is low. Otherwise, Glen Loch should be avoided as a through-route; the Land-Rover track along nearby Gleann Fearnach (see below) provides much easier going, especially for mountain bikers.

The lower reaches of Glen Loch between Daldhu and Ruidh Chuilein form part of the Seven Shielings route (Strathardle to Ruidh Chuilein: 7 miles/11km; 190m/620ft; 3hr/mb:1½hr + halts). The route to upper Glen Loch branches northwards at the top of a rise a few hundred metres east of Ruidh Chuilein hut. There is a cart track across the moor as far as Loch Loch, that most unimaginatively named of lochs, and then a path continues along the lochside and trends downhill to Glen Tilt. The route is only intermittently ridable; even the cart track is too cut up by vehicular traffic to provide easy mountain biking.

The pastures south of Loch Loch were formerly well used for summer cattle grazing and once sported forty shielings; how much more lively and colourful the glen must have been then. Near the ruined shieling of Ruidh na Diollaide at GR 987730 stands the Saddle Stone, which until the last century was visited by women from all over Scotland, as sitting upon it was reputed to promote fertility.

Loch Loch lies in a deep trough between the highest ridges of Beinn a' Ghlo and the steep slopes of Craig an Loch. Along the shoreline are some pleasant bays that make congenial picnic spots when the sun shines, but in dull weather the surroundings can seem very bleak and few would wish to linger here then. The loch's name could derive from that of the glen, Glen Loch being so named because it contains a loch. Less confusingly, its double name could derive from its violin shape, which almost divides it into two. The stretch of water in the middle is so narrow and shallow that it is almost possible to cross from one side to the other dry-shod.

In August 1564 Mary Queen of Scots camped on the shores of this wild loch on the night before a great deer hunt. According to the records, two thousand Highlanders spent nearly two months rounding up two thousand deer on which the royal party could be let loose, but for once, famously, it was the hunted who gained the upper hand. Mary let one of

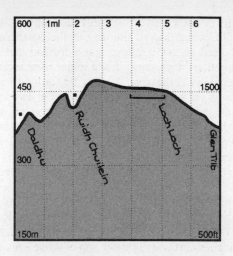

her dogs loose on a wolf and the leading stag bolted, stampeding his herd through the assembled Highlanders. The men threw themselves on the ground to escape injury, but some were trampled to death and others were wounded.

The rocky lochside path gives a pleasant walk and is followed by a gentle descent by the burn of An Lochain to its confluence with the Tilt. No path is marked on the map, but an old path of sorts can still be seen beside the river. Unfortunately, it takes a directissima route, treating the river with disdain and fording it at every bend. It is perhaps better to keep to sheep paths higher up the hillside.

The flat ground at the junction with Glen Tilt was where the second royal visitor, King James V, stayed for three days in 1529. Although it seems improbable, a temporary wooden palace was erected here, three storeys high, with glass windows, tapestries and silk drapes; entry was by drawbridge and portcullis across a pool that was well stocked with fish. Food and wine were so plentiful that the Pope's ambassador, a guest of the king, was astounded by the lavishness of it all. The Glen Tilt Land-Rover track is close at hand, but the swift-flowing river bars the way (Ruidh Chuilein to River Tilt: 4½ miles/7km; 40m/130ft; 2hr/mb:2hr + halts).

GLEANN FEARNACH

North of Kirmichael Strathardle divides into two glens – Glen Brerechan, which carries the A924 westwards across the moors to

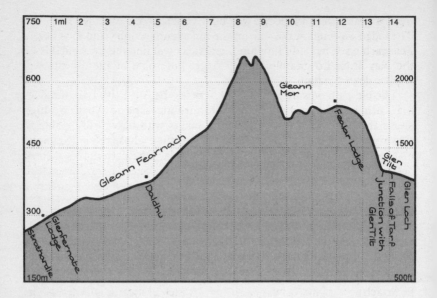

Pitlochry, and Gleann Fearnach, which pushes northwards towards Glen Tilt to provide adventurous walking and cycling opportunities.

In its lower reaches the glen is open and undistinguished, given over to sheep farming; several houses dot the roadside. A tarmaced road penetrates the glen as far as Daldhu (5 miles/8km) and then the glen divides, with Land-Rover tracks continuing up each branch. The left branch leads to Ruidh Chuilein (see above), while the right branch pursues an intricate course across moor and glens for another 7 miles (11km) to one of the highest and remotest habitations in the country: Fealar Lodge (550m/1,800ft). The whole route to Fealar Lodge and beyond to Glen Tilt is a right of way but should be avoided during the stalking season.

The glen begins gently but becomes wilder and more attractive as it progresses. The track climbs to a high point of 660m (2,165ft) on the bleak plateau at the head of the glen and then makes a swift descent into Gleann Mor (Great Glen), whose waterfalls and tree-lined ravine seem particularly pleasant after the bare moors. The track crosses the river at an attractive little gorge (bridge) and eventually veers right up the glen of the Allt Feith Lair to reach the hidden cluster of buildings at Fealar (12 miles/19km; 450m/1,475ft; 5½hr/mb:3hr + halts).

The extensive grazing around Fealar has always been in great demand. Many ruined shielings are scattered about the hillsides, dating from a time before the lodge was built, when access was via Glen Tilt. The lodge was built at the start of the nineteenth century and the Gleann Fearnach track in 1820. Fit mountain bikers will find the track ridable all the way from Strathardle to the lodge, but some of the ascents will require determination.

The old path onward to Glen Tilt crosses the Allt Feith Lair and does a U-turn back towards Gleann Mor, forming a narrow balcony high above the steep-sided river. Mountain bikers with nerve will be able to ride most of it, but as a fall could be serious those whose riding technique matches the author's would do better to walk. The path makes a steep descent to reach the Tilt at the foot of the Garrabuie, where an easy ford gives access to the Glen Tilt path on the far side (from Fealar Lodge: 2 miles/3km; descent of 200m/650ft; 1hr/mb:1hr).

Around Strathardle

Tempting tracks cross the hills both east and west of Strathardle, but they are outside the boundaries of this book and space precludes more than a brief mention of them. Within a few miles of the foot of Gleann Fearnach two rights of way take high routes eastwards to Glen Shee: Enochdu (GR 063628) to Spittal (GR 110699) and Kirkmichael (GR 081601) to Lair (GR 142633). Westwards between Strathardle and Strathay numerous lochans, old paths and newer tracks dot a vast area of moorland whose exploration will appeal especially to mountain bikers; the area is best approached from the A9 between Dunkeld and Pitlochry. Note also the fine network of tracks and paths in Kindrogan Wood at the head of Strathardle.

7

GLEN GELDIE AND
GLEN FESHIE

TRACK RECORD

Nowhere gives such an overwhelming impression of the vastness of the Cairngorm wilderness than this spacious route around the southern flanks of the High Cairngorms between Deeside and Speyside. It is a route of two halves, linking glens of widely differing character. Glen Geldie is unique for its barrenness, its wide horizons and its tundra-like bleakness; in driech weather or in winter it is a considerable undertaking, when stamina and navigational skills will be put sternly to the test. Glen Feshie, contrastingly, is a superb canyon-shaped valley whose beautiful river and woodland scenery make it perhaps the most picturesque glen in the whole Cairngorms. Together the two glens form a route of startling contrasts that shows how much the Cairngorms have to offer besides high mountain scenery.

The watershed between the two glens is the lowest between Speyside and Deeside, reaching a height of only about 560m (1,830ft), and it has long tempted road builders. It was surveyed by Wade in the 1720s, by Telford and Mitchell in 1828, again by Mitchell in more detail in 1837 and by various successors up to and including the twentieth century. Fortunately for wild-land lovers, winter conditions, prohibitive costs and other reasons have seen all these plans abandoned. Glen Fleshie and Glen Geldie are still inviolate, and may they always remain so.

ROUTEPLANNER

OS map: 43/35
Start point: Linn of Dee (GR 062897)
End point: Tolvah at the end of the public road in Glen Feshie (GR 842897)
Total distance: 21 miles (34km)

+ Braemar to Linn of Dee: 6 miles (10km)

+ Glen Feshie (GR 848976, 1½ miles (2km) before Tolvah) to Kingussie: 7 miles (11km); Tolvah to Feshiebridge: 3 miles (5km)

Total ascent: 310m (1,000ft)

in reverse: 380 m (1,250ft)

Total time: 9hr (mb:6½hr) + halts

+ Braemar to Linn of Dee: 2hr (mb:1hr)

+ Glen Feshie to Kingussie: 3hr (mb:1½hr); Tolvah to Feshiebridge: 1hr (mb:½hr)

Braemar: accommodation/provisions/youth hostel/campsite.

Kingussie: accommodation/provisions/station/youth hostel/campsite.

There is also a youth hostel at Inverey near Linn of Dee. Bothies en route: Ruigh Aiteachain (GR 847928).

The route is a right of way. On foot it can be completed in a day if private transport can be arranged at both ends, but it also makes a fine backpacking route, with good paths, gentle ascents and remote vistas. By mountain bike the Land-Rover tracks at each end make a day crossing eminently practicable; the central section across the moors is unridable but the exhilarating descent of Glen Feshie more than compensates. Note, however, that there is an awkward section where a landslide has to be negotiated, and this requires great care with a bike (see p98).

The route is best undertaken in an east-west direction in order to minimise ascent and to enjoy Glen Feshie to the fullest, on descent from the bleak moors of Glen Geldie. In this direction also the route provides a fine return route to the Aviemore area from trans-Cairngorm routes such as the Lairig Ghru (Route 9) and the Lairig an Laoigh (Route 10). In connection with this, note the forest tracks that continue across the Moor of Feshie north-east of Feshiebridge to provide through-routes to

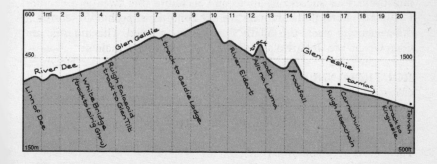

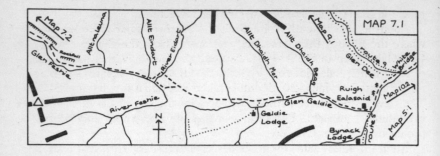

Rothiemurchus. To the south the route can be combined with Glen Tilt (Route 5) or the routes east of Drumochter (Routes 2, 3 and 4) to form longer expeditions or circuits. There are no shorter return routes.

ROUTE DESCRIPTION

From Braemar the route begins as the Lairig Ghru and the Lairig an Laoigh end, with a 6 mile (10km) road section to the Linn of Dee. From here a Land-Rover track, generally well surfaced but quite rough in places, continues westwards on the north side of the Dee. The pines are left behind much sooner than in neighbouring glens and ahead lies a broad green valley delimited by featureless hills. It is a gentle landscape, saved from dullness by the ever-agreeable Dee.

After about a mile look out for the ruins of Dalvorar on the south side of the river, where Viscount Dundee and his troops are said to have camped on their way through Glen Geldie and Glen Feshie to the Battle of Killiecrankie in 1689. On a grassy slope a further mile along are the ruins of Dubrach, where a detachment of government troops was stationed after the '45. One wonders what all the soldiers who came this way over the centuries would think of those who come here now for pleasure.

About 3 miles (5km) beyond the Linn of Dee is a great crossroads in the wilderness where the Geldie Burn parts company with the Dee, and here White Bridge spans the Dee. The bridge is not named after its colour but after the Geldie (Geal Dheidh, White Dee). The Dee turns northwards towards the Lairig Ghru and if time permits it is worth making a short detour along its banks to view the Chest of Dee (see p118). The continuing track along the Geldie becomes much rougher beside a forestry plantation. As you reach the trees cast a glance northwards to distant Cairn Toul and southwards to distant Beinn a' Ghlo; these are the last inspiring mountainscapes you will see for many a mile, for Glen Geldie disdains such visual distractions.

About a mile beyond White Bridge is another major river junction where the Bynack Burn branches southwards from the Geldie towards Glen Tilt. Keep to the main track along the Geldie, which passes the ruins of Ruigh Ealasaid (*Roo-y-Yala*sitch, Elisabeth's Shieling) and rises up the gently curving glen. Mountain bikers will find it rough but ridable. The view is notable for its non-existence, for the rise of the moor blots everything from sight. The feeling of heading into a vast and uncompromising wilderness is acute.

After 4½ miles (7km) the track descends across the river and ends at the sculpted ruins of Geldie Lodge at the foot of An Sgarsoch (The Place of Sharp Rocks; 1,006m/3,300ft) and its western neighbour Carn an Fhidhleir (Carn an *Eel*er, The Fiddler's Cairn; 994m/3,260ft) are two of the remotest Munros in Scotland, but they can be easily bagged from the Linn of Dee with the help of a mountain bike. Although it is hard to believe now, there used to be a cattle tryst on the extensive summit plateau of An Sgarsoch in droving days.

The continuing path to Glen Feshie leaves the track about 200m before it fords the Geldie (7½ miles/12km; 3hr/mb:2hr + halts). It rises gently across the moor well away from the river and is fine to walk but far too rocky to cycle. The view becomes more open, although there is still nothing to see except distant rolling hills, which only make the vast moor seem more boundless. The path is not always easy to follow and if you lose it in bad weather precise compass work will be required to keep on line. In winter, when the path is under snow and the landscape has an Arctic appearance, the crossing of the moor is a major expedition.

From the start of the path it is not much more than 3 miles (5km) to the River Eidart, which marks the start of the descent into Glen Feshie, but it seems much further. You will be glad to cross the almost imperceptible watershed and see the River Feshie before you, rushing down from its upper basin on the left to do a U-turn and disappear down Glen Feshie on the right. At one time the Feshie flowed across the watershed into the Geldie, but down-cutting in Glen Feshie captured it and caused the U-turn.

The Eidart (*Ait*yart) is a considerable river that in former times often required a detour many miles upstream to effect a crossing. Things are easier these days, for in 1957 a dramatic bridge was built astride a beautiful rocky gorge about 500m upstream from the confluence with the Feshie. Below the bridge the rushing waters plunge over a cliff in a spectacular 10m (30ft) waterfall, the largest of several on this stretch of river. Beside the bridge a lovely little mossy stream provides drinking water and itself forms a ribboned waterfall. It is a perfect picnic spot, and a sign that you have left the moors behind for the more picturesque scenery of Glen Feshie. Care is required around the edge of the gorge, especially with a mountain bike.

The descent into the welcoming jaws of Glen Feshie now begins. The path crosses the Allt Eindart (which is normally possible dry-shod) and soon reaches the banks of the Feshie itself. It cuts a beautiful smooth swathe through the heather and is a joy to ride as it swoops down the glen like a mountain biker's dream. The only obstacle is the considerable gorge of the Allt na Leuma (Owlt na L-yaim, Stream of the Leap; GR 886891), whose depths conceal an impressive waterfall, but the gorge is easily negotiated on foot. Beyond the gorge the Feshie enters its own miniature canyon, whose banks are beautifully wooded with birch and pine. The path becomes narrow and requires care; mountain bikers should take to a higher-level Land-Rover track which the path joins a short distance further down.

The beauty of the upper Feshie is legion. The cascading river, the tree-clad banks and hillsides and the teeming waterfalls that tumble from them combine to form an exquisite landscape. At every turn there is something new and picturesque to catch the eye. It is the sort of country that makes you want to find a grassy patch beneath a spreading pine and commune with nature, and it seems even more enchanting after the moors of Glen Geldie. It is also the sort of place that can make you fall in love with mountain biking, as you sweep from one idyllic spot to another for mile after mile.

Mountain bikers will be brought to an abrupt halt, however, when the river takes a sharp left-hand turn beneath the craggy slopes of Creag na Gaibhre (*Gaa*-irra, Goat; GR 863900), for here a major landslide has obliterated the track. With care, walkers can negotiate the narrow, exposed and developing path across the rubble without too much difficulty, but for mountain bikers this section is a major headache. Bikes must be carried, and this is a manoeuvre that should not be attempted without a prior reconnoitre.

On the far side of the landslide the track continues its descent through superb pinewoods beside wide grassy plains where the river flows lazily among shingle beds. After keeping right at a fork and crossing a small stream by stepping-stones, another narrow and exposed section (again affected by landslides) has to be negotiated, and then the track swoops down gloriously to Ruigh Aiteachain (*Roo*-y *Aity*achan, Juniper Shieling), a popular bothy just off the track to the right. It was around here that the Victorian painter Landseer painted many of his Highland

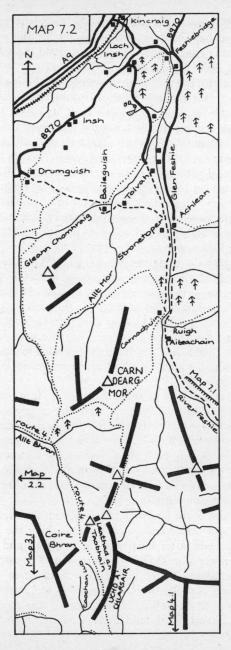

MAP 7.2

N

Kincraig

Loch
Insh

A9

B970

Feshiebridge

B970   Insh

Drumguish

Baileguish

Tolvah

Glen Feshie

Achlean

Gleann Chomhraig

Allt Mor

Stronetoper

Carnachuin

Ruigh
Aiteachain

CARN
DEARG
MOR

Map 7.1

River Feshie

route 4

Allt Bhran

Map
2.2

route 4

Map 3.1

Coire
Bhran

Leachad an
Taobhain

Caochan ua

UCHD A'
CHLARSAIR

Map 4.1

landscapes, and a fresco painted by him used to adorn the wall of one of the ruined huts near the bothy. From here it is less than a mile to the roadside at Carnachuin, where there is a bridge across the Feshie and a notice informs you, sadly, that you are leaving the Cairngorms National Nature Reserve (17 miles/27km; 7½hr/mb:6hr + halts).

From Carnachuin onwards there is a choice of routes, depending on whether you are walking or cycling and whether you are heading westwards towards Kingussie or northwards towards Feshiebridge. If you are making for Feshiebridge the easiest cycling route is a high-gear descent of the (private) tarmaced road from Carnachuin to the public road near Tolvah. Walkers will find more agreeable going on the other side of the river, where a path reaches the public road at Achlean (GR 852976).

If you are making for Kingussie the best route is an old drove road and right of way, now a forest track, that begins 2½ miles (4km) north of Carnachuin opposite Achlean at GR 847976 (note the useful bridge across the Feshie at GR 851965). The track climbs over a ridge into the shallow glen of the Allt Chomhraig, fords the river and climbs over another low ridge on the far side of the glen to descend to Drumguish, from where it is only a few miles along the B970 to Kingussie.

8

AROUND SPEYSIDE

ROTHIEMURCHUS FOREST

Rothiemurchus Forest (OS map: 36) contains some of the most picturesque woodland scenery in the Highlands, with lovely rivers and lochs as well as some superb specimens of old Caledonian pine. A maze of tracks and paths, including a nature trail at Loch an Eilein and a wayfaring trail at Loch Morlich, penetrate the forest to give wonderful walking in the shadow of the High Cairngorms. A useful visitor's guide and footpath map are available from Rothiemurchus visitor centre at Inverdruie, just outside Aviemore on the Cairn Gorm ski road.

The tracks of Rothiemurchus are also an attractive prospect for mountain bikers, and under an enlightened estate management policy some of the best have been linked together to form a wonderful cycling route. The route runs through the forest for 7 miles (11km) from Inverdruie to Loch Morlich and gives splendid cycling, with obstacles such as stiles and water splashes to add spice to the proceedings. If the privilege of cycling in the forest is not to be lost, mountain bikers are asked to please keep to this route and to avoid all other tracks and paths.

From Inverdruie the mountain-biking route takes the road to Blackpark and then bears right on a track to Loch an Eilein car park. Heading westwards from here it follows a track along the north shore of the loch and crosses heathery moorland to a cross roads at Lochan Deo, where the track from Coylumbridge to Loch Einich is crossed; at the fork just before this lovely moorland lochan take either branch.

The route continues along the north side of Lochan Deo and joins the Coylumbridge approach to the Lairig Ghru for a while. It crosses Am Beanaidh at the Cairngorm Club footbridge, follows the banks of the Allt Druidh and then rises away from the stream to the forest crossroads known as Piccadilly (see p 114). The Lairig Ghru track goes right here while the Rothiemurchus mountain-biking route goes straight on, rising through the forest and then descending to the wide dirt road that runs from Loch Morlich to Rothiemurchus Lodge. Turn left to reach the bridge over the River Luineag at the west end of Loch Morlich and join the ski road. From here it is only a few miles back along the road to Inverdruie (round trip by mountain bike from Inverdruie: 11 miles (17km); about 2hr + halts).

A second route through the forest on the south side of Loch Morlich enables another circuit to be made to An Lochan Uaine in the jaws of the Ryvoan Pass. This can be linked to the above route to make a fine figure-of-eight loop that enables a halt to be made for refreshments at Loch Morlich. From Loch Morlich follow Route 11 to An Lochan Uaine, taking the road to Glenmore Lodge and then the fine sandy track to the lochan (see p128). On your return, leave the track just before the bridge over the Allt na Feith Duibhe and branch left on another fine track that runs through the forest to join the ski road above Loch Morlich. At a fork at the first river keep right (ford; bridge upstream), then keep left at the next fork. All rivers are bridged.

On reaching the ski road turn left and after 100m take the track on the right, which takes you up the only real ascent of the day deep into the forest on the south side of Loch Morlich. Keep right at the first two forks, then left at the third to descend to the track along the south shore of the loch. Turn left here to reach the dirt track to Rothiemurchus Lodge (complete circuit by mountain bike from Inverdruie: 17 miles (27km); about 3hr excluding halts).

AN SLUGAIN

An Slugain (An *Slook*an, The Gullet) (OS map: 36) is an old right of way that begins at the west end of Loch Morlich (GR 958096) and runs through Glen More forest to a minor road at Milton of Kincardine (GR 937145; 3½ miles/6km; 1½hr/mb:1hr). The route reaches its high point in the gap to the east of Creag a' Ghreusaiche, and it is this that gives it its name. There is a good Land-Rover track all the way; from Loch Morlich it rises gently through the gap to the edge of the forest and then descends pleasantly to Milton through varied and interesting mixed woodland scenery. It is an excellent short trip whether on foot or by bike and is especially fine in the autumn. From Milton a return by road can be made via the B970 to Coylumbridge. Alternatively, the route can be extended into a longer off-road circuit by returning via Nethy Bridge and the Ryvoan Pass (see p128).

Just before the summit of the track a branch track climbs to near the summit of Creag a' Ghreusaiche (*Ghrey*sich, Shoemaker; 435m/

1,426ft) and from here there is a magnificent view over the Spey valley, Rothiemurchus and Glen More to the Cairngorms.

THE DULNAIN VALLEY

West of Aviemore a vast moorland stretches from Speyside to Strath Errick near the Great Glen. Numerous estate tracks and paths climb high onto the moor, but the scenery is mostly uninteresting and the area is little visited. The lovely Dulnain valley (OS map: 35/36) is an exception, and a visit to the lower glen makes a delightful trip from Aviemore. Walkers with private transport can reach the glen via a minor road from Carrbridge, but the route described below makes a more strenuous circuit from Aviemore that is especially suited to mountain bikes. Note that the route includes a testing ascent and, if a detour is to be avoided, the fording of the Dulnain (which is normally easy).

Of all the tracks and paths that leave the A9 south of Aviemore and cross the moors to the Dulnain, that which reaches the valley at its prettiest stretch begins as a tarmaced road 100m north of the Aviemore turn-off, signposted Lynwilg (GR 811105). Follow the road over the bridge and then left beside a stream. At a fork keep right up a very steep hill – the start of the 440m (1,450ft) ascent. The tarmac soon ends but the continuing track is well engineered, well drained and well gritted. It is known as the Burmah Road and is a right of way. It climbs steadily and relentlessly high above the steep-sided glen of the Allt Dubh (Doo, Black); only tigers will be able to ride it all the way. Fortunately, the view across Rothiemurchus Forest to the high tops of the Cairngorms is worth stopping to see.

The large cairn at the summit is a welcome sight, and beyond lies a swift descent to the peaceful green haven of the Dulnain valley. A bridge across the river deposits you on a riverside track that runs downstream past Caggan Bothy to the ruins of Eil Cottage. Here the track becomes a lovely grassy route across meadows beside the sparkling river, with beautiful woodlands that include a corridor of dwarf juniper. At times the valley is reminiscent of Glen Feshie, and in one or two places it has the look and smell of an Alp.

After crossing a small stream and reaching a gate, keep right at a fork to stay beside the river until you are opposite the house at Dalnahaitnach. Ford the river to reach the road to Carrbridge and take the second track on the right about 400m along. The track climbs to a gate and forks; take the left branch, which crosses the moor to join Wade's road south of Sluggan. To avoid the ford of the Dulnain, follow the track uphill to a junction and turn right to reach Wade's road at Insharn.

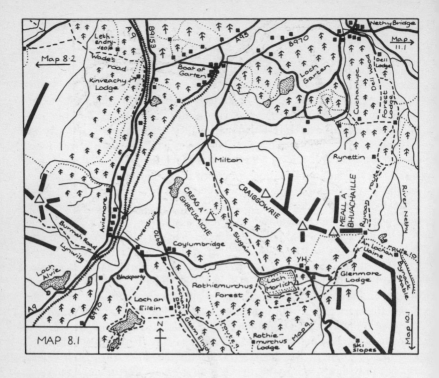

MAP 8.1

Wade's road is described below in an east-to-west direction. To use it as your return route to Lynwilg, follow it over a low bealach and down through Kinveachy Forest to Avielochan, then take to the old or new A9 for the rest of the way (round trip from Lynwilg by mountain bike: 20 miles/32km; about 4hr + halts).

WADE'S ROAD:

Aviemore to the Slochd Mor

The 8½ mile (14km) section of Wade road between Avielochan north of Aviemore and the Slochd Mor further north (OS map: 36/35) is a right of way and is still well used by foresters, pony-trekkers, walkers and mountain bikers. It makes a fine off-road route, intricate, interesting and ridable nearly all the way. Join it just beyond Avielochan (GR 905170), where it runs beside the A9. Go straight over a tarmaced road and past a house and climb to join the Kinveachy Lodge road. Wade's road bears left almost immediately and climbs steadily through the trees, keeping straight on when the main track turns right to Lethendryveole. After

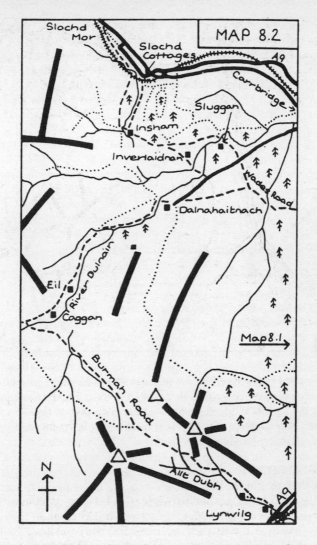

MAP 8.2

Slochd Mor
Slochd Cottages
A9
Carrbridge →
Insham
Sluggan
Inverlaidnan
Wade Road
Dalnahaitnach
Eil
River Dulnain
Caggan
Map 8.1 →
Burmah Road
Allt Dubh
A9
N
Lynwilg

crossing a low bealach it descends onto the vast plains of the lower Dulnain valley, now much afforested.

The track crosses the Carrbridge road and reaches the River Dulnain at Sluggan Bridge, a high humpbacked bridge that was one of Wade's finest constructions. The bridge remains intact and now incongruously spans the river beside the poignant ruins of Sluggan farm. Across the river, Wade's road continues as a green track to a forest fence, which it follows across the shoulder of Inverlaidnan Hill, giving good views up the Dulnain. It next joins the track from Inverlaidnan to Insharn, two still inhabited houses, and when the main track goes right to Insharn it goes straight on over a small Wade bridge. About 100m beyond the bridge it bears right (stile) into the forest and climbs across the hillside into the jaws of the Slochd Mor. In the Slochd Mor (Slochk Moar, Great Pit) four lines of transportation meet: Wade's road, the old A9, the new A9 and the Highland Railway (from Avielochan: 8½ miles/14km; 3½hr/mb:2hr + halts).

Those seeking an off-road return route to Aviemore will find various alternatives on either side of Wade's road, but none is as direct or interesting. Cyclists can return by the A9 or, more pleasantly, by Carrbridge, but note also that there is a fast off-road return route to the Dulnain valley using the track from Slochd Cottages (GR 847238) to Insharn and the track from there past Inverlaidnan to the Dulnain valley road.

WADE'S ROAD:
Etteridge to Kingussie
This beautiful 6 mile (10km) right of way near Kingussie (OS map: 35) lies further south than the other routes in this chapter, but it is many people's favourite bit of Wade road and deserves inclusion. It crosses interesting terrain at the foot of the hills on the east side of Strathspey and for most of the way is out of sight and sound of the A9, as peaceful today as it was for travellers of the eighteenth century. It passes several tranquil lochans, runs through fine birch woods and gives good views across the strath. From the mountain biker's point of view it is above all a lovely, mostly level track that is ridable nearly all the way.

The track is joined at Etteridge farm, which is reached by a track that leaves the A9 just north of the Crubenmore turn-off (GR 685928). The nearby Falls of Truim are worth a visit. Turn left at the farm buildings to pick up Wade's road. Immediately you are in beautiful country as the track passes picturesque Loch Etteridge, beloved by all manner of birds, and continues to the green fields and birch woods around Phones Lodge.

After crossing the Allt Phoineis (bridge) the track becomes a grassy swathe through the trees and passes another loch. At the end of the trees there is a short overgrown section and then a Land-Rover track crosses the route from left to right. The left branch is Wade's road, and it gives excellent going once more as it continues across the empty moors. At GR 725962 it crosses a fine humpbacked bridge, and here you should make a short detour over the rise on the right to view lovely Lochan Dabhaich

(*Dav*ich, Vat or Huge Woman), a lonely, reedy moorland loch surrounded by even lonelier trees and ruined shielings.

Soon Kingussie comes into view and you reach yet another lochan, Lochan Odhar (*Oa*-ar, Dun-coloured), just before which the Land-Rover track descends left to Milton of Nuide and the A9. Wade's road continues straight on as a grassy track across the babbling Milton Burn. A wetting at this awkward little stream can be avoided by turning right at Lochan Odhar, crossing a bridge at Luibleathann Bothy and tramping down the far bank to regain the track.

The track now crosses green fields between an old wall and a new fence, passing countless ruins as it progresses. When it bears left carry straight on through a gate in a fence and then through a narrow band of new forest to reach the A9 at GR 751991. There is a layby nearby and a lochan on the far side of the road. Across the road a stile in a fence gives access to a pleasant back road that tunnels back under the A9 to reach the B970 at Ruthven, from where Kingussie is only a short distance away (6 miles/10km; 2$\frac{1}{2}$hr/mb:1$\frac{1}{2}$hr + halts).

9

THE LAIRIG GHRU

TRACK RECORD
In the north-east of Scotland between Speyside and Deeside is a great tract of mountainous country that contains four of Scotland's seven 1,220m (4,000ft) mountains. This is the Cairngorms, a region of high plateaux, deep corries, remote lochs, swift-flowing rivers, ancient forests and Arctic-like tundra. Here visitors flock to walk, climb, ski, mountain bike, birdwatch or simply to gaze out of the windows of their cars, but here also is a wilderness where it is still possible to be truly alone.

The Cairngorms consist of three major plateaux, running from Braeriach to Cairn Toul in the west, Cairn Gorm to Ben Macdui in the centre and Beinn a'Bhuird to Ben Avon in the east. Between these three plateaux two major corridors cut through the heart of the massif from north to south, forming classic cross-country routes that have been used since time immemorial. These corridors are the Lairig Ghru in the west and the Lairig an Laoigh in the east. The Lairig an Laoigh is described in the following chapter.

The Lairig Ghru is perhaps the most celebrated mountain pass in Scotland and is regarded by many as the finest in Britain. Its scale has to be seen to be appreciated. From the majestic pinewoods of Speyside to the picturesque glens of Deeside – a total distance of 28 miles (45km) from Aviemore to Braemar – it threads its way between the highest mountains in Britain outside of the Ben Nevis group. For grandeur and variety of scenery it is without equal. At its highest point it reaches 833m (2,733ft), higher than any other route in this book except for the Minigaig, and yet even here it remains a deep cleft dwarfed by the great mountainsides of Braeriach (1,296m/4,251ft) and Ben Macdui (1,309m/4,294ft).

Its name is said by some to derive from the Gaelic *ghruamach* (*ghroo-amach*, forbidding or gloomy) and in foul weather, when wind whips

108

through the pass, veils of mist swirl across the hillsides, and rain and sleet sweep and sting and penetrate every inch of exposed flesh, it is easy to sympathise with this view.

At its worst the Lairig can be a killer. Owing to its length, height, and lack of escape-routes a change in the weather can quickly turn a sunny jaunt into a battle for survival. Such was the case one beautiful spring day when I set out from Braemar to cross the Lairig with a companion. We camped overnight near Corrour Bothy and on the following day set out for the summit of the pass. As we gained height the weather closed in, leaving us floundering in deep snow in white-out conditions. Progress became impossible and we were forced to retreat, thoroughly exhausted. As darkness closed in we tried to erect our tent, but as if to test our hill-craft even further the gale ripped it to shreds. It was a chastened pair of hillwalkers who later staggered into Corrour Bothy, a bleak and spartan hooch in the cold light of day, but as welcome a haven as we could have wished for on that night. The following day, having shown us its worst, the Lairig gave of its best as in magnificent snow conditions under a brilliant, brittle sky we completed our journey to Aviemore through a wonderland of glistening fresh snow.

Perhaps because of this adventure the Lairig for me will always be at its most beguiling in the spring, when deep snow still blankets the summit of the pass and the flora and fauna of the glens on each side are poised to

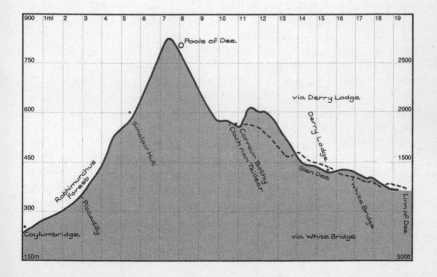

109

welcome the coming of the sun. But each season in the Lairig has its devotees. In winter the pass has an Arctic appearance and a savage charm, although only experienced mountaineers and ski tourers would be wise to venture here then. In summer it presents a startling contrast, filled with the smells and colours of long Highland gloamings. In autumn the colours intensify and there is an air of foreboding as skies darken and the winter storms approach once more.

At all seasons, even in the height of summer, Lairig weather can be capricious; cold winds funnel through the great corridor, making it always necessary to be equipped to guard against exposure. Let it also be said, however, lest this make the Lairig seem too forbidding and gloomy, that in good conditions the route is a magnificent expedition for those who are fit and experienced enough to tackle it, and as the shortest route between Aviemore and Braemar it has become a classic hillwalking challenge. As for the Lairig's gloomy name, the derivation of *ghru* from *ghruamach* is unlikely, for the Highlanders of old rarely named their surroundings so emotively. Other possible derivations are *cruidh* (*croo*-y, cattle, from the Lairig's days as a drove road) and ruadh (*roo*-a, red, from the granite screes at the summit), but the most likely origin of the name is as an aspirated form of the Allt Druidh (*Droo*-y, Flowing), the stream that drains the pass to the north.

The Lairig today gives a rough passage, but this was not always the case. Until the 1870s it was used as a drove road and in those days it was the practice each spring for Rothiemurchus folk to clear the route of any boulders that had been brought down from the heights by winter storms. One wonders whether concerted action by modern travellers could return the Lairig to its former boulder-free state, but perhaps such a clean-up campaign would now be considered an act of vandalism. In any case, modern path maintenance involves the strategic placement of suitable rocks and boulders to form an erosion-resistant surface, a policy that stabilises the ground and improves the route for walkers at the same time as making mountain biking execrable. Large stretches of the north side of the pass have been so repaired by the Scottish Conservation Projects Trust.

In addition to boulder clearance, apparently it was also the custom for the young women of Rothiemurchus to cross to Deeside in groups of three or four, each carrying on her head a basket of fresh eggs to sell; why Deeside folk were less successful at poultry farming remains unclear. Given the current state of the Lairig path it is debatable how many eggs would survive intact after a crossing today.

Apart from its use by drovers and locals the Lairig has few historical associations. Because of its height, length and challenging terrain most travellers between Speyside and Deeside, be they military or civilian, preferred to use one of the routes around the Cairngorms, such as Glen Feshie or the Bealach Dearg. If the Lairig has any history it is the history of the growth of hillwalking and the search for that indeterminable something that draws people to the wild places of the earth.

ROUTEPLANNER
OS map: 36/43
Start point: Coylumbridge (GR 915107)
End point: Linn of Dee (GR 062897)
Total distance: 20 miles (32km)
 + Aviemore to Coylumbridge: 2 miles (3km)
 + Linn of Dee to Braemar: 6 miles (10km)
Total ascent: 690m (2,260ft) via Derry Lodge; in reverse: 830m (2,725ft)
Total time: 9hr (mb:10hr) + halts
 + Aviemore to Coylumbridge: ¾hr (mb:¼hr)
 + Linn of Dee to Braemar: 2hr (mb:1hr)
Aviemore: accommodation/provisions/station/youth hostel/campsite.
Braemar: accommodation/provisions/youth hostel/campsite.

There are also youth hostels at Loch Morlich near Coylumbridge and Inverey near Linn of Dee, campsites at Coylumbridge and Loch Morlich and a shop at Loch Morlich. Bothies en route: Sinclair Hut (GR 958036), Corrour (GR 981958).

The route, including both Derry Lodge and White Bridge variations, is a right of way. Both north-to-south and south-to-north crossings can be recommended. The summit of the pass is 7½ miles (12km) from Coylumbridge and 12½ miles (20km) from Linn of Dee, and choice of direction may well depend upon whether you wish to tackle the climb to the summit or the long walk at the Linn of Dee end first. Remember that snow may hinder progress over the summit of the pass until early summer. The route is described below from north to south, starting at Coylumbridge, in order to connect with other routes in this book.

In the north there are several alternative approaches to the Lairig along the ski road between Aviemore and Cairn Gorm skiers' car park; these are all described below. In the south there are two major route alternatives, one via Derry Lodge and one via White Bridge; each is again described below. At Derry Lodge the Lairig Ghru meets the Lairig

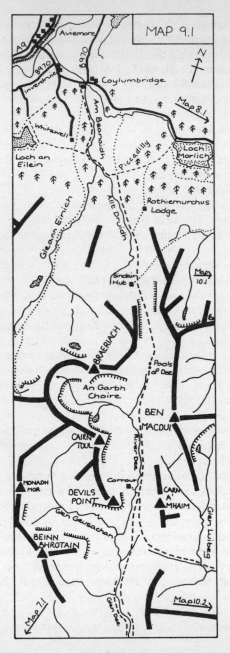

an Laoigh (Route 10), which makes an equally fine return route to Aviemore, thus completing a circumnavigation of Cairn Gorm and Ben Macdui. At White Bridge the Lairig meets the routes to Glen Feshie (Route 7) and Glen Tilt (Route 5), which provide easier routes back to the A9 and the Highland Railway.

On foot in good conditions the Lairig can be completed in a strenuous single day, but a two-day backpack will enable a more leisurely appreciation of the landscape, and even longer will allow some off-route exploration of the surrounding peaks and corries. Always be prepared for a change in the fickle Cairngorm weather and remember that most people get into difficulties by carrying on when they should turn back.

Mountain bikers who are not prepared to carry or man-handle their bikes for great distances over tough and frustrating terrain will find the Lairig a nightmare. The 1928 Scottish Mountaineering Club guidebook stated categorically that 'a bicycle cannot be used with any advantage on this route as the going almost the whole way is very rough and the machine cannot even be wheeled on the path'. Notwithstanding the advent of the mountain bike, this advice still applies; during its central 10 mile (16km) section the route is almost totally unridable, especially with full panniers. Some people will nevertheless find this a challenge, and indeed the Lairig has a cycling tradition that goes back many years, long before the mountain bike was invented.

Any mountain bikers taking up the challenge should undertake the Lairig in a north-to-south direction in order to get the ascent over with in the shortest distance and to avoid tackling the more eroded northern side on descent. From the north the pushing begins at Piccadilly in Rothiemurchus Forest, and the rocky section over the summit of the pass gives very slow going indeed. Beyond Corrour the White Bridge route is easier, but only if the Dee can be forded $2^1{}_2$ miles (4km) further along to reach a Land-Rover track on the far side. The crossing of the deep and fast-flowing Dee should be attempted only by the experienced and only in low-water conditions. The Derry Lodge route involves an extra 60m (200ft) climb but it is safer and from Glen Luibeg onwards is a joy to ride.

Mountain bikers should be ever aware that because the Lairig Ghru is one of Scotland's premier hill tracks any erosion or nuisance value they cause will be especially damaging to their image. If bikes are not to be banned from such places, it is imperative that cyclists behave responsibly.

ROUTE DESCRIPTION

At its northern end the Lairig has several alternative starting points amidst the great forest of Rothiemurchus. The time-honoured approach begins at Coylumbridge, south-west of Aviemore on the B970 Loch Morlich road. A Land-Rover track leaves the roadside beside the camp-site and heads into the forest, eventually reaching Loch Einich many miles distant. At a signposted fork after 700m the Lairig path branches left to the Cairngorm Club footbridge across Am Beanaidh (Am Benny). In places this path is a lovely sandy ribbon through the forest, its beauty enhanced in autumn by swathes of purple heather; the mountains ahead are out of sight and the rigours to come out of mind as you enjoy a serene stroll through the greenwood.

A short distance before the footbridge another track comes in from the right. This is the track from Inverdruie (1 mile west of Coylum-bridge) and Loch an Eilein, an alternative starting point that should be used by mountain bikers (see p98). It is also possible for walkers to shorten the route from Coylumbridge by beginning at Whitewell (GR 915087) at the end of the minor road from Inverdruie. From the car park at Whitewell road-end a path goes down to join the Loch Einich track, which can then be followed to its junction with the Loch an Eilein track. The bewildering number of tracks and paths in Rothiemurchus Forest make attractive short walks and cycle routes (see p101).

Once across the Cairngorm Club footbridge, so called because it was erected by that club in 1912, the path bears away from Am Beanaidh to a crossroads in the forest known as Piccadilly. The paths coming in from the left and from straight ahead begin on the Loch Morlich road and provide yet more starting points for the Lairig; the latter in particular, beginning at GR 956097, is a useful approach route for walkers and mountain bikers staying around Loch Morlich. The Lairig path goes right at Piccadilly to follow the Allt Druidh up into the jaws of the pass, and from hereon it becomes rougher. At first it climbs high above the stream through dense forest, and then the trees begin to thin out until finally only a few gnarled Scots pines remain to turn the path into an obstacle course.

Emerging from the trees, you reach the brow of a hill from where there is a fine view back over the forest to the Spey valley. Ahead the deep cleft of the pass can be seen clearly for the first time, framed by the slabs of Creag an Leth-choin (Craik an *Laich*in, Crag of the Half-dog or Lurcher) and Sron na Lairige (Strawn na *Lahr*ika, Nose of the Pass). The name Creag an Leth-choin commemorates a lurcher that fell to its death here during a great deer hunt. Hidden on the far side is the narrow corrie known as Lurcher's Gully, an area of dispute between ski developers and conservationists for many a year. At the foot of Sron na Lairige stands the Sinclair Hut, beautifully sited on a grassy knoll high above the Druidh.

Within the forest tree roots help to stabilise the path, but once you are out of the trees the going becomes boggier and rockier. Soon another path comes in from the left from Rothiemurchus Lodge, and from here to the Sinclair Hut is perhaps the most eroded section of the route. Much work has been done on path restoration and you should keep to the path to prevent further erosion.

NB The Rothiemurchus Lodge approach to the Lairig is peaty and not a right of way; Rothiemurchus Estate wishes that it be avoided.

The path rises little as it follows the Druidh up to and through a narrow defile below the Sinclair Hut, where yet another approach route to the Lairig comes in from the left from the ski road. This path leaves the ski road at the hairpin bend at GR 985073 and climbs through the gap between Creag a' Chalamain and Creag an Leth-choin. With private transport it is the shortest of all the approach routes to the Lairig, but it involves an extra 110m (360ft) of ascent and misses Rothiemurchus Forest.

The Lairig path used to cross the Druidh in the depths of the defile and climb now dangerously eroded slopes up to the Sinclair Hut, which is hidden above. The new improved path crosses the stream further along, and you can then double back to the hut if you so desire. The small, spartan but welcoming refuge was built in 1957 as a memorial to Angus Sinclair, an Edinburgh philosophy lecturer who died on the slopes of Cairn Gorm in 1954. It has a spectacular situation opposite the crags of Creag an Leth-choin, with views both up to the jaws of the pass and down across Rothiemurchus Forest to the Spey valley. The accommodation it affords is primitive, but like Corrour Bothy it can be a lifesaver, and it is certainly a welcome sight to those coming over the Lairig from the opposite direction ($5\frac{1}{2}$ miles/9km; 3hr/mb:$3\frac{1}{2}$hr + halts).

Beyond the hut the path climbs into the stony wilderness of the upper Lairig. The worst of the erosion is behind you now, owing to the increasingly rough terrain and the diminishing number of people who venture here. Even flies, which can be a nuisance in the forest on a hot day, shy away from the higher reaches of the pass. The ascent is surprisingly gentle and finally flattens out onto the extensive summit boulder-field, where all streams disappear underground. The crags on either side peter out into steep slopes of red granite scree, with tongues of grass and boulders that give access to the peaks above.

The summit is an undistinguished spot among the boulders, but the view down both sides is terrific. Northwards lies the now distant Spey valley, framed between the jaws of the pass; the renowned naturalist Seton Gordon believed that he once saw mist above the Pentland Firth from here. Southwards the valley of the Dee lies at your feet, with Cairn Toul and the Devil's Point prominent.

As you continue across the summit boulderfield the Allt na Criche (Owlt na *Creech*-ya, March or Boundary Burn) tumbles down from the Cairngorm–Ben Macdui plateau in a series of waterfalls on the left, to disappear underground and perhaps to feed the Pools of Dee ahead. Despite its mad dash down the mountainside, the March Burn is not named after the month but from the days when boundaries were walked or marched to demarcate territory.

The four beautifully clear Pools of Dee, two large and two small, lie in hollows among the boulders. They are connected underground and water can just be detected seeping in and out of their ends. They are said never to freeze over, which is difficult to believe given the volume of snow that is dumped here each winter; when snow covers the ground their presence underfoot should not be forgotten. The old name for the pools was Lochan Dubh na Lairige (Black Lochans of the Pass), and it is a shame that this more vivid and evocative name has been superseded.

The path undulates and twists around the pools before leaving the summit boulderfield behind for easier terrain beside the infant Dee. The path does become rockier again in places, but it is never as consistently rough as it is on the northern side. As you descend, the vast U-shaped trench of Glen Dee opens out before you and the scale of the surroundings becomes increasingly impressive. On the left are the massive slopes of Ben Macdui, while on the right is one of the great corries of the Highlands – An Garbh Choire (An *Garra* Chorra, The Rough Corrie), which in scale, grandeur and wildness is rivalled in the Cairngorms only by the head of Loch Avon and Slochd Mor of Ben Avon (see Route 12). The walk across the Braeriach–Cairn Toul plateau around the rim of the corrie is one of the great expeditions of the Highlands, especially magnificent (but requiring especial care) when the corrie rim is corniced.

As you pass the enormous corrie entrance the subsidiary corries that line its sides come into view one by one. Facing you is Coire an Lochain Uaine (*Oo*-anya, Green), its lochan hidden from view but its great waterslide clearly visible. Next right are the deep, shaded recesses of upper Garbh Coire, whose snowbeds normally last all year round. Further right the upper part of the Falls of Dee can be seen tumbling from the lip of the plateau, and further right again is Coire Bhrochain (*Vroch*in,

116

Porridge), with the summit of Braeriach perched on the rim of its impressive headwall. Some stray cattle are said to have plunged to their deaths from this rim, and according to tradition the corrie is named after the consistency of their remains.

Continuing along the flat bottom of Glen Dee, the mountains on each side begin to soar skywards in a most un-Cairngorm-like fashion. At the corner of An Garbh Choire, Cairn Toul has been gouged to a point by numerous corries, while further down the glen the Devil's Point is unmistakable. Opposite the Devil's Point the featureless slopes of Ben MacDui also give way to the fine-pointed peak of Carn a'Mhaim (*Va*-im, Breast). The corrie on the near (north) side of the Devil's Point is Coire Odhar (*Oa*-ar, Dun-coloured), and it is this that gives the bothy at its foot, Corrour Bothy, its name.

Shortly after Corrour Bothy comes into view a large group of rocks is passed beside the path on the left. The largest and flattest of these is the Clach nan Taillear (the Tailors' Stone). It was here that three tailors died sheltering from a storm; one Hogmanay they had drunkenly boasted that on a single winter's day they could dance a reel in Abernethy, Rothiemurchus and Mar, but en route to their last reel they were overtaken by bad weather.

Corrour Bothy, perhaps the most renowned bothy in Scotland, stands in the heart of the Lairig, 13 miles (21km) from Aviemore and 15 miles (24km) from Braemar. The Devil's Point, which towers above it, is a monolith of rock whose prim name is a euphemism for the Gaelic Bod an Deamhain (Boat an *Jaw*-an, Devil's Penis). The bothy was built in 1877 for the use of deer stalkers and watchers and was reconstructed by the Cairngorm Club in 1950 for the use of Lairig travellers. It lies a few hundred metres off-route across the Dee which is here bridged by a footbridge built by the Nature Conservancy Council in 1959 (11 miles/ 18km; 5½hr/mb:7½hr + halts). One frosty August night I had the privilege of seeing the aurora borealis from here; curtains of soft rippling light reached out across the sky, silhouetting the surrounding peaks and making their outlines seem to shimmer. I stood mesmerised.

Beyond the bothy is a fork where you must choose between two paths that do not meet again until the Linn of Dee 9 miles (14km) distant. The more scenic route veers left around Carn a'Mhaim into Glen Luibeg and Glen Lui. The path climbs 60m (200ft) and tends to channel water after rain, but once it reaches Glen Luibeg it becomes a beautiful sandy ribbon through the pines to Derry Lodge, where Glen Luibeg and Glen Derry join to form Glen Lui. The Scots pines at Derry Lodge are among the finest in the country.

117

From the lodge a Land-Rover track continues down gentle Glen Lui beside the broad flats of the Lui Water to reach the roadside near Linn of Dee. The many ruins in the glen testify to more populous times. The Earl of Mar's estates were forfeited following the failure of the 1715 Jacobite rebellion, and it was then perhaps only a matter of time before the local people were evicted; the clearances took place in 1726.

The alternative route out from Corrour Bothy continues down Glen Dee to White Bridge at the junction of the Dee and the Geldie. Its more open scenery is less attractive than the Derry Lodge route, but it involves no further ascent and after avoiding the boggy ground at the gaping entrance to Glen Geusachan it stays close to the Dee, which at the Chest of Dee especially has some fine small waterfalls and pools. The route will be used mainly by mountain bikers intending to ford the Dee and reach the Land-Rover track on the far side and by travellers continuing to Glen Feshie or Glen Tilt. From White Bridge another Land-Rover track heads eastwards to Linn of Dee (see p96 for description).

10

THE LAIRIG AN LAOIGH

TRACK RECORD

The Lairig an Laoigh (*Lahr*ik an *Loo*-y, Pass of the Calves) is the more easterly of the two great passes that cut through the heart of the Cairngorm massif from Speyside to Deeside. You would expect it to have much in common with its western neighbour the Lairig Ghru (Route 9), and in terms of spectacular mountain scenery and challenging terrain they are indeed in a class of their own. The Lairig an Laoigh is often undeservedly regarded as the poor relation of the two because it lacks the Lairig Ghru's classic simplicity of line and the grandeur and scale of its mountain and corrie scenery, but this does an injustice to a magnificent trans-Cairngorm route that many find as equally rewarding as its more celebrated neighbour.

The route follows an intricate itinerary through a stunning variety of landscapes and close to a number of beauty spots that would attract tourists in droves were there a road to take them there. The traveller is lured ever onwards to discover what is around the next corner and over the next horizon: eastwards past the sandy shores of Loch Morlich and jewel-like An Lochan Uaine, then southwards across the shoulder of Bynack More, passing close by that most secret of all Cairngorm treasures, Loch Avon, to descend finally onto the serene, pine-studded plains of Glen Derry. Such is the variety, beauty and spaciousness of the landscape that it seems a world away from the contrasting attractions of the corridor-like Lairig Ghru.

From the north the Lairig an Laoigh can be approached from the Spey valley either by going eastwards from Aviemore or southwards from Grantown and Nethy Bridge. As a through-route from Aviemore to Deeside it was never as popular as the Lairig Ghru because of its indirectness and length, but from further down the Spey towards Grantown it was the shorter and easier of the two routes and was formerly well used by local inhabitants. It was also an especially attractive route to drovers who came this way with calves that were not strong enough to tackle the screes of the Lairig Ghru – hence the name of the pass.

Lest this explanation imply that the Lairig an Laoigh is a somewhat easier proposition than the Lairig Ghru, be advised that it would be prudent to treat it with equal respect. The central section is very rough, the open terrain makes navigation awkward in mist, there is a major river crossing at the Fords of Avon and on the shoulder of Bynack More the route attains a height of 792m (*c*2,600ft), scarcely lower than the summit of the Lairig Ghru. Only well-equipped and experienced walkers and mountain bikers should tackle it.

ROUTEPLANNER
OS map: 36/43
Start point: Glenmore Lodge (GR 987095)
End point: Linn of Dee (GR 062897)
Total distance: 18½ miles (30km)
　　+ Aviemore to Glenmore Lodge: 7 miles (11km)
　　+ Linn of Dee to Braemar: 6 miles (10km)
Total ascent: 620m (2,030ft)
　　in reverse: 640m (2,100ft)
Total time: 8½hr (mb:8hr) + halts
　　+ Aviemore to Glenmore Lodge: 2½hr (mb:1hr)
　　+ Linn of Dee to Braemar: 2hr (mb:1hr)
Aviemore: accommodation/provisions/station/youth hostel/campsite.
Braemar: accommodation/provisions/youth hostel/campsite.

There are also youth hostels at Loch Morlich near Glenmore Lodge and Inverey near Linn of Dee, campsites at Loch Morlich and Coylumbridge and a shop at Loch Morlich. Bothies en route: Ryvoan (GR 006115), Bynack Stable (GR 021105), Hutchison Memorial Hut (GR 023997, 1 mile off-route). There is also a small stone refuge at the Fords of Avon (GR 042032).

The route, including both Glenmore Lodge and Nethy Bridge variations, is a right of way.

Like the Lairig Ghru, the Lairig an Laoigh is described in a north-to-south direction in order that the most difficult section is tackled early on and travellers wishing to extend the trip can return to Atholl or Speyside by easier routes through Glen Tilt (Route 5) or Glen Feshie (Route 7). At the Fords of Avon half-way along the Lairig crosses Glen Avon (Route 12), which can be used to extend the route eastwards towards Tomintoul

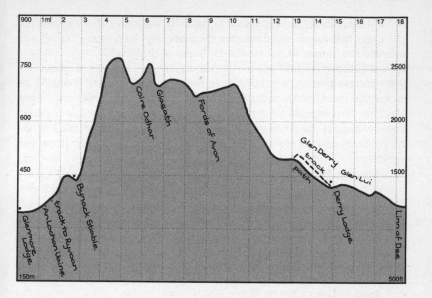

or the Bealach Dearg (Route 13) to explore the remote eastern Cairngorms.

Again, like the Lairig Ghru, the Lairig an Laoigh is a tough but practicable single-day proposition for fit walkers and mountain bikers, but an overnight wilderness camp has its attractions and would make the journey less of a rush. The path is in excellent condition, with walkers being able to skip lightheartedly over bouldery sections that will reduce mountain bikers to gibbering impotence, but the length and seriousness of the route should not be underestimated. NB The Fords of Avon can be impassable when the river is in spate and there is no practicable way round.

From the mountain biker's point of view the Lairig an Laoigh is almost as tough as the Lairig Ghru. Land-Rover tracks penetrate each end of it, but the central 8 mile (13km) section is mostly unridable and in some instances so rough that a bike is no more than an encumbrance. Only fit, determined, skilful and unflappable mountain bikers will enjoy it, but the rewards are commensurate with the effort and, one way or another, the experience will be unforgettable. The crossing is easier in a north-to-south direction as better paths on the northern side of the pass give easier pushing. Especially fit mountain bikers can combine the Lairig with Glen Tilt (Route 5) or Glen Feshie (Route 7), ending at Blair

121

Atholl or Kingussie respectively, to make a weekend trip by rail using the Highland Railway an attractive proposition.

ROUTE DESCRIPTION

From the road-end at Glenmore Lodge east of Aviemore the route begins as per the route to Abernethy (Route 11), following an excellent sandy track through beautifully wooded country to a fork beyond An Lochan Uaine (see p129 for description). The left branch continues past Ryvoan Bothy to Abernethy and is the approach route to the Lairig from that direction.

The Lairig an Laoigh branches right at the fork, making a short climb across a low plateau where ancient pines cluster around the lovely moorland loch of Loch a' Gharbh-choire (*Ghar*av, Rough). Some short sections of track have the consistency of a stream bed, but they cannot detract from the picturesqueness of the scene.

A short descent brings you to Bynack Stable, a rough corrugated iron shelter on another lovely site beside the bustling River Nethy. To the right Strath Nethy cuts a long and deep corridor between Cairn Gorm and Bynack More, but the Lairig takes a less obvious route, crossing the river (bridge) and climbing 350m (1,000ft) across heathery moorland onto the north shoulder of Bynack More. The path is good and gritty but the ascent is an especially tough one for mountain bikers; as distraction there is a commanding northern panorama over the forests and plains of Strathspey, and until late spring there may be snowdrifts to ease the fevered brow.

Once the shoulder of Bynack More is reached the path levels off and contours around to the east side of the mountain. In parts the track has several strands, perhaps a relic of droving days when herds fanned out on easier ground. Immediately ahead is the summit of Bynack More (1,090m/3,574ft), whose rocky north ridge provides an interesting 300m (1,000ft) ascent to the tumble of granite boulders that mark the summit. Strong walkers may wish to bag the summit and continue past the Barns of Bynack to A'Choinneach (A *Choan*-yach, The Boggy Place; 1,017m/3,336ft) and the Saddle, and then descend to Loch Avon and the Fords of Avon to rejoin the Lairig.

On the east side of Bynack More the Lairig makes an adventurous descent into shallow Coire Odhar (*Oa*-ar, Dun-coloured), the path liberally spiced with boulders for te delectation of mountain bikers. To the east Ben Avon and Beinn a'Bhuird come into view, and in between featureless moors roll for mile upon mile to Glen Avon and Tomintoul. The place has a bleak outlook and in poor visibility disoriented travellers

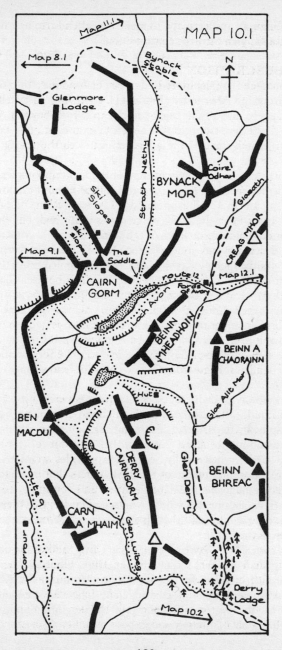

MAP 10.1

N

Map 11.1

Map 8.1

Bynack Stable

Glenmore Lodge

Coire Odhar

Strath Nethy

BYNACK MOR

Ski Slopes

Glaeath

CREAG MHOR

Ski Slopes

Map 9.1

The Saddle

CAIRN GORM

route 12

Map 12.1

Loch Avon

Fords of Avon

BEINN MHEADHOIN

BEINN A CHAORAINN

Glas Allt Mor

Hut

BEN MACDUI

DERRY CAIRNGORM

Glen Derry

BEINN BHREAC

route 9

Corrour

CARN A'MHAIM

Glen Luibeg

Derry Lodge

Map 10.2

have lost their way and their lives here. The path crosses the floor of the corrie, fords the awkward little stream of the Uisge Dubh Poll a' Choin (*Oosh*ka *Doo* Pola *Choin*, Black Water of the Dog's Pool) and climbs out the far side of the corrie.

Another steep boulder-strewn descent follows to the glen of the Glasath (*Glass*ah, Green Ford), and then the Lairig at last begins to look something like a mountain pass should as a broad corridor opens up southwards between Bynack More and Creag Mhor (895m/2,937ft, Craik Voar, Big Crag). On the right-hand skyline are the Barns of Bynack, giant haystacks of rock some 30m (100ft) high. In high winds walking around the Barns can be a disconcerting experience, for competing currents of air buffet you this way and that with amusing but unsettling randomness. Other granite tors dot the skyline like warts.

The path crosses the Glasath on stepping-stones and climbs gently to the head of its glen, where Lochan a'Bhainne (*Van*-ya, Milk) nestles on the watershed, bleak or inviting depending on the weather. Over the watershed the corridor through the mountains continues, the path trending downhill by the banks of the Allt Dearg (Owlt *Jerr*ack, Red Stream) to arrive at the Ath nam Fiann (Ah nam *Fee*-an, Ford of the Fingalians), otherwise known as the Fords of Avon, that great crossroads in the wilderness where Glen Avon cuts from right to left across the Lairig. On the near side of the River Avon is a small stone bothy that makes a useful emergency shelter; beside it is the only patch of grass in the whole rugged area that could conceivably serve as a rough pitch for a small tent (8¼ miles/13km; 4½hr/mb: 4½hr + halts). One mile to the right up Glen Avon lies Loch Avon, and it would be a travesty if you were not to make the half-hour walk to see it. There can be few more dramatic sights in the British Isles (see p137).

The crossing of the Avon can be difficult; in spate it is impossible. There has been controversy in recent years about whether to erect a bridge here. Those in favour say it could save lives, those against say it might have the opposite effect because an easier crossing might attract into this remote area people who are not competent to be there. My love of wild places and my wish to keep them wild gives me some sympathy with the latter view.

I once arrived here late one evening in early May, intending to cross the Avon while I was still warm from exertion, but I succumbed to the patch of greenery beside the shelter and made camp. I justified this to myself with a piece of river-crossing lore I had learned in the Alps, reasoning that the river would be lower in the morning because the snow that swelled it would freeze overnight.

It was certainly a cold night, with a star-studded sky over-head and frost forming on the inside of my bivi tent. The following morning dawned bright and clear, with glorious streaming sunlight etching the surrounding mountains in exquisite detail and making me feel privileged to be there. While the sun was low in the east I raced up to Loch Avon to obtain an early morning view of that spectacular loch that is vouchsafed to few and that will remain with me for ever. As for the actual ford of the river, the water level was not visibly lower, but the invigoratingly cold water and the snowbank on the far side that made exit precarious only seemed an affirmation of a supreme wilderness experience. No, let no bridge be built at the Fords of Avon. As Gerard Manley Hopkins put it so aptly in his haunting poem 'Inversnaid', 'O let them be left, wildness and wet; Long live the weeds and wilderness yet.'

Beyond the Fords of Avon the Lairig continues its way southwards between Beinn Mheadhoin (Vane, Middle; 1,182m/3,883ft) and Beinn Chaorainn (*Hoor*in, Rowan; 1,082m/3,553ft). Almost immediately

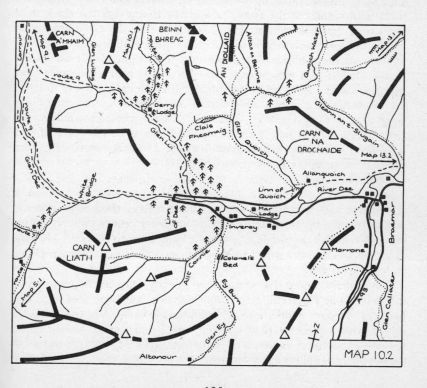

MAP 10.2

there is another stream to be forded, the Allt an t-Seallaidh (Owlt an *Tyolly*, Stream of the View), but you can keep your boots on this time. The going improves for a while beside the elongated Dubh Lochan (Doo Lochan, Black Lochs), but just when mountain bikers may think it safe to get back in the saddle the bouldery wastes return with a vengeance on the next and last ascent of the route, to the 740m (2,450ft) bealach between Beinn Mheadhoin and Beinn a'Chaorainn.

While walkers will skip lightheartedly from boulder to boulder, mountain bikers will find this section a real struggle, especially with loaded panniers. With progress becoming as slow as coastal erosion, mountain bikers may find themselves wistfully recalling the days of droving, when paths were cleared of rocks to protect the hooves of cattle. Those finding themselves pinned beneath their supposed mode of transport for the umpteenth time will perhaps find laughter the best policy and wonder, not for the first time, whether this particular form of masochism should be called bike mountaineering rather than mountain biking.

The bealach itself is a pleasant spot, with a few reedy lochans, a waterfall tumbling down from Beinn Mheadhoin and grand views along the Lairig in both directions. The Dubh Lochan makes a fine foreground for the view back to the Barns of Bynack, and it becomes obvious why the Allt an t-Seallaidh was so named. Ahead lies the broad vale of Glen Derry with its first welcoming pines. The descent is initially indistinct, steep and boggy, becoming bouldery again lower down, but the roughest terrain is now past and many stretches are ridable. To the right is the gaping mouth of Coire Etchachan (*Ait*shachan, Juniper), with its impressive 120m (400ft) rock headwall. A well-worn path can be seen ascending the back of the corrie towards Loch Etchachan and Ben Macdui, a magnificent hillwalking route to the summit of the highest Cairngorm.

Approaching the flats of Glen Derry the junction with the Coire Etchachan path is passed and the Glas Allt Mor (Glass Owlt More, Big Green Stream) is forded (this is easy unless it is in spate). The Hutchison Memorial Hut is 1 mile away along the Coire Etchachan path, deep in the heart of the corrie. Once across the Glas Allt Mor the path sudddenly improves beyond a mountain biker's wildest dreams to give a lovely grassy ride across the flats of upper Glen Derry. It reaches an excellent Land-Rover track that gives a further exhilarating 6 miles (10km) through the pines, past Derry Lodge and down Glen Lui all the way to the roadside near the Linn of Dee.

Walkers also will find much to wonder at along this lovely final stretch of the Lairig. The pines of Glen Derry must be among the most magnificent trees in the country and the walk through them is enchanting. There is one section especially that should not be missed – the old path to Derry Lodge that pre-dates the Land-Rover track, leaving it about 1 mile after its start, at the point where it bears left and climbs away from the Derry Burn. The path goes straight on at this point to cross the river at a bridge (GR 039958). NB This variation is impracticable to mountain bikers.

Just above the bridge is the site of the old Derry dam, one of many that were built on Deeside and Speyside in the early nineteenth century to aid the transportation of timber; water was impounded behind the dam, then suddenly released to float logs down the river. On the far side of the river the path meanders through the forest on a carpet of pine needles. It is a delightful walk, with the tumbling river never far away. Just above the point where the path rejoins the riverside are some picturesque waterfalls that are worth making a detour to view. Further on is the knoll of An Toman Dearg (An *Tooman Jerrack*, The Red Knoll) which is fenced against deer to enable regeneration of trees; without such measures the old pine forests of the Cairngorms will die.

The hillsides on each side of Glen Derry have little of interest to distract from the woodland and river scenery. On the west side of the glen are three high corries, but only Coire an Lochain Uaine (*Oo*-an-ya, Green), the hanging corrie next to Coire Etchachan, has any depth and its hidden lochan cannot be seen from the path. On a curious historical note, the renowned eighteenth-century poacher-cum-poet William Smith built a hut here and wrote a poem about the corrie that for several generations was the most popular song in the eastern Highlands.

At Derry Lodge the path recrosses the Derry Burn (bridge) and rejoins the Land-Rover track. The last 3 mile (5km) section to the Linn of Dee is as per the Lairig Ghru (see p117).

11

THE BRAES OF ABERNETHY

TRACK RECORD

The River Nethy rises on the slopes of Cairn Gorm and flows northwards to join the Spey, and the outlying hills on the north side of the Cairn-gorms are therefore known as the Braes of Abernethy. The flanks of the Braes are crossed by a number of tracks and paths, and these can be linked to form an interesting cross-country route between Aviemore and Tomintoul. This route does not have the classic dimensions of the neigh-bouring Cairngorm passes, but its more intimate and charming scenery is in its own way equally appealing.

Beginning amidst the pine forests of Glen More, the route first crosses the picturesque Ryvoan Pass, which once formed part of the Thieves' Road to the west coast (see p154). It then penetrates the glorious Abernethy Forest, the largest remaining tract of natural pine forest in Britain, and crosses from glen to glen across the valleys of the River Nethy, the Dorback Burn and the Burn of Brown as it skirts the Braes to Tomintoul. It is a route of near horizons, of corners and surprises, a route to savour for its individual parts.

ROUTEPLANNER

OS map: 36
Start point: Glenmore Lodge (GR 987095)
End point: Tomintoul (GR 168187)
Total distance: 17½ miles (28km)
    + Aviemore to Glenmore Lodge: 7 miles (11km)
Total ascent: 350m (1,150ft)
    in reverse: 340m (1,120ft)
Total time: 8hr (mb:4½hr) + halts
    + Aviemore to Glenmore Lodge: 2½hr (mb:1hr)
Aviemore: accommodation/provisions/station/youth hostel/campsite.
Tomintoul: accommodation/provisions/youth hostel.

There is also a youth hostel at Loch Morlich near Glenmore Lodge, campsites at Loch Morlich and Coylumbridge and a shop at Loch Morlich. Bothies en route: Ryvoan (GR 006115).

The route is a right of way except for the section between the Crom Allt and Attinlea.

The route makes an attractive connecting route between the central Cairngorm passes (Route 9 and 10) and those further to the east (Routes 12 and 13), and it can be completed in a single day. The only problematical section, from the point of view of terrain and navigation, is between the Crom Allt and Attinlea, where good map-reading skills are required. Those seeking shorter circuits will find the many individual parts of the route well worth exploring in their own right. The whole route makes a pleasing mountain-biking expedition, with some testing little ascents, some exhilarating descents and ever-changing scenery and terrain that add spice to the enterprise.

ROUTE DESCRIPTION

From the road-end at Glenmore Lodge east of Aviemore, continue along the lovely sandy track that cuts a swathe through beautiful mixed woodland to the Pass of Ryvoan. In the jaws of the pass lies lovely An Lochan Uaine (An Lochan Oo-*an*-ya. The Green Lochan), whose translucent

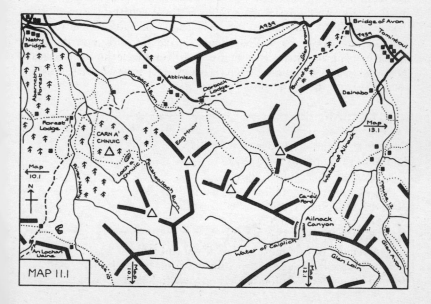

waters, sandy shores and waterside trees make it, with a little stretch of the imagination, seem more like a tropical lagoon or a desert oasis than a Scottish lochan. Here, according to legend, the fairies washed their clothes. On a sunny day, when the water mirrors the trees that cling to the rocky hillsides above, it can be a difficult place to leave behind. NB An Lochan Uaine can also be reached from Aviemore by an off-road route through Rothiemurchus Forest (see p102).

Beyond the lochan the track rises to a fork where the Lairig an Laoigh track (Route 10) branches right. Keeping left, the track to Abernethy veers north and rises onto the open moor past Ryvoan Bothy and its two reedy lochans. It is very rough in places but soon improves again as it enters Abernethy Forest and descends through the trees. At one point you cross a short stretch of heathery moor, and just before here (look for cairns on the left) stands a now tree-engulfed and poignant memorial to James Maxwell, a 22 year old hillwalker who was killed in World War I.

Beyond the moor the track re-enters the wood and keeps left at a fork to descend to Forest Lodge. In the spring the scent of the pines here is almost intoxicating. The Forest Lodge area is now owned by the Royal Society for the Protection of Birds; cars may be driven to the lodge from the minor road to the west (GR 998167). A track continues northwards through the forest to Nethy Bridge, passing some magnificent specimens of Caledonian pine, and this makes a fine mountain-biking circuit in combination with the An Slugain a few miles down the road from Nethy Bridge (see p102).

If you are continuing to Tomintoul, a maze of tracks and paths cross the open country to the east between Forest Lodge and the road to Dorback Lodge. However, it is recommended that you keep to the

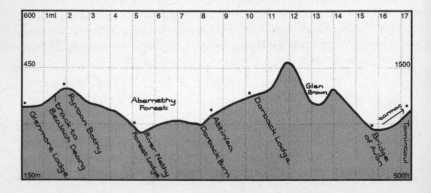

following route as the RSPB are anxious that nesting birds elsewhere are not disturbed. Continuing northwards past Forest Lodge, follow the main track right across the River Nethy (bridge). When the main track turns right again, keep straight on and bear immediately left to follow another track beside a small stream. Turn sharp left to follow this track across the Crom Allt and Faesheallach Burn (both of which can normally be forded dry-shod) to a fork at some ruins (GR 032164).

Take the right branch, which curves right across pleasant, wide-open moorland to meet another track across the stream to its end at a T-junction. Go straight on beside a wall to join another good track, which eventually degenerates and becomes lost in the heather as you approach the Dorback Burn. This is the only pathless, boggy section en route, with the ford of the Dorback Burn finally putting an end to any aspirations to dry feet. Aim for Attinlea, the largest building seen ahead, picking up sheep paths and eventually a track that leads past the house to the Dorback Lodge road.

From the road-end at Dorback Lodge two tracks lead on across wild moorland country that is in sharp contrast to the woodland landscapes of the first part of the route. The right branch is the old right of way to Glen Avon, which also provides an approach route to the Ailnack Canyon (see p139). To continue to Tomintoul take the left branch, which goes around the lodge and climbs across a low ridge to descend steeply into the claustrophobic confines of Glen Brown (from the Gaelic *bruthainn*, *broo*-in, sultry heat). Note the many ruined cottages that are a feature of this section of the route and testify to its importance in pre-clearance times.

Once you are into Glen Brown follow a path downstream, crossing and recrossing the Burn of Brown several times, to reach a track out the far side (look for an old iron gate in the fence about 100m past the end of the forestry plantation on the right). This track climbs over another low ridge and descends through trees once again (where it becomes horribly stony) to reach picturesque Kylnadrochit Lodge and the A939 at Bridge of Avon, 2 miles (3km) from Tomintoul.

12

GLEN AVON

TRACK RECORD

'The Avon, regarded from the point of view of river and mountain scenery, is perhaps the most perfect glen in Scotland, for in the whole 38 miles from its source above Loch Avon to the Spey, there is not a single dull passage,' wrote Henry Alexander in the 1928 Scottish Mountaineering Club Cairngorms guidebook. No one who follows the course of the Avon (pronounced 'Aan') over this distance can fail to agree with this judgement, for the variety and stature of the scenery are breathtaking. Upstream from its confluence with the Spey the Avon leads nowhere except into the heart of the wilderness, yet there is a track all the way and no route more deserves a chapter to itself; it is the only major route described in this book that is not a through-route from one road to another.

In its lower reaches below Tomintoul roads follow the banks of the Avon throughout its course, but above Tomintoul roads and towns are left behind for a magnificent 20 mile (30km) corridor that cuts deep into the heart of the Cairngorms massif, ending at the remote mountain fastness of Loch Avon. The Avon itself is a beautiful river that has long been famous for the purity and clarity of its water, resulting from the lack of peat in its catchment area. The water is sometimes so clear that it appears deceptively shallow, so take heed that people have drowned in it in the past. An old legend tells how Fingal's wife drowned in it, causing the river to be named after her as the Ath Fhionn or Fair One. As the old couplet says, 'The water of Avon, it runs sae clear, 'Twad beguile a man o'a hundred year.'

The track up Glen Avon keeps close to the river throughout its length, from the peaceful meadows of the lower glen, through a turbulent central section where the water rushes through the Linn of Avon beneath the spectacular ridges and corries of Ben Avon, to the wild upper glen, where

On the Devil's Staircase in the shadow of Buachaille Etive Mor *(Route 1)*

Evening shadows on Conic Hill *(Route 1)*

Approaching Glen Coe *(Route 1)*

Weir crossing en route to Sronphadruig Lodge *(Route 2)*

Loch an t-Seilich from the final section of Comyn's Road *(Routes 2, 3 and 4)*

Watersplash near Carn Dearg *(Route 6)*

A vast and uncompromising wilderness: the view west from Ruigh Ealasaid *(Route 7)*

Superb mountain biking in Rothiemurchus Forest *(Route 8)*

In the jaws of the Lairig Ghru *(Route 9)*

Riding techniques (1): the normal position (the climb over into Glen Derry, *Route 10*)

Glen Builg bivi *(Route 13)*

Ben Alder Cottage and Loch Bricht *(Route 15)*

The natural bridge over the Burn of Agie *(Route 18)*

The path along Loch Affric at sunset *(Route 20)*

The long and winding road to Alltbeithe *(Route 20)*

dramatic Loch Avon lies in a crag-girt trench between Ben Macdui and Cairn Gorm. There can be no more impressive end to a glen. Of its kind, perhaps only Loch Coruisk on Skye surpasses Loch Avon, and there can be no greater commendation than that. In all, the many guises of Glen Avon add up to an irresistible route that demands superlatives.

ROUTEPLANNER
OS map: 36
Start point: Tomintoul (GR 168187)
End point: Loch Avon (GR 026033)
Total distance: 20 miles (32km)
Total ascent: 540m (1,770ft)
    in reverse: 150m (500ft)
Total time: 8hr (mb:6hr) + halts
Tomintoul: accommodation/provisions/youth hostel.
Loch Avon: no facilities, and may it ever remain so.

Bothies en route: the Ponymen's Hut (GR 129061), Faindouran Lodge (GR 082062). There is also a small stone refuge at the Fords of Avon (GR 042032) and shelter can also be found beneath the Shelter Stone at the head of Loch Avon (see below).

The route is a right of way. For the first 5½ miles (9km), as far as Dalestie there is a (private) tarmaced road. An excellent Land-Rover track continues for another 10½ miles (18km) to just beyond Faindouran Lodge and then a path goes the rest of the way to the head of Loch Avon and beyond.

As the upper end of the route reaches no road and offers no easy ways out of the wilderness, most walkers and mountain bikers will choose to return along the glen to Tomintoul. The complete return trip to the mouth of Loch Avon is a considerable journey of 40 miles (64km) that only mountain marathoners will contemplate completing on foot in a single day. Ordinary mortals should settle for an over-night halt in tent or bothy.

At the Fords of Avon, Glen Avon crosses the Lairig an Laoigh, and this gives backpackers and bikepackers an opportunity to vary the route; either direction along the Lairig reaches civilisation in a shorter distance than the return trip to Tomintoul, but the going is much harder (see Route 10). At Inchrory Glen Avon also connects with the Bealach Dearg (Route 13) and Donside (Route 14), giving yet more options for the exploration of this fascinating area. A day spent exploring the vicinity of Loch Avon, perhaps including an ascent of Ben Macdui via Loch

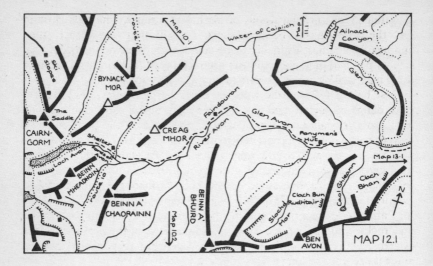

MAP 12.1

Etchachan, is also recommended, while hillwalking routes out from Loch Avon are discussed below.

Mountain bikers can do the return trip from Tomintoul in a very long and eventful day, but would be advised to leave their bikes at the end of the Land-Rover track and walk the last few miles to Loch Avon as the path becomes increasingly impracticable to cycle. It is on routes such as this that the mountain bike really comes into its own, enabling exhilarating access to magnificent country.

ROUTE DESCRIPTION

From Tomintoul the route to Glen Avon heads south-eastwards out of town along the A939. Leave the main road when it turns left to Braemar and carry straight on, turning right after a few hundred metres on a road signposted Delnabo. When this road bears right to descend across the Avon to Delnabo, branch left on a Land-Rover track signposted Queen Victoria's Viewpoint (car park). The viewpoint is a short distance along and boasts a fine view across the verdant pastures of lower Glen Avon to the summit ridge of Ben Avon. The track continues past the viewpoint and joins the private road along the glen at the bridge near Delavorar. This road comes from the end of the public road at Delnabo, and with private transport to Delnabo can be used to shorten the route by 1½ miles (2km).

Beyond Delavorar the road holds to the lush green banks of the sparkling Avon through woods of birch and juniper. The hills close in and the river snakes between them, first around one corner, then another. It is almost Rhine-like; one could easily imagine the occasional schloss perched high above on the brow of a hill. In spring and summer there may well be oystercatchers to pipe you on your way.

· Just before Dalestie the Burn of Little Fergie comes down from a steep defile on the left, and an old drove road, now a path, climbs beside it to cross a bealach to Donside. Near the bealach the path passes a curious rocky notch appropriately named The Eag (Aik, Notch), which is worth a look if you have the time and energy. At Dalestie the tarmaced road gives way to a good Land-Rover track that continues to still-used Inchrory Lodge, a fine stone edifice built around the middle of last century (8 miles/13km; 3hr/mb:1½hr + halts). Inch is the Scots word for flat land beside a river, and Inchrory is indeed a pleasant oasis in the now rocky confines of Glen Avon, with fine views of the northern ridges of Ben Avon. The identity of Rory has been lost to posterity, but his name is recorded as long ago as 1546.

Inchrory is a crossroads. Eastwards the small gorge of the Allt Roderick carries a track over a low pass to Donside. Southwards a Land-Rover track continues up Glen Builg towards the Bealach Dearg and Deeside. Glen Avon, however, does a right-angled turn and heads westwards into the heart of the Cairngorms. In droving days Inchrory was a hive of activity as herds arrived and dispersed along the various glens (see p140).

At Inchrory you are already 8 miles (13km) from Tomintoul yet still barely beginning to make an impression on this long glen, for the best of the route is still to come. For the next 7 miles (11km), as far as Faindouran Lodge, the well-gritted Land-Rover track gives easy walking and excellent cycling, with the numerous corries, ridges and tors of Ben Avon competing for attention as they come into view one by one. The initial short section from Inchrory to the Glen Avon/Glen Builg junction is pleasantly lined with birches, and then the glen beckons westwards with its finest stretch of river scenery – the Linn of Avon. This picturesque wooded gorge lies hidden beside the track at the top of the rise a few hundred metres beyond the Glen Builg junction; its deep pools and waterfalls show the Avon's purity and clarity to perfection.

Beyond the Linn the track makes a gradual climb away from the narrow glen bottom before descending again to cross the river at the bridge at the foot of Glen Loin, a deep narrow side glen that cuts into the plateau to the north (see below). There are so many new estate tracks here that even the most committed of mountain bikers must find them a regrettable intrusion in the landscape.

On the far side of the bridge a path comes up the other side of the Avon from Inchrory, where another bridge makes possible a fine short circuit of some 4 miles (6km) along both sides of the Linn. Continuing up the glen a steep 90m (300ft) climb carries the track high above the river, only to descend again further along. Cyclists will find this a stiff climb; walkers can avoid it by taking a short cut along the old riverside path that pre-dates the track.

From hereon the vast northern corries of Ben Avon rivet the attention. First into view is the Caol Ghleann (Kail, Narrow), a deep corrie with several spurs leading up to Ben Avon's summit plateau. It seems inappropriately named, for it can be considered narrow only in comparison with the huge corries still to come. Conspicuous tors adorn the spurs. On the left is Clach Bhan (Clach Vahn, Stone of Women), whose chair-like rocky hollows were visited by pregnant women until late into the nineteenth century in the belief that sitting in their icy waters would ensure an easy birth. Further right is Clach Fiaraidh, and further right still is the most prominent tor of all, the 25m (80ft) high Clach Bun Rudhtair (Boon *Roo*tir, Foot of the Mounds).

The next corrie along is the massive Slochd Mor (Slochk Moar, Big Pit), which forms a huge amphitheatre between Ben Avon and Beinn a' Bhuird. At its entrance, beside the track, stands the Ponymen's Hut, and below the hut a bridge crosses the Avon to give access to the corrie. The hut was formerly used by travellers en route to Faindouran Lodge; it still makes a useful shelter on bad days, while on good days it is a fine spot for sitting and contemplating the wide open spaces of the corrie.

Beyond the Slochd Mor the river snakes between heathery spurs and the track is never far away from it. The next corrie reached is again enormous but more shallow and backed by the more gentle slopes of Beinn a' Bhuird; again there is a bridge across the Avon at the mouth of the corrie. The glen then becomes more gorge-like and the track is forced to climb away from the river to contour across the hillside. A bend is rounded and the ruins of Faindouran Lodge are reached at last (15 miles/24km; 6hr/mb:3½hr + halts). The hill top above the bend is called Cnapan a' Mheirlich (*Crap*an a *Vare*lich, Robber's Hill), a reminder of the days when cattle thieves used Glen Avon and Glen Derry as a route from Speyside to Deeside. How much the thieves seemed to view cattle raiding as their right can be seen from an incident of 1633, when they murdered a local laird and his son in the Coal Ghleann as a reprisal for measures taken against them.

Beyond Faindouran Lodge, whose end portion has been restored as a bothy, the glen surprisingly widens again to form a huge plain. The scale and character of the landscape become almost Norwegian; one expects to see glaciers tumbling down the glens. Ben Avon and Beinn a' Bhuird are left behind and the twin Beinn a' Chaorainns (Hoorin, Rowan) rise ahead. The track immediately becomes much rougher, fords a couple of streams and ends less than a mile beyond the lodge at GR 077051.

An alternatively boggy and rocky path continues up the glen and from hereon a mountain bike becomes more of an impediment than an aid to progress. The scenery is less dramatic than in the lower glen (and in the upper reaches still to come), yet it is an astonishing and mysterious part of the glen, for it seems inconceivable that such a spacious plain could exist in the heart of the hills. If this were the Himalayas one would expect to find a lost kingdom here.

The path stays close beside the bustling river, except for one section where it takes a short cut across the plain and where in mist it is easy to lose all sense of direction despite the numerous cairns. The plain ends when it meets the slopes of the Beinn a' Chaorainns, which force the river into a twisting heathery ravine. Drovers and thieves who brought cattle up Glen Avon usually avoided this ravine by crossing the hills to the north between Faindouran Lodge and the Lairig an Laoigh.

Ahead now is Beinn Mheadhoin (Vane, Middle; 1,182m/3,883ft) with its conspicuous summit tor. The path climbs well above the river and exits from the ravine onto yet another wide plain – the great crossroads where the Lairig an Laoigh crosses Glen Avon from north to south. Here are the Fords of Avon and its small stone refuge (19 miles/31km; 7½hr/mb:5½hr + halts; see p122 for a description of the area).

The glen is now nearing its end but the best is still to come, for a further mile of rough path leads to that most dramatic of lochs, Loch Avon, which bursts into view as you surmount the last moraine at its mouth. The view is breathtaking in its suddenness and magnificence, with this most inaccessible of lochs encircled by towering crags such as the eye-catching monolith of Shelter Stone Crag at its head. Shoreline paths combine to make an attractive 3½ mile (6km) circuit that passes several fine golden sand beaches (although the river has to be forded at both ends).

A short distance beyond the head of the loch, at the foot of the crag that is named after it, lies the Shelter Stone, a huge rectangular boulder that has quite a history and beneath which many a climber has spent a memorable night (it shelters five to six people comfortably). In the eighteenth century it was known as a retreat for thieves, and in 1887 the Cairngorm Club, Scotland's first climbing club, was founded here.

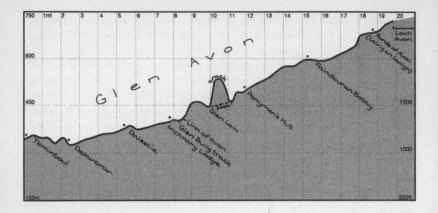

Routes out from Loch Avon

From the head of Glen Avon it is a long way back to Tomintoul, but if you are not constrained by having to return to your starting point there are other routes that lead onwards out of the wilderness. The most straightforward of these routes is the Lairig an Laoigh, which can be followed from the Fords of Avon northwards to Aviemore and Speyside or southwards to Braemar and Deeside, but it is still a much more strenuous route than Glen Avon and should not be undertaken lightly (see Route 10).

From the amphitheatre at the head of Loch Avon there are numerous walking and scrambling routes up to the Cairn Gorm–Ben Macdui plateau, from where the skiers' car park on the north side of Cairn Gorm is within reach. The easiest path up to the plateau goes south-eastwards via Loch Etchachan, another large and spectacular loch at a higher elevation on Macdui. More strenuous and awkward routes ascend directly to Cairn Gorm either via Coire Raibeirt or from the Saddle between Cairn Gorm and A' Choinneach. These routes require care; anyone contemplating them should consult a hillwalker's guidebook.

Ben Avon

Those intent on the ascent of Ben Avon (1,171m/3,841ft), a massive mountain bristling with granite tors and with more ground over 900m (3,000ft) than any other mountain in Scotland, will find Glen Avon by far the most spectacular approach. The normal route ascends a bulldozed track that begins 200m beyond the Glen Builg junction; this becomes a path over several subsidiary tops leading directly to the distant summit.

138

Maze-like Clach Bhan is passed on the ascent, and by descending the north ridge of Stob Bac an Fhurain to complete a circuit of the Caol Ghleann, Clach Bun Rudhtair can also be visited.

A worthwhile extension to the ascent would be to continue beyond the summit across the Sneck and around the Slochd Mor; the summit of Beinn a' Bhuird (Voort, Table Mountain; 1,196m/3,923ft) could be taken in on the way, thus completing the ascent of the two major summits of the eastern Cairngorms. A path on the far side of the Slochd Mor descends to the bridge across the Avon at the Ponymen's Hut; alternatively, it is possible to descend scree slopes from the Sneck into the heart of the Slochd Mor. From any approach all ascents of Ben Avon are a considerable undertaking unless you cycle in or camp.

The Ailnack Canyon

The rolling moorland plateau to the north of Glen Avon barely rates a second glance beside the dramatic scenery of Ben Avon, but in the heart of the moors lies one of the hidden wonders of the Cairngorms – the Ailnack Canyon. Here great walls of broken rock dwarf the Water of Ailnack far below and the curious pyramid of rock called the Castle juts out from the rock face. It is an awesome spot, startling in its unexpectedness, more like a Colorado landscape than the Scottish Highlands.

There are several ways of reaching the canyon but it is rarely visited owing to its remoteness. The easiest approach is via the Glen Loin Land-Rover track, but Glenavon Estate wish this route not to be used in order not to disturb deer. The easiest alternative approach begins at Dorback Lodge to the north-west (GR 077168, see p131). From here an old right of way crosses the moors to the Water of Ailnack, crosses the river at the Ca-du Ford or another ford about a mile further south and continues to Dalestie in Glen Avon; this used to be part of the main route from Abernethy to Donside. There is a Land-Rover track for the first 5 miles (8km) and then a further mile of trackless moorland leads to the Castle. Great care is required around the edges of the canyon and the steep hillsides above, and only experienced hillwalkers should venture here. Another approach to the canyon follows the course of the Water of Ailnack from Delnabo in Glen Avon and has the added interest of passing a second canyon just above Delnabo; there is a Land-Rover track part of the way.

13

THE BEALACH DEARG

TRACK RECORD
It is ironic that while there are two major corridors through the heart of the Cairngorm massif (the Lairig Ghru and the Lairig an Laoigh), there is no immediately obvious route from Speyside to Deeside across the lower hills to the east. Even the A939 Tomintoul-Ballater road, which runs some 11 miles (18km) east of the summit of Ben Avon, has to climb to a height of 644m (2,013ft), making it the second highest road in the country after the Cairnwell. Coming from the north, as did the Highland cattle drovers on their way to the markets of the south, Glen Avon provides an initially tempting route southwards from Tomintoul, but at Inchrory after 8 miles (13km) it takes an abrupt right-angled turn and heads westwards to come to an abrupt halt at wild Loch Avon in the heart of the Cairngorms.

Inchrory therefore became an important crossroads in the days of cattle droving and thieving. Cattle arrived here, legitimately or otherwise, from Strath Avon to the north, Abernethy to the north-west (crossing the Water of Ailnack at the Ca-du Ford; see p139) and Donside to the east (crossing the low pass at the head of the Don; see p151). They then dispersed southwards along Glen Builg or westwards along Glen Avon and through the Lairig an Laoigh to Glen Derry. All these routes are still rights of way. After the '45, when the government attempted to clamp down on cattle thieving, military patrols were stationed near Inchrory and they immediately recovered forty-three head of cattle from some Rannoch thieves.

Most drovers pushed southwards from Inchrory along Glen Builg, whose lush grazings lured the cattle onwards to Loch Builg at the head of the glen. Only here, on the moors east of Ben Avon, does it become apparent that Glen Avon and Glen Builg have flattered to deceive, for there is now no obvious way forward. South of Loch Builg, Glen Gairn cuts from left to right across the line of march, and ahead, blocking the way to Deeside, lies a barrier of high hills, culminating in the 900m (2,953ft) peak of Culardoch (Cul*ard*och, Back High Place).

One possible route onwards for drovers was to go up Glen Gairn and over the bealach at its head, but this passed through the rocky defile between Creag an Dail Mhor and Creag an Dail Bheag and did not make for easy droving. Some drovers turned eastwards and headed down Glen Gairn towards Ballater, and this was also the route taken by Queen Victoria on her 'great expedition' from Tomintoul to Balmoral in 1860. The shortest route from Loch Builg to Deeside, however, goes straight over the mountains to Keiloch and Invercauld, crossing the 650m (2,030ft) Bealach Dearg (*Byal*och *Jerr*ack, Red Pass) between Culardoch and Carn Liath, and despite its height this became the main route for drovers and other travellers.

Drovers continued to use the Bealach Dearg until droving died out in the late nineteenth century, but by that time the pass had been superseded by Caulfield's military road (now the A939) further east, built in the 1750s. In 1832 an Edinburgh civil engineer named James Flint drew up proposals for a road over the Bealach Dearg as a shorter alternative to Caulfield's route, but the plan came to nothing and today only an occasional walker or mountain biker comes this way to explore the old hill track and discover the back country of the Cairngorms.

Scenically as well as historically the route has much to offer the cross-country traveller, from the glorious river scenery of Glen Avon to the wilder loch, moorland and mountain scenery of the central section and the picturesque forest tracks of Deeside. Above all there is the high bealach that gives the route its name, the Bealach Dearg itself, a bleak spot on a wintry day, but at other times a stunning viewpoint from which to survey the hills of Deeside. The route is less trodden than its more celebrated neighbours the Lairig Ghru and the Lairig an Laoigh but it has much to recommend it. These eastern reaches of the Cairngorms deserve to be better known.

ROUTEPLANNER
OS map: 36/43
Start point: Tomintoul (GR 168187)
End point: Keiloch (GR 186915)
Total distance: 19½ miles (31km)
    + Keiloch to Braemar: 3½ miles (6km)
Total ascent: 390m (1,280ft) + 80m (260ft) using Land-Rover track;
    in reverse 400m (1,310ft) + 80m (260ft) using Land-Rover track

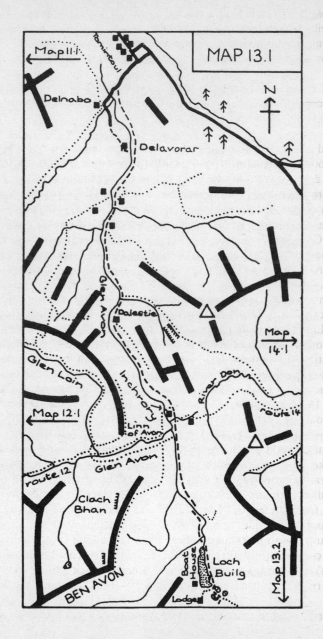

MAP 13.1

N

Map 11.1

Delnabo

Tomintoul

Delavorar

Glen Avon

Dalestie

Map 14.1

Glen Loin

Inchrory

Map 12.1

River Don

route 14

Linn of Avon

route 12

Glen Avon

Map 13.2

Clach Bhan

BEN AVON

Boat House

Loch Builg

Lodge

Total time: 8½hr (mb:5½hr) + halts
   + Keiloch to Braemar: 1hr (mb:½hr)
Tomintoul: accommodation/provisions/youth hostel.
Braemar: accommodation/provisions/youth hostel/campsite.

Bothies en route: Lochbuilg Boathouse (GR 186029). Emergency shelter can also be found at the stable on the Bealach Dearg (GR 180981).

Provided conditions are good at the bealach the route, which is a right of way, provides a straightforward trip that strong walkers can complete in a single day. As ever, an overnight halt in tent or bothy gives more time to explore and take in the atmosphere. The route is described in a north-to-south direction, following in the footsteps of the drovers and linking with the descriptions of the Braes of Abernethy (Route 11) and Glen Geldie/Glen Feshie (Route 7) to form a Grand Tour that amounts to a circumnavigation of the High Cairngorms. By mountain bike this three-route circuit gives wonderful cycling, with some idyllic campsites along the way.

   From Deeside it is also possible to extend the route to Blair Atholl via Glen tilt (Route 5) or to return northwards by the Lairig Ghru (Route 9) or the Lairig an Laoigh (Route 10), branching eastwards down Glen Avon from the Fords of Avon if you wish to return to Tomintoul. The possibilities are endless for both backpackers and bikepackers. The quickest return route to Tomintoul for mountain bikers is the interesting hilly road route via the A93, B976 and A939, perhaps using the Gairn-side or Donside tracks as off-road alternatives to rejoin the Bealach Dearg route at Loch Builg or Inchrory respectively (see Route 14). On a north-to-south crossing Glen Gairn provides a useful escape route from Loch Builg should conditions on the higher part of the route deteriorate.

   Unlike most of the other routes in this book the Bealach Dearg considerately provides both walking and cycling variations, with both a directissima path and a less steep Land-Rover track on the ascent to the bealach from the north. The Land-Rover track goes all the way from Tomintoul to Deeside, apart from a short section along the shores of Loch Builg, and makes an excellent mountain-biking route. At its high point it climbs 80m (250ft) above the bealach to reach a height of 730m (2,400ft), making it second only to the Corrieyairack (Route 18) as the highest ridable off-road pass in the country (for those with pistons for legs!).

   A north-to-south crossing has the advantage of a more leisurely ascent to the bealach, but a south-to-north crossing may be preferred by those who like to get all the ascent over and done with in the first few miles while they are fresh, leaving 15 miles (24km) of mostly downhill or level going from the summit of the pass to Tomintoul. The ascent from the south involves a 5 mile (8km) 400m (1,300ft) climb, however, and for mountain bikers at least, this is not the most appealing of starts.

ROUTE DESCRIPTION

From Tomintoul to the junction of the River Avon and the Builg Burn above Inchrory the route heads southwards along the banks of the Avon on tarmaced road and Land-Rover track (8 miles/13km; 3hr/mb:1½hr + halts). This section corresponds with the route along Glen Avon described as Route 12. When the Avon turns westwards at Inchrory the route to the Bealach Dearg continues southwards along Glen Builg. If time permits you should make a detour a few hundred metres up the Glen Avon track to the top of the first rise to view the picturesque Linn of Avon.

Glen Builg continues green and lush beneath broken limestone outcrops. The bothies used by the military patrols after the '45 are said to have been on the slopes of Meall Gaineimh on the west side of the glen. The track stays on the left (east) side (despite indications to the contrary on some maps), crossing grassy riverside haughs. After about a mile it climbs steeply away from the river and then descends to ford it before climbing again to emerge onto the moors. The ford is not difficult but it may require you to take off your boots. The final ascent passes a fine little birch-studded gorge whose pools and waterfalls are worth a diversion.

Once out of the confines of Glen Builg the main track swings right and climbs the hillside. Leave it to continue straight ahead on another track that deteriorates to a path almost immediately and cross two streams to reach the shores of Loch Builg. The first crossing is of the Feith Laoigh (Fay *Loo*-y, Stream of the Calf), a major tributary of the Builg Burn; it is usually possible to cross it dry-shod using large boulders for stepping-stones, although this is more awkward with a bike. The second, easy, crossing is of the Builg Burn again, taking you back to the left (east) side of the loch.

Loch Builg lies in a scoop of moor between rolling heather-clad hills and is noted more for its bleakness than its beauty, well suiting its Gaelic name (*Bool*ig, Bag). The 1 mile (1½km) path along its shore is the only section of the whole route where there is no track for mountain bikers. It is a typical lochside path, alternately rocky and boggy, easy for walkers to skip along but considerably more frustrating to cycle. The head of the loch, with its fine sandy beach, its boathouse and the ruins of Lochbuilg Lodge is a picturesque spot dominated by pyramid-shaped Culardoch (11 miles/18km; 4¾hr/mb:3hr + halts). At the almost imperceptible watershed immediately beyond the loch the moor bristles with lochans, and beyond these is Glen Gairn, which cuts from left to right across the route. A Land-Rover track comes up Glen Gairn to the lodge (see p150) and the path threads its way between two of the lochans to join it. The lochan on the left (Lochan Feurach – *Fay*rach, Grassy) is the largest of the lochans.

The route onwards goes left along the track but it is worth taking a short detour right to view the sculpted ruins of the lodge. A path continues behind the lodge up Carn Dearg, from where the summit of Ben Avon is within reach. The boathouse is now used as a bothy by backpackers and, increasingly in summer, by mountain bikers coming up Glen Gairn.

To continue to the Bealach Dearg go left along the track, passing by two smaller lochans and then between two larger ones to reach another junction where the Bealach Dearg track branches right. The lochans are interesting for several reasons, but most obviously for their abundant bird population. Some of them are fed by water from Loch Builg that escapes underground against the northward drainage of the loch into Glen Builg. In one of them the water is said to bubble up as a spring, although I have yet to discover where. Another is the Lochan Oir, (*Oa*-ir, Gold), where, according to tradition, a water horse guards a cache of gold hidden in the depths.

For the next couple of miles the Bealach Dearg track follows the broad heathery glen of the River Gairn upstream beneath Culardoch before cutting back left to climb to the bealach itself between Culardoch and Carn Liath (*Lee*-a, Grey). The northern shoulder of Culardoch blocks views of the ascent (perhaps fortunately!), and initially the track is pleasant and grassy as it descends into the glen to cross the Gairn (bridge). Half-way down a small stream is crossed, below which, in a grassy field on the left, is a curious collection of large boulders, like a dilapidated stone circle.

About 50m before the stream the old Bealach Dearg path branches right to stay on the right (west) side of the Gairn, and this makes a more interesting route for walkers than the newer Land-Rover track. The path holds to the west bank for about 2 miles (3km), passing a bridge over the Gairn near its confluence with the Allt Phouple (Owlt *Foop*il) and crossing at another bridge further along to leave the glen and climb beside the Allt na Claise Moire (Owlt na *Clash*a *Moa*-ira, Stream of the Big Trench) directly up to the Bealach Dearg.

Other paths branch off in all directions. The Allt Phouple and the Allt an Eas Mhoir (Owlt an Aiss Voir, Stream of the Big Waterfall) further up the glen both carry paths that climb towards the summit of Ben Avon. Another path continues up Glen Gairn through the rocky gap between Creag an Dail Mhor and Creag an Dail Bheag to cross the watershed into Glen Quoich and Gleann an t-Slugain at the foot of Beinn a' Bhuird; this makes a useful walking route if you are heading towards the Linn of Dee. Note also the paths that cross the rarely visited country to the east of the Bealach Dearg. One path in particular is a right of way that leaves the Land-Rover track at the point where it crosses the Gairn, climbs around the eastern flanks of Culardoch and descends past Carn Moine an Tighearn and Leac Ghorm to Balnoe (GR 214938). From here you can either go left to Inver or right around the back of Meall Avie to Keiloch. The whole area is marvellous wild walking country.

Mountain bikers aiming for the Bealach Dearg should keep to the Land-Rover track up Glen Gairn, which continues pleasantly along the east bank of the river until it rounds a corner and climbs across the face of Culardoch to the bealach. The ascent is long, rough and quite steep in parts but sections of it, especially the great final sweep to the summit, are ridable if your legs are up to it. On the other hand, like your intrepid author, you may decide to walk to give you more time to admire the view of Ben Avon, whose bristling summit tors dot the skyline across the glen (at least, that's my story).

Mountain bikers pay for their use of the track by having to follow it to its summit at the foot of the heathery summit dome of Culardoch, 80m (250ft) above the bealach; the summit of Culardoch is only 170m (550ft) higher. The view from the high point of either the track or the path is extensive enough to be worth any effort on ascent, for before you the mountains of the Mounth stretch southwards to the horizon above the forests of Deeside, with majestic Lochnagar displaying its attractions to perfection. If you have the energy it is worth climbing to the summit of Culardoch, the highest point between the Gairn and the Dee, for the equally spacious view back to Loch Builg (is it really that far away?) and the north.

Mountain bikers will now be eager to claim the reward for their toils with a swift descent to Deeside, but they will have to wait a little longer because the immediate descent to the bealach from the high point of the track is very rough and steep and needs care if a head plant onto the track is to be avoided. At the bealach stands an old wooden stable that on a wintry day, when the view is non-existent and the pass is a very bleak

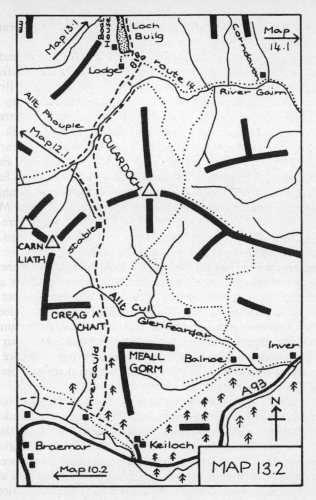

place indeed, provides rudimentary but welcome shelter. The very existence of a stable in this remote spot gives some indication of the volume of traffic that once came this way. The old path by the Allt na Claise Mhoir rejoins the track about 30m before the stable (15 miles/24km; 6½hr/mb:4½hr + halts).

The track now improves to become merely rough as it skirts the vast basin of upper Glen Feardar (*Fyar*der, Bog of the High Water), a beautifully green and wooded glen that was well populated before the clearances. Improving all the time, the track soon becomes a beautiful

147

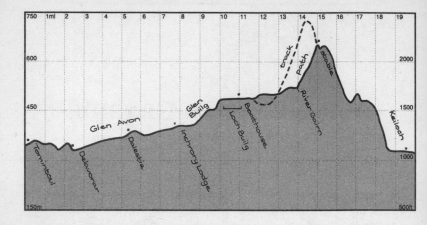

mountain-biking route as it crosses the Allt Cul (Cool, Back) at a bridge and enters the forests of Deeside, which form perhaps the most picturesque section of the whole route. Passing the first pines, a short, sharp climb takes the track up to the low bealach between Creag a' Chait and Meall Gorm, and then it is downhill through the trees all the way to Keiloch. The forest track is excellent, and never too steep to be enjoyable for mountain bikers as they get their just rewards at last for having surmounted the heights. If you arrive here late in the evening the slanting sunlight forms wonderful dappled patterns on the forest floor, making the descent a delightful way to end the day.

At the foot of the descent you join a dirt track that runs from Keiloch to the Linn of Quoich. The drovers turned right here and forded the Dee near Braemar Castle, but such exploits are not recommended to travellers today. Turn right if you wish to avoid Braemar and head for the Linn of Quoich and the Linn of Dee, otherwise the road-end at Keiloch is less than a mile down the track to the left. From Keiloch it is a few hundred metres to the A93, with Braemar a further 3 miles (5km) down the road.

If you are heading for the Linn of Quoich keep straight on at every junction until you cross the Allt Dourie, then branch immediately left to follow a pleasant track through fields and beside the Dee, with fine views up and down the glen and across the river to Braemar. It is 5 miles (8km) from Keiloch to the road-end at Linn of Quoich. The Linn is a popular picnic spot where the tumbling Quoich Water plunges between great plates of rock, and the track up beautiful Glen Quoich gives one of the most attractive short excursions on Deeside.

148

14

DONSIDE AND GAIRNSIDE

East of the Bealach Dearg the trend of the river systems is eastwards towards the North Sea. The mighty Dee carries the A93 all the way to Aberdeen, but to the north of this are two rivers whose upper reaches are roadless: the River Don and the River Gairn. Both carry good tracks that are rights of way and give excellent short trips on foot or by mountain bike. They begin on the A939/B976 Tomintoul–Deeside road and end in the heart of the hills on the route to the Bealach Dearg (see Route 13). Start points and end points can be linked to form an enterprising circuit. There are inns on the A939 at the foot of each track (Cock Bridge Inn on Donside, Gairnshiel Lodge on Gairnside), but otherwise Tomintoul and Ballater offer the nearest facilities.

DONSIDE

ROUTEPLANNER
OS map: 37/36
Start point: Cock Bridge (GR 257090)
End point: Inchrory Lodge (GR 179081)
Total distance: 6 miles (10km)
Total ascent: 90m (300ft)
   in reverse: 100m (330ft)
Total time: 2½hr (mb:1½hr) + halts

Route description
The Don rises on the high moors east of Ben Avon and follows a parallel course to the Dee, flowing eastwards away from the Cairngorms towards Aberdeen. The twisting lower glen has variety and charm, giving ever-changing views on a more intimate scale than that found on Deeside. Roads follow the course of the river more or less all the way upstream from Aberdeen to Cock Bridge, and then a Land-Rover track continues past the source of the Don to Inchrory in Glen Avon. It is this last 6 mile

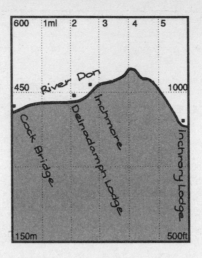

(10km) section that is of interest to walkers and mountain bikers; as a cycling route the track is mostly in excellent condition and has little ascent.

The original Ballater–Tomintoul road was built by Caulfeild's soldiers in the 1750s, and it was they who gave Cock Bridge its curious English name, after the sign of the Red Cock that adorned the inn at the bridge over the Don. The inn survives to this day as a useful watering hole, and also worth visiting here is historic Corgarff Castle. The track to Inchrory leaves the road on the south side of the bridge, following the signs to the castle, and continues straight on past the castle car park.

The glen remains broad and tame nearly all the way to the source of the river, with a pleasant frieze of rolling hills on each side that give scant preparation for the dramatic mountainscapes of Glen Avon beyond the watershed. Everywhere ruins testify to more populous days, before the people left the glen in search of a better living elsewhere. For 2 miles (3km), as far as the cluster of cottages at Delnadamph Lodge, the track is tarmaced. Further along is Inchmore, a pleasant spot with a small lochan and restored bothy where another track branches left onto the moor towards the source of the River Don at the Well of Don. Shortly afterwards a right branch heads across the hillside in the opposite direction to the Eag and Glen Avon, and then the only appreciable climb en route takes the track up 40m (130ft) around a spur to reveal the dramatic outline of Ben Avon ahead. The prominent tor is Clach Bun Rudhtair.

Below the track at this point is the huge grassy basin of the Feith Bhait (Fay Vatsh), whose grazing rights were long disputed by

150

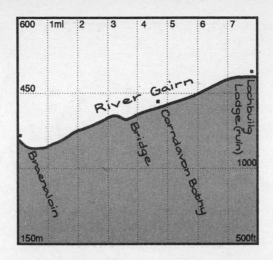

Strathavon and Corgarff people. In the eighteenth century as many as twenty shielings were in use here. It seems improbable that the infant Don could excavate such a hollow, and the geological truth of the matter is that it did not. The River Avon originally flowed eastwards from Inchrory through the Feith Bhait, until glacial down-cutting in the direction of Tomintoul captured it; this also accounts for the curious right-angled bend in the Avon at Inchrory.

Beyond the Feith Bhait the track crosses the Don, which is now just a small stream, and begins its short descent to the more intimate surroundings of Glen Avon. Half-way down is the still-used house at Lagganauld, which served as a lodge in the 1840s before the construction of Inchrory Lodge, and then the small gorge of the Allt Roderick carries the track pleasantly down to Inchrory.

GLEN GAIRN

ROUTEPLANNER
OS map: 37/36
Start point: Braenaloin (GR 281999)
End point: Lochbuilg Lodge (GR 187027)
Total distance: 8 miles (13km)
Total ascent: 150m (500ft)
  in reverse: 20m (65ft)
Total time: 3½hr (mb:2hr) + halts

151

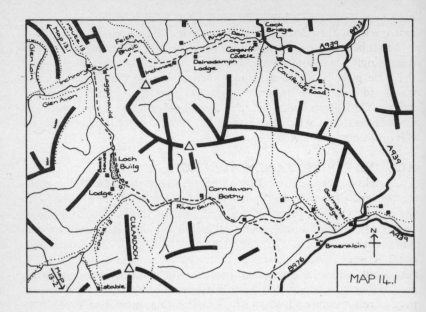

Route description

The Gairn rises on the slopes of Ben Avon and flows eastwards for about 20 miles (32km) to join the Dee at Ballater. Its name means 'rough water', but this belies the tranquil beauty of its glen, which is as green and gentle as its neighbour the Don and which in former times was densely populated and beloved by its inhabitants.

As on Donside roads follow the course of the lower glen and an excellent Land-Rover track continues to the upper reaches. The time-honoured start of the track is at Braenaloin, near the junction of the B976 and A939. At first the track is rough in patches, but after 3 miles (5km) it joins a newer and better surfaced track that begins just below the high point of the B976 south of Braenaloin and is now the main vehicular approach to the glen. Further south, just above Bush Lawsie, another track leaves the road to join the new track, and this (also a right of way) may be useful to walkers approaching from Deeside; it is less suitable for cycling.

At Braenaloin Glen Gairn is so broad and indeterminate that it is surprisingly difficult to distinguish among the rolling hills. The track crosses flat land that in the nineteenth century housed a sizable community, including a weaver, a tailor and a minister; only sheep graze here now. Rounding a bend the track takes to high ground to join the new track and then descend again to cross the river (bridge).

From hereon the track hugs the riverbank as it makes its way up the increasingly corridor-like and picturesque glen, emerging eventually onto the wide plain beside Loch Builg, where it crosses the Bealach Dearg track and ends at the ruins of Lochbuilg Lodge. En route the imposing ruins of Corndavon Lodge are passed at a bend in the glen, and nearby is Corndavon Bothy, which was restored in 1988. Otherwise all is empty in this now uninhabited glen.

AROUND DONSIDE AND GAIRNSIDE

The tracks beside the River Don and River Gairn can be linked at their western ends by a $5\frac{1}{2}$ mile (9km) run along Glen Builg (see p144) and in the east by $5\frac{1}{2}$ miles (9km) of road and 3 miles (5km) of track (old military road), making a total circuit of 28 miles (45km) that gives a good day's mountain biking. The road section involves a stiff climb to its high point between the two glens. The military road (a right of way) is fairly rough but it remains one of the most delightful stretches of Caulfeild road still in existence, with lovely old single-arched bridges (some in dire need of restoration) and the air of a secret and forgotten byway.

Walkers can avoid most of the A939 by using either of two pleasant old drove roads that cross the hills between Gairnside and Donside west of the road. One of these tracks (The Ca) begins at Tullochmacarrick (GR 277015) in Glen Gairn and climbs over the bealach west of Carn a' Bhacain to meet the old military road near Delavine (GR 285068); the other (The Camock) begins further up Glen Gairn at Easter Sleach (GR 263019) and climbs west of Camock Hill before descending to meet the old military road at Ordgarff (GR 263083). Both routes are rights of way.

Further east, beyond the A939, are some considerable stretches of wild hill and moorland country crossed by several important paths, but unfortunately lack of space precludes their inclusion here.

153

15

THE THIEVES' ROAD (1)

TRACK RECORD

When the clansmen of Lochaber journeyed eastwards to plunder the fertile lands of Moray they chose a route that avoided major centres of population. The route became known as the Rathad nam Meirlach (*Rah*-ad nam *Mare*lach) or Thieves' Road, a long-distance cross-country route across the breadth of Scotland that passed through the heart of the Grampian Mountains. Even today it crosses only one road (the A9) in its nearly 100 miles (160km) journey and it remains one of the most historic and challenging expeditions in the Highlands.

From east to west the Thieves' Road went from Abernethy through the Ryvoan Pass to Glen More and Strathspey, down to Dalwhinnie and along Loch Ericht, across the Bealach Dubh to Ossian, Corrour and the head of Loch Treig, and finally into Lochaber via the Lairig Leacach or Glen Nevis. Owing to its length it is described in this book in three sections. The easy eastern section through the Ryvoan Pass forms part of Route 11. The wild western section between Strath Ossian and the west coast is described as Route 16. The complex central section between Dalwhinnie and Strath Ossian, together with a number of variations, is described here.

The area is bounded by Loch Ericht in the east, Strath Ossian in the west and Loch Laggan in the north. In combination with Route 16 it contains the most remote country in the Central Highlands. From Dalwhinnie at the north end of Loch Ericht it is possible to follow hill tracks westwards for some 40 miles (60km) and not touch a road until one reaches the west coast near Fort William. The land is wild and rugged, criss-crossed by ancient tracks, endowed with well-placed bothies and superbly suited to backpacking and bikepacking.

The route along Loch Ericht into the interior is quiet and peaceful today, but when it formed part of the Thieves' Road it saw many a skirmish. Perhaps the most famous clash was a running battle between the MacPhersons and the Camerons who were beaten back along the loch-side. The best archers on each side, although friends, were forced to engage in combat until they mortally wounded each other. It is to be hoped that no such bloody incidents await the traveller today, for this is country where it is still possible to find peace. It is a land where a person can disappear for a week or more and barely begin to know its remote mountains and vast plateaux, its sharp ridges and rock faces, its beautiful rivers and hidden lochans. It is an area to savour.

ROUTEPLANNER

OS map: 42
Start point: Dalwhinnie station (GR 634849)
End points: (north): A86 near Kinloch Laggan (GR 554898)
        (west): north end of Loch Ossian (GR 411698)
        (south): B846 at west end of Loch Rannoch (GR 506577)
Dalwhinnie: accommodation/provisions/station.
Kinloch Laggan: no facilities; shop at Laggan Bridge (5 miles/8km)
Loch Ossian: no facilities; youth hostel at south end of loch (3½ miles/ 6km), station and bunkhouse at Corrour (4½ miles/7km).
Loch Rannoch: no facilities; station/hotel at Rannoch Station (6 miles/ 10km), accommodation/provisions/campsite at Kinloch Rannoch (9 miles/14km).

The complete Thieves' Road is a multi-day expedition. As it crosses the breadth of Scotland connections are possible with many of the other routes in this book, but owing to its length there are no simple return routes.

Distances, ascents and times for the central section described in this chapter are given below. Bothies within the area: Blackburn of Pattack (GR 544818), Culra (GR 523762), Ben Alder Cottage (GR 498680).

From the east the route into the heartland begins at Dalwhinnie. A Land-Rover track runs down Loch Erichtside for 5 miles (8km) to Ben Alder Lodge and the Boathouse, and from here tracks and paths fan out in all directions. Thanks to the enlightened access policy of Ben Alder Estate, cars have long been allowed to use the Loch Ericht track to reach the Boathouse, from where generations of hillwalkers have set out for the sharp ridges and great plateau summits of magnificent mountains such as Ben Alder and Geal Charn. Cyclists used the track long before the advent of the mountain bike. A locked gate after 1½ miles (2km) stops cars but a key can be obtained by telephoning 052-82-224.

Details of routes within this area, return routes, extensions and suggested itineraries are given below. The easiest route connects Dalwhinnie with Kinloch Laggan via Loch Ericht and the beautiful valley of the River Pattack. There is a Land-Rover track all the way and Ardverikie Estate have agreed to approve the use of the tracks along Lochan na h-Earba and the south side of Loch Laggan for mountain biking, thus opening up a connection to Route 16 and a superb off-road cycling route all the way from Dalwhinnie to Loch Ossian, Corrour and beyond. The track to be used at any one time depends upon estate management considerations; contact the estate office at Kinloch Laggan (052-83-300) for advice. If the privilege of cycling these tracks is not to be lost mountain bikers are asked to avoid all other estate tracks around Ardverikie and the paths over the hills west of the River Pattack.

ROUTE DESCRIPTION

Dalwhinnie to Kinloch Laggan via Ben Alder Lodge, the Boathouse and the Pattack Valley

The track along Loch Ericht to Ben Alder Lodge begins at Dalwhinnie Station and crosses the line just south of the platform. It is a good track (a right of way) through pleasant lochside woods, but quite undulating and bumpy to cycle, more suited to car than bicycle suspension (5 miles/ 8km;50m/160ft; 2hr/mb:1hr + halts).

At the lodge the track branches away from the lochside to climb gently over a low rise into the Pattack valley. Just over the rise stands the old shed known as the Boathouse, which is the time-honoured start of the path to Culra Bothy, Ben Alder and the other fine peaks in the area, whose soaring summits are not strung out across the moor in front of you. Cars are often to be found parked at the Boathouse and horses sometimes congregate here for shelter and titbits (7 miles/11km; 150m/ 500ft; 3hr/mb:1½hr + halts).

Beyond the Boathouse the track descends to Loch Pattack and enters the broad, open valley of the River Pattack. It becomes grassy for a while before crossing the river and improving again as it makes its way gently down the valley. Many stands of trees are passed along the way, giving the place an air of seclusion. In the first small wood stands Blackburn of Pattack Bothy, a useful base for walks in the area but not as well-sited or as popular as Culra. There are also many waterfalls, and the whole adds up to one of the loveliest excursions in the Central Highlands. The first series of waterfalls enliven a small gorge about 1 mile past Blackburn of Pattack; walk down to the old bridge across the river to get the best view.

The next fork reached is an important one for mountain bikers

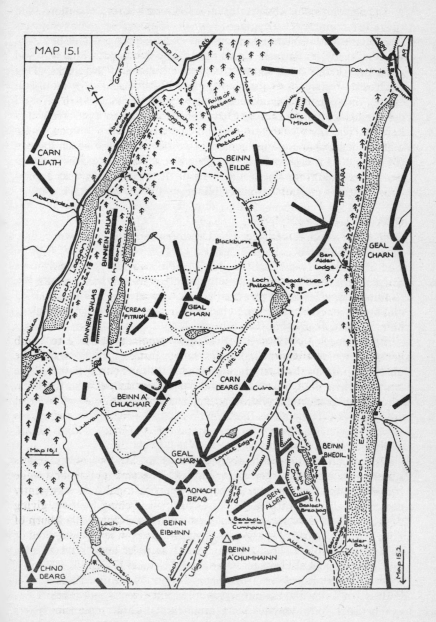

MAP 15.1

heading westwards, for the left branch here cuts across the moor to Ardverikie on south Loch Lagganside (for details see p164). The route to Kinloch Laggan bears right and soon reaches perhaps the most beautiful waterfalls on the whole river, hidden deep in a small gorge well to the right of the track. Passing another left branch to Loch Laggan the main track crosses the river and then recrosses it at the Linn of Pattack, where the river tumbles through a narrowing between rocks. Soon a forest fence is reached, and on the right here is the Pattack's most spectacular waterfall, the Falls of Pattack, which plunge 12m (40ft) into a gorge flanked with sharp and perpendicular cliffs. It is an impressive place but extreme caution is required at the cliff edge, which is vertiginous and often waterlogged from spray; take heed of the danger notices. Beyond the falls a steep descent leads past Gallovie to the roadside about a mile east of Kinloch Laggan (14 miles/2km; 170m/550ft; 6hr/mb:3hr + halts).

Those seeking a return route to Dalwhinnie have, considering the relatively short distance, surprisingly no easy off-road options. Cyclists can return to Dalwhinnie by road. Adventurous walkers seeking a cross-country return route can use either of two paths up onto the moors north or south of Beinn Eilde (leaving the Pattack track at GR 554869 and GR 548834 respectively), but when the paths end the going gets tough. There are some impressive sights to see along the way, notably the fine waterfall on the River Mashie at GR 571869 and the great rocky gaps on either side of Creag nan Adhaircean: the southern gap, known as the Dirc Mhor (Great Slash), is an impressive 130m (400ft) cleft that has some fine cliffs, while the northern gap contains an elongated loch and an enormous boulderfall riddled with caves – a great contrast to the gentle Pattack valley.

Ben Alder Lodge to Ben Alder Cottage via Loch Erichtside

At Ben Alder Lodge a side track branches left from the Dalwhinnie-Pattack track and continues past the lodge to become a path along Loch Erichtside for another 9 miles (14km) to Ben Alder Cottage (a right of way). The loch is a hydrological curiosity for it cuts right through the watershed east of the Ben Alder group, and its steep-sided shores provide an obvious corridor through the hills. The path is excellent, well built and well drained, and it can be continued southwards to Loch Rannoch or westwards to the Bealach Dubh (see below).

To avoid the grounds at Ben Alder Lodge do not fork left at the driveway but follow the main track uphill to a bridge and take the rough track that cuts back down to the shoreline. The track continues beside the loch for another couple of miles and then the path takes over, so close to the shoreline in places that there are gaps where it has slipped into the water. Further along, the path deteriorates as it squeezes along the foot of the steep craggy slopes of Beinn Bheoil and Sron Coire na h-Iolaire, but even here it continues to give good walking for the most part and is a fine route along the narrows of the loch.

There is one place, however, where care is required, for as the path approaches the corner of Alder Bay there is an awkward section on shoreline crags and eroded ground where it is necessary to put hand to rock. It is barely a scramble but caution should be exercised. At the corner itself the old path climbs right beside an old fence, but this is now becoming overgrown as most people prefer to go straight on along the shore (from Ben Alder Lodge: 9 miles/14km; c200m/650ft; 4hr/mb:3hr + halts).

The route is a problematical one for mountain bikers. It is ridable for a good way, and even when the path becomes rougher along the narrows of the loch the pushing is easy. The corner of Ben Alder Bay, however, is extremely awkward and a slip would land you in deep water in more ways than one. Only experts should venture here.

The Boathouse to Ben Alder Cottage via the Bealach Breabag

This route crosses the Bealach Breabag (*Bya*loch Brepak, Pass of the Little Kick, ie Cleft) between Beinn Bheoil and Ben Alder. It provides a direct connection between Culra Bothy and Ben Alder Cottage and passes through outstanding mountain scenery, but it also climbs much higher than the Loch Erichtside and Bealach Dubh paths and is much rougher.

From the Boathouse the path crosses the moor to follow the east bank of the Allt a' Chaoil-reidhe past Culra Lodge and bothy. It is a wonderful path, a tribute to the path-building expertise of its makers. Beyond the bothy (which stands on the far side of the river and can be reached by a bridge – see below) the path climbs steeply up the hillside into the great mountain basin between Ben Alder and Beinn Bheoil, wer Loch a' Bhealaich Bheithe nestles. En route excellent views are to be had of the dramatic Lancet Edge of Sgor Iutharn opposite and the rocky bounding ridges of Coire na Lethchois of Ben Alder, known as the Long and Short Leachas. All these ridges give excellent scrambles.

The path deteriorates and becomes very boggy as it skirts the loch but the surroundings continue to compensate, for at the head of the loch is Garbh Choire of Ben Alder (*Garra* Chorra, Rough Corrie), whose massive broken rock walls are very impressive, especially in winter when cornices teeter over their rims. At the end of the loch the path improves again and climbs towards the Bealach Breabag; it ends below the bealach but the remainder of the climb is easy.

The Bealach is broad and can be confusing in mist. On the descent of the far (south) side the going becomes much rougher and boggier, but throughout there is a wonderful view over the waters of Loch Ericht to the distant mountains of the Southern Highlands. Steepening convex slopes lead down to Alder bay and bothy but a path develops on the left (east) bank of the stream to ease the descent. When you reach a point about 100m (330ft) above the bay, look left for a lone rowan tree that marks Prince Charlie's Cave, a small howf formed by leaning rocks where Prince Charlie really did stay when he was on the run from the Redcoats.

The route over the Bealach Breabag is not an easy mountain-biking route. From the Boathouse to Culra the path provides wonderful cycling, but once it begins to climb to Loch a' Bhealaich Bheithe it becomes to steep to ride, and later it becomes too rough. From the start of the climb you will probably walk most of the way to Ben Alder Cottage, with the final descent to Alder Bay being particularly rough (8 miles/13km; 440m/1,450ft; 5hr/mb: 5hr + halts).

The Boathouse to Ben Alder Cottage via the Bealach Dubh and the Bealach Cumhann

Owing to the height and roughness of the Bealach Breabag the normal route from the Boathouse to Ben Alder Cottage takes the longer route around the west side of Ben Alder over the Bealach Dubh (*Byal*och Doo, Black Pass), where there is a fine path (a right of way) all the way. A newer Land-Rover track goes from Loch Pattack to Culra Lodge, but it is an undulating, bumpy and extremely unpleasant way of getting to Culra compared to the old path from the Boathouse mentioned above. So much for progress. Avoid the track and take the path to Culra, crossing the Allt a'Chaoil-reidhe by a bridge at GR 525764 (look for the fork where the Culra path cuts back right from the Bealach Breabag path).

Beyond the bothy the path continues up the narrowing and increasingly steep-sided glen between the craggy north-west face of Ben Alder and the steep slopes falling from Sgor Iutharn, whose dramatic pointed summit towers overhead. Apart from places where it was washed away by the floods of early 1900, the path remains excellent as it follows the picturesque stream up the glen, barely rising until it makes its final climb to the bealach at the head of the glen.

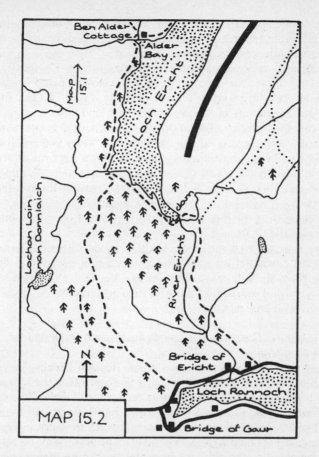

MAP 15.2

Over the bealach is the green and boggy glen of the Uisge Labhair (see opposite), with Loch Ossian visible in the distance at its foot. The path deteriorates somewhat but still gives excellent walking for the most part. It contours left out of the glen, descending and reascending to the Bealach Cumhann (*Byal*och *Coo*-an, Narrow Pass) between Ben Alder and Beinn a' Chumhainn, and then descends the more open glen of the Alder Burn to Alder Bay and bothy (10 miles/16km; 350m/1,150ft; 4½hr/mb:3½hr + halts).

Mountain bikers will find much of this route ridable and exciting. It can be ridden most of the way to the foot of the Bealach Dubh, although it is very narrow and runs close beside the river in places, requiring skill and nerve. After a push to the bealach the descent of the far side crosses a steep hillside where care is required; many will prefer to walk. The ascent to the Bealach Cumhann requires further pushing before the path again becomes ridable on descent to Alder Bay. Only the last part of the path, which is overgrown and broken, is frustrating to negotiate with a bike.

Ben Alder Cottage to Loch Rannoch

Ben Alder Cottage has a magnificent site on Alder Bay at the foot of Ben Alder and is well situated for the ascent of Ben Alder and other walks in the Ben Alder region. Southwards it is a long way out to Loch Rannoch and the B846 but the way is eased, especially for mountain bikers, by a good track (a right of way) for much of the way. There is a bridge over the Alder Burn upstream of the cottage, but it is normally easy to cross on stepping-stones directly below the cottage, where there are some fine small water-slides and pools.

The initial route down the lochside is problematical. After crossing the Alder Burn you are faced with incredibly tussocky grass beside the loch or peat bogs further right. It is probably best to keep left through the trees to find the best going, and once around the headland at the southern corner of Alder Bay there is much to be said for taking to the sandy shore of the loch if the water is low. Half-way along the loch is the start of a path that is worth going to some trouble to find. On reaching the small stream that enters the loch at the bay at GR 494662, walk upstream to the remnants of what might once have been a bridge. The path starts here; it is not obvious at first but soon develops into an excellent path that is ridable for much of its length.

On reaching the south-west corner of the loch the Cam Chriochan is crossed by a bridge and the path turns along the south shore. The track to Loch Rannoch soon branches off to the right, but the ground around here has been so devastated by motorised stalking vehicles that the junction may not be easy to see, so check the map and watch the ground. The track is a fine moorland track that improves all the time and is never less than interesting. It rises 90m (300ft) before making a long gradual descent in and out of forestry plantations to reach the B846 near the west end of Loch Rannoch, and it is ridable nearly all the way (9 miles/14km; 180m/600ft; 4hr/mb:3hr + halts). At one point a good path bypasses one of the plantations to shorten the route slightly for walkers. A feature of the route is the marvellous view westwards to the Blackwater Reservoir and the Glencoe hills, and across Rannoch Moor to the Blackmount Range. If you are heading for Rannoch Station it is possible to take a short cut past Lochan Loin nan Donnlaich and Lochan Sron Smeur to reach the Corrour–Rannoch track described on p177.

Tired mountain bikers may prefer to avoid the Loch Rannock track by continuing along the south shore of Loch Ericht to the dam at the south-east corner. There used to be a path but vehicular traffic has ploughed it into a mudslide. From the dam a tarmaced road descends the enclosed and uninteresting glen of the River Ericht to reach the roadside at Bridge of Ericht. The route is far less interesting than the Loch Rannoch track but involves no further ascent and has a tarmaced road to finish.

The Boathouse/Ben Alder Cottage to Loch Ossian via the Uisge Labhair, connecting with Route 16

From Dalwhinnie the Thieves' Road went via Ben Alder Lodge, the Boathouse, Culra and the Bealach Dubh into the glen of the Uisge Labhair (*Ooshka Lah*-ir, Loud Water) and so to Loch Ossian (a right of way). Today, the glen of the Uisge Labhair remains by far the shortest route from the Boathouse or Ben Alder Cottage to Loch Ossian, but it is very boggy. To reach it follow the path over the Bealach Dubh from Culra Bothy or the path over the Bealach Cumhann from Ben Alder Cottage. A path develops on the right (west) bank of the stream (from the Boathouse to Loch Ossian: 10½ miles/17km; 300m 1,000ft; 4½hr/mb:4hr + halts).

Loch Pattack to the A86 at the west end of Loch Laggan (via hill paths), connecting with Routes 16 and 18

A number of fine paths cross the hills between Loch Pattack and Loch Laggan. A very rough Land-Rover track branches right from the Loch Pattack-Culra Land-Rover track mentioned above and climbs across a shoulder into the glen of the Allt Cam. From here paths shoot off in all directions. The obvious way forward is up the valley of the Allt Cam into a deep trough through the hills known as An Lairig (An *Lahr*ik, The Pass). Apart from a short section in the middle there is a path all the way, which beyond the ruins of Lubvan (GR 445790) becomes a Land-Rover track.

A more direct and hilly path fords the Allt Cam and climbs into the depression between the Munros of Beinn a' Chlachair and Geal Charn, where Loch a' Bhealaich Leamhain lies. The path divides to send a branch along each side of the loch and then around each side of Creag Pitridh to descend to Lochan na h-Earba, from where Land-Rover tracks lead to Lagganside. On the north side of Geal Charn another path crosses from near Blackburn of Pattack to Lochan na h-Earba. This whole area is wonderful walking country. Mountain bikers will find better going on the route described next.

River Pattack to the A86 at the west end of Loch Laggan (via Land-Rover tracks), connecting with Routes 16 and 18

At the fork at GR 546852 a track branches left from the Pattack valley track to take a more or less level route across the moor past a beautiful old birch wood (Coille Doir-ath) and descend to turreted Ardverikie House on the south side of Loch Laggan.

From this track two further tracks branch west to the west end of Loch Laggan, one via the shores of Lochan na h-Earba and one via the shores of Loch Laggan. The former is the more interesting and better surfaced. It branches left at GR 516868 to ford a stream and end at a T-junction. Go left and then immediately right on a path through an unpromising-looking forest clearing; if you lose the path when the trees thin out, make directly for Binnein Shios, which rises ahead, until you join the track from Ardverikie to Lochan na h-Earba. The track along the shores of the twin lochs provides excellent going through a great trench hemmed in by rocky mountains; pause to contemplate the massive slabs and over-hangs of Binnein Shuas and wonder at the rock athletes who climb them. Beyond the lochs the track descends around the shoulder of Binnein Shuas to a junction with the south Loch Laggan track, from where a left branch descends to Luiblea and the A86.

The south Loch Laggan track, which runs along the wooded lochside from Kinloch Laggan and Ardverikie to the junction with the Lochan na h-Earba track, is much cut up by forestry vehicles and is rougher than the Lochan na h-Earba track. The two tracks provide longer routes from the Pattack valley to the west end of Loch Laggan than the hill paths described above, but they are the recommended routes for mountain bikers, as noted in the Routeplanner.

16

THE THIEVES' ROAD (2)

TRACK RECORD

The western section of the Thieves' Road between Loch Ossian and the west coast passes through remote and beautiful country in the shadow of some of the finest and highest mountains in Scotland, including Ben Nevis (1,344m/4,409ft). The route itself consists of a number of sections that are quite distinct in terms of both terrain and scenery. The first section described in this chapter is a connecting route from the A86 at the west end of Loch Laggan to the Thieves' Road at Loch Ossian. This is a pleasant and mainly wooded approach route to the interior that follows an excellent Land-Rover track along broad glens and beneath sweeping hillsides, continuing past Loch Ossian to Corrour. From Corrour onwards the going is much rougher as a path negotiates the complex country around the head of the Loch Treig and south of the Grey Corries (a tough section for mountain bikers). The final section takes walkers through the dramatic Nevis gorge or the Lairig Leacach, while bikers can detour around the southern flanks of the Mamore Range for an equally scenic high-level route above Loch Leven.

At the heart of the route lies Corrour, an insignificant dot on the map at the northern edge of Rannoch Moor, as remote and as desolate a spot as any wilderness lover could wish for. Yet to approach the wilderness that is Corrour demands a redefinition of terms because Corrour is a railway station – at 410m (1,347ft) the highest station in the British Rail network and the only station inaccessible by public road. Apart from the station there is nothing here but moor and bog – 'a wide and wasted desert, old and unreclaimed as time', as Principal Shairp well described the area in his poem on Rannoch.

The West Highland Railway on which Corrour stands was opened in 1894 and the station was supposedly built to allow north-bound and south-bound trains to cross. The fact that Sir John Stirling Maxwell, the

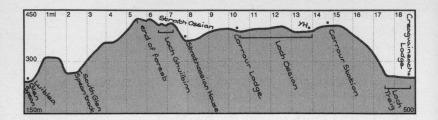

Director of the railway, had a lodge on the nearby hillside is said to be mere coincidence! Little has changed since those days. A photograph of the station taken in the early years and which used to sit in the station-master's office could easily have been taken yesterday.

The only people detraining at Courrour these days are walkers, back-packers and mountain bikers, who come to climb the clutch of Munros or to walk or cycle the ancient tracks. Most come in summer when the days are warm, the gloamings long and the only blight on the landscape is the over-friendly midge. Yet Corrour is at its wildest and most beautiful at other times of the year. In autumn, for instance, when the first chill of winter is in the air, the hillsides are golden and the sycamores at Loch Ossian turn a ravishing red and yellow. Or in spring, with new growth on the moor, the peaks flecked with snow, the hillsides glistening after a shower and an exhilarating freshness in the air. Or winter, when the snow lies deep and walking can become a test of survival.

Never was the wildness of Corrour brought home to me more than on May Day 1982, when, in search of an early summer walk, I detrained here in a blizzard. The largest snowflakes I have ever seen silently turned the green trees of Loch Ossian to pristine white, and only by crawling on my stomach to distribute my weight on waist-deep snow like quicksand did I manage to reach the top of the insignificant Meall na Lice above the youth hostel.

Even in the heart of winter a steady stream of hardy walkers arrive by train at Corrour. 'They like the challenge,' says Jim Morgan, the ex-station-master here. In summer they can stay at Loch Ossian youth hostel and in winter they can now stay in the old station building, which Jim and his wife Christine have converted into a bunkhouse since the halt became unmanned in 1987. The greatest challenge of all, however, is to walk or to cycle in along the Thieves' Road. Corrour then truly does seem like a mirage on the moor. No matter how many people come here, to pass through or to stay, man will never seem more than an intrusion in this vast and wild landscape.

ROUTEPLANNER

OS map: 42/41

Start point: A86 near west end of Loch Laggan (GR 432830)

End points: (north): Spean Bridge (GR 221815)

(west): Fort William (GR 105742) or Kinlochleven (GR 188619)

(south): Rannoch Station (GR 422579)

Loch Laggan: no facilities; accommodation/provisions/campsite/ station at Roybridge (10½ miles/17km); station at Tulloch (5 miles/ 8km).

Spean Bridge: accommodation/provisions/station.

Fort William: accommodation/provisions/station; youth hostel and campsite in Glen Nevis.

Kinlochleven: accommodation/provisions; campsite nearby.

Distances, ascents and times are given below for individual sections of the route. Accommodation within the area: youth hostel at Loch Ossian (GR 371671), bunkhouse at Corrour (GR 356664; ring 039785-236 for details); bothies at Staioneag (GR 295678), Meanach (GR 266685), Lairig Leacach (GR 282736).

The western section of the Thieves' Road and its off-shoots are mostly straightforward routes in terms of terrain and navigation. There are few significant ascents and good Land-Rover tracks or paths everywhere, except for a short section around Tom an Eite on the Glen Nevis route (see below). Do not let this lure you into treating the area lightly, however, for its scale, remoteness and lack of quick escape routes demand experience and good equipment.

Corrour Station offers the only easy way out of the interior; many a winter's day sees walkers huddled on the platform awaiting rescue by the great 'iron horse'. Beyond Corrour it is a long way to the next outpost of civilisation and the going is tough; mountain bikers especially should not let the good track from Lagganside to Corrour lead them into under-estimating the size of the task ahead.

The site of Corrour Station enables some remote country to be explored in a single day using the train; popular trips include Corrour to Rannoch Station via Corrour Old Lodge (see below) and Corrour to Tulloch Station over the Munros on either side of Loch Treig. Only by arriving at Corrour by train is it possible to walk back to civilisation in a day, those crossing the area on foot, including those completing the Thieves' Road, should prepare for a multi-day trip. It is possible to mountain bike in and out in a day, but it would be a tough proposition.

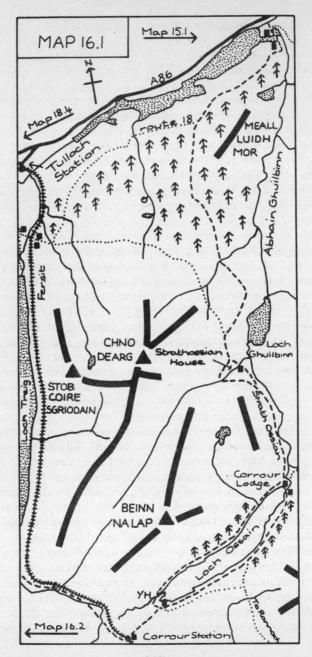

MAP 16.1

Map 15.1 →

N

A86

route 18

← Map 18.4

MEALL
LUIDH
MOR

Tulloch
Station

Abhain Ghuilbinn

Fersit

CHNO
DEARG

Strathossian
House

Loch
Ghuilbinn

Loch Treig

STOB
COIRE
SGRIODAIN

Srath Ossian

Corrour
Lodge

BEINN
NA LAP

Loch Ossain

YH

To Rannoch

← Map 16.2

Corrour Station

168

Details of routes and suggested itineraries are given below.

ROUTE DESCRIPTION
West end of Loch Laggan to head of Loch Treig via Strath Ossian, Loch Ossian and Corrour

The track to Strath Ossian is Forestry Commission approved and there is a right of way beyond. At the west end of Loch Laggan a track crosses a bridge over the River Spean and forks. The left branch is the track to Loch Laggan and Lochan na h-Earba (see p164). Take the right branch past some houses and climb steadily through forestry plantations, with good views along Glen Spean. After passing some minor left branches the track levels out and descends to a major fork where the route to Corrour branches left; the right branch continues along Glen Spean (see p198).

The Corrour track climbs steadily around Meall Luidh Mor to a low bealach in the woods and then makes a long gradual descent and reascent to the forest edge. Out onto the open hillside at last, the first stream reached is a lovely place to linger on a hot day, with water-slides to cool the fevered brow and other parts of the anatomy after a long ascent. You are now high above Strath Ossian. Across the strath Beinn a' Chlachair and the sweeping ridges of the Geal Charn group fill the skyline, with sandy-shored Loch Ghuilbinn nestling at their foot. The winding River Ossian leads the eye up the strath past the loch and the clump of trees that shelter Strathossian House to the distant trees of Loch Ossian.

The main track rises across the hillside to take a broad sweep around still-used Strathossian House. A side track takes a short cut past the house, saving a lot of time and effort. The main track then continues along the broad trench of the strath beside grassy riverside haughs that provide many fine picnic spots. When the strath was inhabited every pool and island in the river had a name. There was, for example, a Sorley's Pool, an Alasdair's Pool, a Mairi's Pool and even an Island of the Maltman's Son, whoever he was. Such names, now long forgotten and recorded only on ancient maps, remind one that before the clearances places as isolated as Strath Ossian were once home to many people.

Soon the woods that fringe Loch Ossian and shelter Corrour Lodge are reached. The lodge was built in the early twentieth century to replace Corrour Old Lodge (see p177). A track completely encircles the loch and either side makes a good route onwards. The right (west) side avoids the grounds of Corrour Lodge and its associated cottages, passing blooming rhododendrons in early summer and golden sycamores in autumn. Both sides make lovely serene routes beside the wooded shores of the loch. The

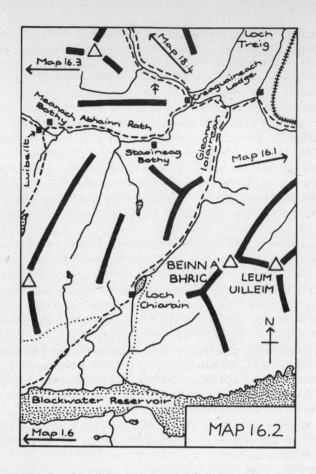

MAP 16.2

two tracks reunite at the south end of the loch, where Loch Ossian Youth Hostel stands picturesquely on a small wooded peninsula surrounded by tree-clad islets. This is very pleasant country, not dramatic, but peaceful, uncluttered, wild. A further mile across the moor lies Corrour Station, and here the track ends (15 miles/24km; 340m/1,120ft; 6hr/mb:3hr + halts).

If Loch Ossian seems remote, the lonely outpost of Corrour seems even more so, and the station and incongruous railway line only seem to heighten the feeling that man is an intrusion here. Leaving Corrour, there is a real feeling of leaving civilisation behind. Ahead lies wilderness. The path onwards crosses the railway line just north of the platform and turns right to run beside the line. It is a finely engineered route across the moor between peat hags, glacial moraines and reedy lochans, raised to keep it as dry as possible. Much of it is ridable, but it gets boggy in wet weather and to prevent erosion mountain bikers should walk it then. NB Another path from Loch Ossian bypasses Corrour and makes a useful short cut for walkers.

The path follows the railway down the glen of the Allt a' Chamabhreac, eventually becoming a rough track that descends to the head of Loch Treig (Traig, Forsaken). The railway bears right to contour along the eastern shore of the loch some 100m (330ft) up the hillside; the sight of a train that far above you in that great wilderness is truly surreal.

At the lochside the track crosses the Allt a' Chamabhreac, here a lovely wooded stream with some fine pools and waterfalls near the bridge. On a hot day the cool waters are tempting, but in typical Highland weather immersion will be the last thing on your mind. An old tale of Loch Treig tells of an old trout recalling a cold May Day (seemingly similar to the one I encountered in 1982), when he was young and foolish and leaped high into the air, only to find his body arched and frozen before it touched water again. Such stories were probably told to the children of the community that once lived here before the damming of the loch and the raising of the water-level in the 1930s.

The rough track undulates around the shoreline to reach the wide Abhainn Rath that flows into the loch at its south-west corner. There is a bridge over the river and on the far side stands still-used Creaguaineach Lodge. Above the loch tower Stob Coire Easain and Stob a' Choire Mheadhoin, and to their west rise the first of the Grey Corries – that marvellous twisting ridge of peaks that, together with the equally fine Mamore, Aonach and Nevis ranges, form a dramatic backdrop to the remainder of the journey.

From this remote spot no less than four routes lead out of the wilderness. In clockwise direction these are the Blackwater Reservoir, Loch Eilde Mor, Glen Nevis and the Lairig Leacach. Each is described below in turn.

To Kinlochleven via the Blackwater Reservoir

Perhaps the least useful of the four routes when making for the west coast, and certainly not part of the Thieves' Road, this route (a right of way) heads southwards from the shores of Loch Treig along Gleann Iolairean. It climbs into the steep-sided defile between Beinn na Cloiche and Beinn a' Bhric, descends past Loch Chiarain to the dam at the west end of the huge Blackwater Reservoir and then drops down into the steep-sided glen of the River Leven to reach Kinlochleven (from Corrour: 14½ miles/23km; 150m/500ft; 6hr + halts). The main item of interest en route, apart from the sight of the massive reservoir resting on the moor, is the Grey Mare's Tail waterfall near Kinlochleven.

To Fort William via Loch Eilde Mor and the Lairig Mor

This route (a right of way) is the easiest of the four routes for mountain bikers but still involves a fair amount of pushing before you reach a ridable track. Once you are onto the track a long, rough ride awaits, but it is the sort of track for which mountain bikes were made. From Creaguaineach Lodge a rough path continues westwards along the north bank of the Abhainn Rath. After about a mile it climbs onto a broad plain and in the distance can be seen Aonach Beag and Ben Nevis, cleaving the skyline like a great prow. Across the river is Staoineag Bothy, looking like an Alpine hut on its rocky bluff; stepping-stones enable the river to be crossed dry-shod in normal conditions.

The river winds across the plain in deep, still pools and at the far end the path climbs out beside a series of waterfalls to emerge into a huge basin where Meanach Bothy stands. This is big country, the continuing glen heading westwards between the Mamores and the Grey Corries all the way to Glen Nevis. The Loch Eilde Mor route leaves the main glen at Meanach and turns southwards. The Abhainn Rath is crossed on stepping-stones to pick up a Land-Rover track at the ruined buildings of Luibeilt. NB Outside of the summer months or after heavy rain the stepping-stones at Staoineag and Luibeilt may be unusable; at such times it is prudent to follow the south bank of the Abhainn Rath from Creaguaineach Lodge. A signpost beside the bridge at the lodge now indicates the south bank as the main route, and a rough path has developed here.

At Luibeilt take one last look at the majestic mountains all around, then follow the rough track up to a grassy bealach beneath featureless hillsides. Over the bealach lies a great trough filled by Loch Eilde Beag (*Ail*-ja Baig, Little Hind) and Loch Eilde Mor (Moar, Big), along whose shores the track continues at the foot of the Mamores. The going and scenery improve as the summits of the Mamores come into view one by one. A number of fine paths leave the trackside to climb towards the tops, and some reach the main Mamore ridge itself, giving wonderful ridge wandering. Other paths descend from the track to Kinlochleven.

At the end of Loch Eilde Mor the track rises over a low bealach to reveal a tremendous view over Loch Leven, framed between the Pap of Glencoe and Beinn na Caillich. A long descent follows to Mamore Lodge,

172

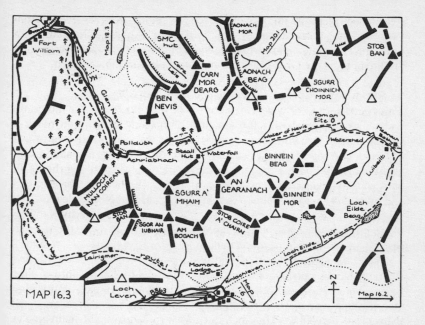

MAP 16.3

where refreshments can be had and where the lodge driveway descends left to give access to Kinlochleven for cyclists. Beyond the lodge the track climbs again to become a level balcony above Loch Leven, giving an eagle's eye view of the loch and Kinlochleven. Soon the West Highland Way is joined and the remainder of the route is as per Route 1, following the rough track across the southern flanks of the Mamores, over the Lairig Mor and down to Fort William (see p45 for description); (from Corrour: 28 miles/45km; 390m/1,780ft; 12hr/mb (by road from end of Lairig Mor):7½hr + halts).

To Fort William via Glen Nevis

The route beside the Abhainn Rath continues westwards as a right of way past Luibeilt up the great corridor between the Mamores and the Grey Corries to form perhaps the most magnificent of all the routes out from the head of Loch Treig (and the toughest with a mountain bike). From Luibeilt a track runs along the south bank of the river for a short distance and then a grassy path continues across extensive riverside plains. The going is good if somewhat boggy in places. At the head of the glen the river does a right-angled turn in front of Tom an Eite, an insignificant lump in the middle of the moor. The path crosses the Allt Coire a' Bhinnein and leaves the banks of the Abhainn Rath to cross to Tom an Eite, becoming very indistinct. This featureless area can be awkward in mist; if in doubt, you should follow the Allt Coire a' Bhinnein upstream for a few hundred metres as far as a ramshackle old shed known as the Watershed (GR 238691). Here there is a small dam from where it is possible to follow the infant Water of Nevis northwards to rejoin the path along its bank.

The going continues rough beside the Water of Nevis until the path contours away from the river and begins its descent into the confined glen between the sharp peaks of the Mamores and the Grey Corries. From hereon the path is much improved and the scenery is nothing short of spectacular, increasing in scale and grandeur as you go. Rounding a corner, the beautiful hidden mountain sanctuary of Steall (Shtyowl, Waterfall) appears below you, with Ben Nevis towering behind. The Steall itself is a mighty 110m (350ft) waterfall that tumbles onto the plain near Steall Hut, a private (locked) hut that may be reached by a swaying wire bridge over the fast flowing water.

At the far end of Steall plain the excitement continues as you enter the unique Nevis Gorge, a remarkable gorge of Himalayan character where the river surges over a tangle of enormous boulders between rocky walls. Care is needed on the rocky and occasionally vertiginous path, until you emerge from the gorge and suddenly find yourself at the start of the Glen Nevis road (from Corrour: 14 miles /23km; 140m/460ft; 6hr/mb:6¹/2hr + halts).

It is still another 7 miles (11km) to Fort William, but the beauty and character of Glen Nevis is such that even walking along the road is a pleasant experience. Much of the tarmac can be avoided by taking a forest track that runs parallel to the road from Achriabhach (GR 142684) nearly all the way to Fort William. More interestingly for adven-

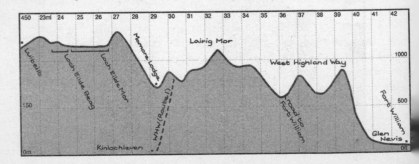

turous walkers and mountain bikers, a path leaves the road a short distance beyond Achriabhach at GR 139691 to follow the river most of the way to the youth hostel. By crossing the bridge at the youth hostel another path can be followed along the far riverbank to the roadside at Claggan on the outskirts of Fort William. NB From Fort William it is possible to return to Loch Laggan by a mainly off-road route along Glen Spean (see p197).

To Spean Bridge via the Lairig Leacach

The Lairig Leacach (*Lah*rik *Lyech*kach, Slabby or Granite Pass) is the most northerly of the four routes out from the head of Loch Treig (a right of way). It is the true Thieves' Road and was later a major drove road, for, unlike in Glen Nevis, there are no awkward narrow places where cattle could get into difficulty. There are no Himalayan-like gorges here and no 1,220m (4,000ft) peaks, but the scenery is none the less stunning and the route certainly deserves consideration as an alternative to Glen Nevis, especially if you are heading in the direction of the Great Glen. As a mountain-biking route the path on the south side of the Lairig is not ridable (in either direction), but the rough track that descends from the summit to Glen Spean gives an exhilarating descent.

The path begins below Creaguaineach Lodge and follows the shore of Loch Treig to the Allt na Lairige, where there is a bridge, and then for the next 3½ miles (6km) there are paths on each side of the river. Above the bridge a wooded gorge conceals a number of waterfalls, including the

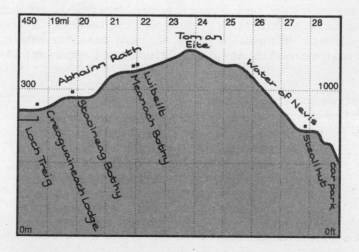

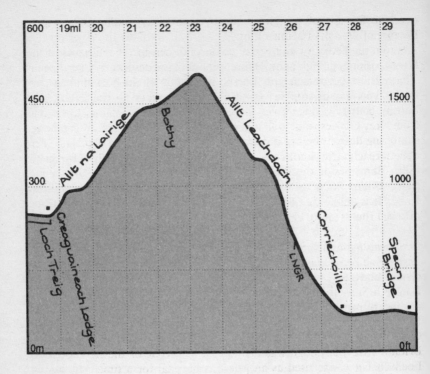

6m (20ft) Easan Dubh (Aissan Doo, Black Waterfall), and this is worth a visit even if you do not intend to continue across the Lairig. The best view of the waterfall is obtained from the right side (left bank) of the river, where the Alpine-like path clings to the side of the gorge among trees; care is required and this is no place to be encumbered with a mountain bike. The main path goes up the other side of the gorge through a fine small gorge of its own where slabs of rock have been laid to form a staircase, but the Easan Dubh is not visible from here.

Above the gorge you enter a fine 'lost valley' where occasional trees dot the hillsides and the river gurgles between grassy haughs that once provided good grazing for drovers and thieves. The paths on each side are poor in this section but improve as the route veers right up the broad green valley that leads to the summit of the Lairig. The scenery becomes ever more dramatic until you reach the Lairig Leacach bothy in a terrific position at the foot of the north-east ridge of Stob Ban (White Mountain), whose cone-shaped summit towers overhead. Even more impressive is the great craggy lump of Sgurr Innse (*Een*sha, Sign) that hovers over the far side of the glen, unjustly ignored as a hillwalking target because of its lack of Munro status.

From the bothy a Land-Rover track continues into the narrows of the Lairig, rising to a high point before beginning the descent to Glen Spean. The hillsides become steeper on the north side of the pass and in particular you should stop to view Coire na Ceannain on the left, whose narrow bounding ridge gives some indication of the delights to be had from Grey Corries ridge walking. On a bike the rough track gives a bone-shattering descent before it deposits you on the wide open plains of Glen Spean, reaching a minor road at Corriechoille. From here it is a further 2 miles (3km) beside the River Spean to Spean Bridge (from Corrour: 15 miles/24km; 260m/800ft; 7hr/mb:4½hr + halts). NB From Spean Bridge it is possible to reach Fort William or return to Loch Laggan by off-road routes (see p196).

To Rannoch Station via Corrour Old Lodge

This off-shoot to the main routes westwards strikes south-east from Loch Ossian and makes a fine station-to-station walk between Corrour and Rannoch Station (a right of way). From the east side of Loch Ossian a number of paths converge to cross the hillside to the ruins of Corrour Old Lodge, situated on an exposed site at 523m (1,723ft) on the slopes of Carn Dearg. At one time this was the highest inhabited residence in Britain. After the lodge was abandoned in favour of the new lodge at Loch Ossian it was used as an isolation hospital for a time, but now it stands ruined and forgotten high up the hillside, its gaunt and striking ruins conjuring up thoughts of a latter-day Stonehenge. The shallow corrie behind it is the Coire Odhar (*Oa*-ar, Dun-coloured) after which the lodge and station are named. From the lodge the path descends to a Land-Rover track that reaches the B846 Rannoch road 1½ miles (2km) from Rannoch Station (Corrour to Rannoch: 11 miles/18km; 200m/650ft; 4½hr + halts).

17

THE CORRIEYAIRACK PASS

TRACK RECORD

Viewed from the junction of the A889 Dalwhinnie road and the A86 Newtonmore road in Strath Mashie, the obvious route westwards to the Great Glen is not south-westwards along the line of the present road by Loch Laggan and Glen Spean but north-westwards beside the waters of the Spey. From here the broad strath that carries that great river stretches invitingly into the distance like some great Alaskan valley, but as a through-route to the Great Glen it is a cul-de-sac. Once it has lured travellers into the interior, the Spey turns south-westwards, and across its watershed lies not the Great Glen but Glen Roy, which in turn leads back to Glen Spean.

To reach the Great Glen from the upper Spey it is necessary to climb the high mountain barrier to the north, which forms one of the great watersheds of the Highlands. The low point on this skyline is a 764m (2,507ft) bealach from where the Allt Yairack descends to Coire Yairack and the Spey, and hence the route over the bealach has become known as the Corrieyairack Pass (Corrie Yairack is an anglicisation of the Gaelic *coire dheirg*, meaning red corrie).

Travellers have used the pass as a summer route for centuries and its history is perhaps better documented than that of any other Scottish hill track. Notable among early users were drovers who crossed from north to south on their way from the islands and the north of Scotland to the trysts at Crieff and Falkirk. For several months each year the pass was blocked by snow and impassable, but in those days no one travelled in winter unless it was absolutely necessary.

In the eighteenth century the pass achieved greater prominence when General Wade arrived in Scotland and built a road over it to link his bases at Ruthven and Fort Augustus, thus accomplishing one of the greatest feats of engineering ever attempted in the Highlands. Never was

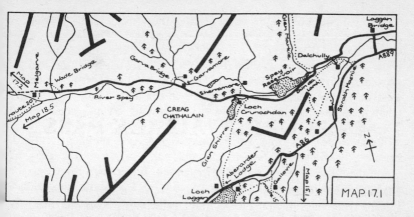

Sarah Murray's 1799 opinion that Wade built his roads 'up and down mountains, never dreaming that he could wind round the bases of them' more justified than in the case of the Corrieyairack.

Wade applied himself with vigour to the construction of the road, and using 510 men the 28 miles (45km) from Dalwhinnie to Fort Augustus were completed in one summer, between April and October 1731. Eighteen traverses or zigzags (later reduced to thirteen) were required for the climb out of Corrie Yairack to the bealach. Numerous bridges were built, some of them among Wade's most beautiful and some of which survive to this day. Poles marked the route in winter, as they still do.

For almost exactly a hundred years Wade's Corrieyairack Pass road remained the highest maintained public road in Britain, in its heyday carrying troops, drovers, traders and other civilians, including the first tourists. For the first few decades of its existence it carried heavy military traffic as government troops moved around the Highlands to counteract the Jacobite threat. One report describes a military column almost 2 miles (3km) long descending the zigzags, 'their arms glittering in the summer sunbeams'.

In 1745 the road almost saw the first battle of Bonnie Prince Charlie's rebellion, a battle that, had it taken place, might have changed the course of British history. Having raised his standard at Glenfinnan, Charlie marched to Fort Augustus and set out southwards over the Corrieyairack. Meanwhile, General Sir John Cope, commander of the government forces, set out northwards from Stirling to meet the threat. Charlie's plan was to place twenty field guns that he had brought from France at the head of the pass and bombard Cope's men as they struggled up the zigzags.

The vanguard of Cope's army reached the vicinity of Sherramore at the foot of the Corrieyairack but then turned back. This seeming indecision resulted in Cope's court martial, but he was acquitted when the court decided that any attempt to confront the rebel army in the wilds of the Corrieyairack would have been disastrous. Had the battle taken place and the Jacobite cause been seen to be in the ascendancy, who knows what new support Charlie would have attracted on his way south to London?

As more peaceful times reached the Highlands in the late eighteenth century the first tourists arrived, and many of them left dramatic accounts of the crossing of the Corrieyairack. Wade had reported to the government that his road was 'as easy and practicable for wheeled carriages as any road in the country'. Few travellers agreed, and the rigours of the crossing became legion. Carriages were broken or blown over. Civilians, especially those on foot, died from exposure. Soldiers numbed themselves with liquor at Garvamore King's House at the foot of the pass, foolishly hoping to immune themselves from the cold and exertion.

One traveller reported the route to be 'inexpressibly arduous ... elevated to a height truly terrific – springing sometimes from point to point over alpine bridges and at other times pursuing narrow ridges of rock frightfully impending over tremendous precipices'. Another, equally unsmitten by a love of wild places, 'thought it almost a miracle to escape unhurt from such horrid wastes, roaring torrents, unwholesome vapour and frightful fogs; drenched from top to toe, frozen with cold, and half-dead with fatigue'.

Such was the account (sounding very much like a typical Highland day on the hill!) given in the inn at Fort Augustus to Sarah Murray, a redoubtable woman in her fifties who was perhaps the first visitor to appreciate the beauty of the Highlands. She crossed the Corrieyairack by horse and carriage the following day, a good day, and declared herself disappointed by its tameness. At the summit she underwent a seemingly spiritual experience, and one way or another one could perhaps still agree with the sentiments she recorded later, that there is 'always something to contemplate' on the Corrieyairack.

The road was maintained until the early nineteenth century but by then its difficulties were considered out of step with the times. It was not built for and was never suitable for civilian traffic; Telford considered it 'so inconveniently steep as to be nearly unfit for the purposes of civil life'. His Loch Laggan road, completed in 1818, offered an easier, if more roundabout, route between the Central Highlands and the Great Glen, and after 1830 the Commission for Highland Roads and Bridges decided that only the 8 mile (13km) section of road between Dalwhinnie and the junction with the new Loch Laggan road near Laggan Bridge would be maintained. The remainder reverted to a drove road, although it is still roughly tarmaced as far as Melgarve. Bridges continued to be repaired until 1850 and many survive to this day, some left high and dry by modern river and road realignments. The 12 mile (19km) section between Melgarve and the outskirts of Fort Augustus is now the longest stretch of original Wade road still surviving.

The military occupation of Scotland in the eighteenth century had tragic consequences for Highland people and Highland culture, but it also bequeathed to hill-track enthusiasts a beautiful route through the wilderness and a spectacular piece of road engineering that, even in ruin, is a fitting memorial to eighteenth-century road-building skills and Wade's vision of a Highland road network. If the road was tarmaced and opened to vehicular traffic it would overnight become an essential tourist attraction. Instead, thankfully, its secrets remain the preserve of those who wish to travel through the wild places under their own steam.

ROUTEPLANNER
OS map: 35/34
Start Point: Melgarve (GR 463961)
End Point: Fort Augustus (GR 378093)
Total distance: 13½ miles (22km) + Laggan Bridge to Melgarve: 10½ miles (17km)
Total ascent: 500m (1,650ft)
   In reverse: 840m (2,750ft)
Total time: 7hr (mb:4½hr) + halts + Laggan Bridge to Melgarve: 4hr (mb:2hr) + halts
Melgarve: no facilities; shop at Lagggan Bridge.
Fort Augustus: accommodation/provisions/campsite.

Despite the opinions of travellers of yesteryear, the Corrieyairack Pass (a right of way) is not a difficult route by Scottish hill-track standards. In foul weather the summit of the pass is a desolate place indeed, but there is an obvious track all the way and it is difficult to lose unless it is covered in snow. With private transport to Melgarve the route is easily walked in a day in good conditions. By mountain bike it is becoming a classic expedition, although the Melgarve side of the pass is so rough that some sections have to be walked, and good luck to anyone who attempts to ride up the zigzags.

The route is described in a south-to-north direction in order to minimise ascent and link with descriptions of other routes in this book. In the south it connects with Lagganside and the Pattack valley (Route 15) and in the north with Caulfeild's Road to Glen Moriston (Route 19). There are no short return routes from Fort Augustus to Melgarve, but a long, mainly off-road low-level return route is possible via the Great Glen and Glen Spean, and the path from Glen Roy to Melgarve is especially recommended (Route 18). In reverse the route requires an extra 340m (1,100ft) of ascent and is a much tougher proposition.

ROUTE DESCRIPTION

The first 8 miles (13km) or so of Wade's road from Dalwhinnie now form the A889 to near Laggan Bridge in Strath Mashie. From Laggan Bridge a minor road continues westwards beside the Spey to the farm at Melgarve. Much of this road follows the line of Wade's road, but there are some interesting variations. One such variation is at the beginning, where Wade's original road followed the south side of the river whereas the present road keeps to the north side as far as the Spey Dam. The original road leaves the A86 about a mile west of Laggan Bridge at GR 605936, signposted Dalchully. It is very gritty until it joins the main driveway to Dalchully, which is tarmaced. The drive crosses a renovated single-arched Wade bridge and when it turns left Wade's road goes straight on beside the Spey. This section makes a fascinating walk for Wade scholars, with the left-hand bank of the road clearly visible and the carriageway in places eroded to an almost archaeological depth and cobbled with stones from the river; it is totally unridable. Eventually it rises through fields to join the present road.

Further down the A86 towards Loch Laggan two other tracks cross to the Melgarve road, making useful approach routes from that direction. One leaves the A86 2 miles (3km) west of Laggan Bridge (GR 594925) and reaches the road near the Spey Dam. It is an excellent track that runs directly beneath Dun da Lamh (see below). The other track begins just east of Aberarder Lodge at the east end of Loch Laggan (GR 532897; OS map 42). Take the rightmost of the two tracks that leave the roadside, then fork left to climb steeply over the moors into Glen Shirra and reach the Melgarve road just below Loch Crunachdan. This 3 mile (5km) track is a useful link route from Lagganside or the Pattack valley (route 15), but it begins with a stiff 80m (250ft) climb that is especially tough on a mountain bike.

Another variation from Wade's original line had to be made when the Spey reservoir was built, and this has left a curious relic. The reservoir was dammed at its eastern end to raise its level to that of Loch

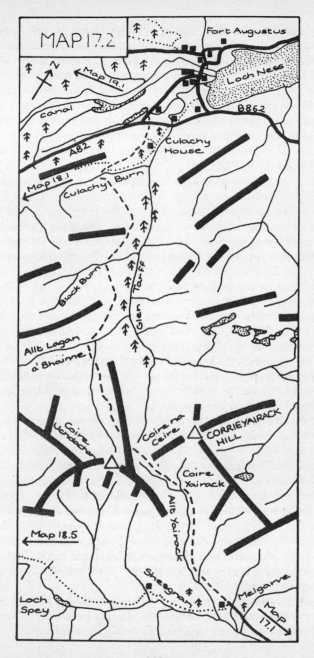

MAP 17.2

Fort Augustus

Loch Ness

Map 19.1

canal

B862

A82

Culachy House

Map 18.1

Culachy Burn

Black Burn

Glen Tarff

Allt Lagan a'Bhaine

Coire Uchdachan

Coire na Ceire

CORRIEYAIRACK HILL

Coire Yairack

Allt Yairack

Map 18.5

Shesgnan

Melgarve

Loch Spey

Map 17.1

Crunachdan, so that the waters of the upper Spey now flow eastwards into the reservoir and then back westwards along a canal into Loch Crunachdan, from where they flow by underground channels into the Lochaber hydro-electric scheme. The present road runs pleasantly along the south shore of the reservoir and the canal, beside which a curiously sited humpback Wade bridge stands defiantly in a field. The position of the bridge is explained by the old stream, now non-existent, that formerly drained from Loch Crunachdan into the Spey before the canal was built.

The road crosses the canal and continues westwards past Sherramore, where Cope retreated from confrontation with the Jacobite army. It rises through a wood and descends to cross the Spey at Garva Bridge, one of Wade's finest constructions. This two-arched bridge is 55m (180ft) long, its two buttresses built on an island in the river, giving it the appearance of two one-arched bridges joined together. The grand but dilapidated building on the right of the road at Garvamore a short distance before the bridge was formerly a kingshouse, built to serve troops working on the bridge, and a fine site for an inn it is too. What better place to refresh oneself before or after tackling the pass?

Beyond Garva Bridge the road deteriorates, becoming progressively rougher and increasingly pot-holed. It is drivable as far as the bridge over the Allt Luaidhe (Loo-eye, lead) and some cars might even make the farm buildings at Melgarve a short distance further along. In this section the line is unmistakably Wade's, proceeding in a series of long straights linked by dog-legs. Beside the road is a line of pylons that will accompany you for the rest of the journey; their maintenance is currently the only commercial use of the Corrieyairack.

The present wooden bridge over the Allt Luaidhe is not Wade's. That, restored in 1984 by the Association for the Rural Preservation of Scotland, stands 200m upstream, hidden deep within the forest like a relic of some vanished culture, which in fact is exactly what it is. It is worth a look. The original road over it leaves the present road a few hundred metres before the stream beside some old ruins; there is a gate in the forest fence and (at the time of writing) a signpost well back from the road.

On the opposite side of the road to the ruins, in the middle of a field, is a standing stone that commemorates a tale of the sixteenth century. Cathalan, an Irish warrior, fell in love with the daughter of Cluny MacPherson of Speyside and eloped with her towards the Corrieyairack. They spent the night in a small cave on the south side of the Spey, on the hill ever since called Creag Cathalan and named as such on the OS map. An overnight fall of snow enabled pursuing clansmen to track the lovers the next day. Cathalan was killed, and in a fit of remorse Cluny MacPherson had the standing stone erected over his grave. Although nearly a metre high, the stone is now weathered and not easy to spot from a distance; to find it from the roadside ruins walk towards the Spey, aiming midway between the cottage and the wood seen across the river.

The road ends at Melgarve, where there is yet another bypassed Wade bridge, and from hereon the route remains much as it was in Wade's day. On the left a fine approach route comes in from Glen Roy (see p199), but the Corrieyairack continues straight on as a rough track into the hills, rising gently, much of it like a stream bed. In places a path suitable for walkers has developed alongside it but mountain bikers should not expect to stay in the saddle for long. If the state of the track was like this two hundred years ago it is no wonder that there were so many complaints from travellers; the prospect of attempting it in a carriage is enough to bring tears to the eyes.

With uncompromising directness the track cuts across the hillside to the Allt Yairack, takes a single right turn to follow the stream up into Coíre Yairack, then a single left turn to cross the floor of the corrie to the foot of the zigzags. Once it reaches the Allt Yairack it levels off and improves slightly, becoming intermittently ridable as it makes its way into the great grassy bowl of the corrie, which is completely floored with hummocky glacial moraines like giant anthills. Never was a corrie more misnamed, for everywhere it is green not red. The track cuts left across the corrie to follow the main stream up to the skyline, becoming rougher and steeper as the zigzags rise ahead. The zigzags themselves are an easy walk by Scottish hill-track standards, but it would take a superhuman effort to ride them on a mountain bike. There are thirteen traverses – lucky for some.

Above the zigzags keep an eye open for a small well a few metres to the right, from where a mossy rivulet runs across the track. The gradient soon eases off and you reach a large cairn and VHF transmitter that mark the summit of the bealach. On a warm summer's day this is a green and pleasant spot, but go there when the wind is blowing and the mists are swirling and you will not linger long. Northwards is a spacious view which is best described by Sarah Murray 'No lakes, no glens, no plains; all is a boundless space of a rough ocean of mountains, whose tops seem to wave one behind the other, to the distant sea in the west and on every other side, as far as the eye can reach.' To the north-east of the bealach lies Corrieyairack Hill (896m/2,940ft), and further round the ridge enclosing Corrie Yairack is Geal Charn (876m/2,874ft), from where a bird's-eye view of the zigzags can be obtained.

For some reason Wade did not route his road immediately northwards down Coire na Ceire into Glen Tarff but crossed the western shoulder of the corrie to take a more roundabout route down Coire Uchdachan, the next corrie to the west. The highest point of the route is therefore not the bealach but the crest of the shoulder, which lies a short distance further along the 11m (36ft) higher at a height of 775m (2,543ft).

From this high point the track takes a diagonal line down into Coire Uchdachan (*Uch*kachan, Hillside), eventually to cross the Allt Coire Uchdachan. The going remains pretty rough but is an improvement on

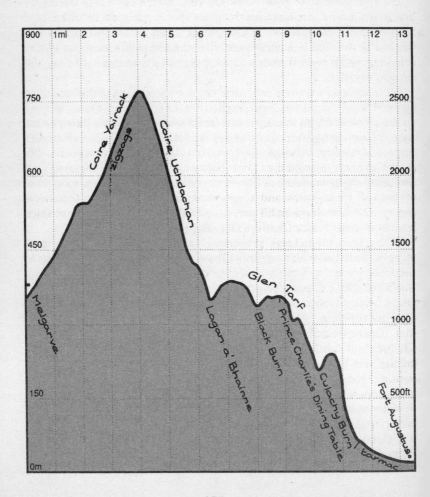

the ascent and is not as steep; it is ridable if taken slowly and carefully. Again, a path for walkers has developed beside the track.

The track crosses the Allt Coire Uchdachan by a wooden bridge that stands beside the now disused Wade bridge. Continuing across the hillside it then descends steeply in zigzags to cross the Allt Lagan a' Bhainne by a Bailey bridge built by the Royal Engineers in 1961. Wade's original road crossed upstream from here, and the remains of his bridge, a later suspension bridge and another bridge across the stream on the far side can clearly be seen.

The flat expanse of grass beside the river on the far side of the Bailey bridge is a prime candidate for the place that Wade's troops nicknamed Snugburgh. It was here, on 30 October 1731, on the king's birthday and the end of the road-building season, that the completion of the road was celebrated with roasted oxen and alcohol, and it was reported that 'the joy was great'.

Keeping well above the river the track now rises around a corner to descend the west side of Glen Tarff whose wooded gorge is a pleasant change from the bare moors. It descends to cross the Black Burn, where a ruined cottage can be seen upstream, and then rises left around another corner. The going is very pleasant; in parts the track is almost reasonable in comparison to what has gone before. At the top of the rise Fort Augustus comes into view at last. It was here, on a small flat area in view of both Fort Augustus and the summit of the pass, that Charlie is reported to have dined on his way to meet Cope. The spot has ever since been known as 'Prince Charlie's Dining Table'.

A short descent and reascent lead to the start of the final steep descent to Fort Augustus, which begins with a series of zigzags leading down to the Culachy Burn. Once across this stream Wade's original road goes sharp right as a grassy riverside track that descends past Culachy Falls and Culachy House but the main track today avoids the grounds of Culachy House by bearing left away from the stream to join a new track that climbs from Fort Augustus to a radio transmitter on Meall a' Cholumain. Shortly after joining the Meall a' Cholumain track a spectacular view opens up along the length of Loch Ness. NB The view is even more stunning from the summit of Meall a' Cholumain, if you have the energy to make the detour up there (see p190).

Wade's road is rejoined on the far side of Culachy House and the minor road that links the A82 and B862 is reached soon afterwards. Wade's road crosses this road and continues as a boulder ruckle of a path to reach the A82 at the driveway to Lochunagan house. This last short section is difficult to walk, never mind cycle, and most people will opt to take back roads for the last mile or two into Fort Augustus. The quietest route follows the minor road right to the B862 then left into town; note also that there is a good short cut along the track past Ardachy Lodge. The fleshpots of Fort Augustus will never have seemed more inviting.

DUN DA LAMH

Dun da Lamh (Doon da Laav, Fort of the Two Hands) is an ancient Iron Age fort that crowns the rocky tree-clad hill-top immediately south of the Spey Dam, about 180m (600ft) above the valley floor. Although dilapidated, it remains one of the largest, most spectacularly situated and, owing to its isolation, best preserved duns in Scotland, and it is well worth a visit. Its name perhaps derives from the difficulty of reaching it, although a modern forestry track has considerably eased access.

The forestry track begins half-way along the track described earlier which links the A86 with the Spey Dam about 2 miles (3km) west of Laggan Bridge. Follow the track as it climbs steadily through the trees, then turn right at a junction to reach the track-end just below the skyline. The ascent is a real tester for mountain bikers. A narrow path continues through the heather to the top of the hill and the dun (leave bikes at the end of the track).

Although ruinous, the dun still impresses on account of its size and situation. Follow the perimeter wall around the summit plateau to get some idea of its layout; it is 130m (420ft) long by 75m (250ft) wide at its greatest extent, and in the north-west corner the wall is still 4m (13ft) high and 7½m (25ft) thick. There are fine views both up and down Strath Mashie, but it is the glorious vista across the Spey reservoir to the wilds of the Corrieyairack that will hold your attention. Should you wish to await a sunrise, there is a rough shelter built from stones from the dun. Allow at least a couple of hours on wheels and a further hour on foot for the visit.

18

THE GREAT GLEN and GLEN SPEAN

This chapter describes off-road excursions in the area around the foot of The Great Glen (Glen More) and Glen Spean, thus linking Fort William and Spean Bridge to Fort Augustus and Loch Laggan. Although not all of the tracks described below can be considered hill tracks, many of them make fine short walks and rides and can be linked to provide connections between some of the major routes described elsewhere in this book. In the near future the Countryside Commission for Scotland hopes to open a Great Glen Way using many of these tracks.

FORT AUGUSTUS TO LOCH OICH

There are a surprisingly large number of tracks to explore in the Fort Augustus area, thanks to the historically important strategic position of the town, which is situated at the foot of Loch Ness, half-way along the Great Glen between Fort William and Inverness, and commands the gateway to the west coast and the islands via Glen Moriston.

Wade routed his Great Glen and Corrieyairack Pass roads through Fort Augustus and Caulfeild added a road westwards to Glen Moriston and Bernera Barracks. When these military roads fell into disuse other lines of communication replaced them, notably Telford's new road west via Invermoriston and the Caledonian Canal, which ran through the heart of the town. In 1903 Fort Augustus also became a rail-head for a brief period, but generally the twentieth century has seen its strategic importance decline. The railway has long closed and the main road west now quits the Great Glen at Invergarry. This is good news for walkers and cyclists, who have thus been bequeathed a variety of interesting off-road routes.

Wade's road over the Corrieyairack Pass is described as Route 17. The first section of it, as far as 'Prince Charlie's Dining Table' offers a

189

steep ascent to a viewpoint from where both Fort Augustus and the summit of the pass are visible (see also Meall a' Cholumain, below). Caulfeild's road to Glen Moriston is described as Route 19. The initial zigzags above Jenkins Park are worth exploring and offer fine views up and down the Great Glen, especially of Fort Augustus and Loch Ness, with distant Ben Nevis visible on a good day. To make a longer circuit through Inchnacardoch Forest take the left branch at a fork above the zigzags, turn left at the next junction, then keep straight on to return to Jenkins Park (4 miles/6km).

Meall a' Cholumain

This insignificant little hill (315m/1,034ft) on the east side of the Great Glen half-way between Loch Ness and Loch Oich is one of the best viewpoints in the glen (GR 360049). Moreover, an access track that serves the radio transmitter at the summit makes an ascent straightforward. The track begins as for the Corrieyairack Pass on a minor road south of Fort Augustus at GR 373072; keep right at all forks to reach the summit. On a mountain bike the ascent is quite steep and rough in parts.

The view from the summit is stunning. It includes both Caulfeild's road to Glen Moriston and Wade's road over the Corrieyairack, but it is the bird's-eye view along Loch Ness that will wrest your attention. For an equally stunning view in the other direction along the Great Glen, walk a few hundred metres along the summit plateau, until Lochs Oich and Lochy come into view in the trench at the foot of the Munros of the Glengarry Forest.

Forest Tracks

Inchnacardoch Forest to the west of Fort Augustus provides a number of splendid woodland walks and rides on each side of the Jenkins Park–Auchteraw road. Between the road and the River Oich a 6 mile (10km) track goes all the way from Fort Augustus to Bridge of Oich, and in combination with the Caledonian Canal towpath (see below) this makes perhaps the best round trip in the area either on foot or by bicycle. The track is described beginning at Loch Oich.

On the west side of Bridge of Oich the track goes north through a gate and past a number of cottages. When it bears left beside the Invervigar Burn take a right branch that crosses the stream (the bridge is down but the crossing is easy). Keeping left at a fork, the main track then climbs high above the floor of the Great Glen before descending to another fork just beyond the bridge at GR 348074. The left branch here reaches the Auchteraw road in a few hundred metres; the right branch takes a

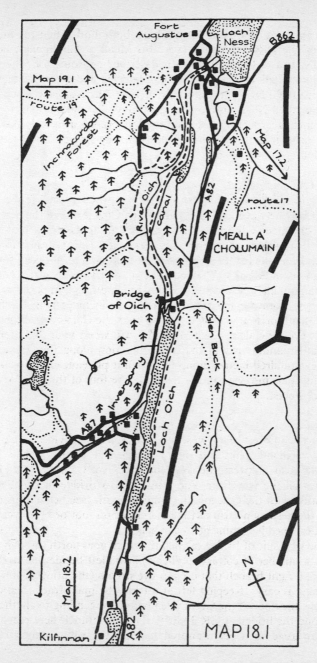

MAP 18.1

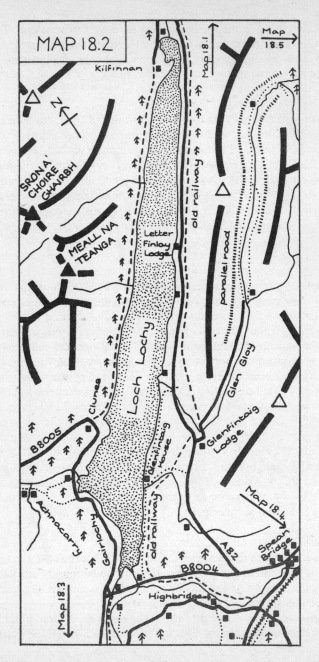

MAP 18.2

Kilfinnan

Map 18.1

Map 18.5 →

SRON A' CHOIRE GHAIRBH

MEALL NA TEANGA

old railway

parallel road

Letter Finlay Lodge

Loch Lochy

Glen Gloy

Glenfintaig Lodge

B8005

Clunes

Map 18.4

Achnacarry

old railway

Gusairn

Glasdrum House

A82

Spean Bridge

B8004

Map 18.3

Highbridge

192

pleasant route through the forest to reach the road further along. To the right of this latter track are a number of colour-coded riverside forest trails that make pleasant walks; an information leaflet can be obtained at Fort Augustus tourist office.

Caledonian Canal Towpath (West Side)

The canal towpath from Fort Augustus to Bridge of Oich was built in the early nineteenth century and is probably used as much today as it ever was. It winds its way like a causeway between the canal and the wooded banks of the River Oich and provides a lovely 5 mile (8km) excursion out of sight and sound of the main road. It is a route of constant delight, to be taken slowly and savoured, at its best in late spring and early summer when the canalside broom is at its most colourful (circuit from Fort Augustus via towpath and forest track: 11 miles/18km; 4½hr/mb:2hr + halts).

Fort William–Fort Augustus Railway

Railway engineers first began investigating the Great Glen in the 1840s, and a line from Fort William to Fort Augustus was eventually opened in 1903, but it was never a commercial success. Locals used it and were fiercely loyal to it, but the tourists who had been expected to flock to it preferred to sail up the Caledonian Canal. Had political machinations and railway rivalries not prevented the line from reaching Inverness, the story might have been different, but as it was the line was ill-conceived and doomed to failure. It first closed in 1911 but reopened in 1913. Passenger services were suspended in 1933 and the track was dismantled in 1947.

For some years thereafter the line provided a good walking and cycling route, but time has taken its toll and today only certain sections remain practicable. Between Fort Augustus and Bridge of Oich a few sections are still passable on foot, especially beside Loch Uanagan, but mostly the line is overgrown or crosses farmland and its exploration is best left to industrial archaeologists.

LOCH OICH

The west side of Loch Oich carries the busy A82, but the east side is still wonderfully peaceful and picturesque. Here are to be found both Wade's road along the great Glen and the old railway line, running side by side to offer a splendid alternative to the main road.

The route begins at the first track on the east side of Bridge of Oich, signposted Aberchalder Farm (NB, not Aberchalder Lodge). The track goes past the farm, over a bridge and pleasantly through woods beside the Calder Burn. Soon the railway line comes in from the right across a substantial bridge, whose rusted ironwork and grassy surface make a colourful contrast. Immediately beyond is the beach at the north end of Loch Oich.

The railway is overgrown and very boggy in parts, although at the time of writing some drainage is being undertaken. The track (Wade's route) remains a delight to walk or ride. At first the railway runs below the track and then it cuts through a tunnel to the other side of it; the castellated towers at the tunnel entrance rear out of the greenwood like some lost jungle temple. Beyond the tunnel the track runs beside the lapping waters of the loch, at times so close to the water that it is undercut. Care is required, especially by mountain bikers, who should not let tree roots distract their attention from decapitating overhead branches. It is a beautiful route, one of Wade's finest.

At a fork near the loch end keep left to climb onto the railway, here a good track, and follow it past an old platform to descend past holiday chalets to the main road (4 miles/7km; 1½hr/mb:1hr + halts).

LOCH LOCHY

There are off-road routes along each side of Loch Lochy. On the east side an adventurous path follows the line of the old railway, while on the west side a forest track (a right of way) provides easier going, especially for mountain bikers.

On the east side the railway line continues straight on past the old platform at the south end of Loch Oich mentioned above. The first 5½ miles (9km) to Letterfinlay Lodge provide excellent going, grassy at first, then resurfaced as a forest track, then grassy again. Above the lodge a maze of fallen trees that is awkward to negotiate almost blocks the way at the time of writing. Beyond, a more overgrown and obstacle-strewn path continues to a Land-Rover track at GR 230886, ending as a beautiful tunnel through rhododendrons.

Beyond here the line is impassable, but a way southwards continues along the Land-Rover track, which climbs to join a surviving section of Wade road high above the loch. This leads to the foot of Glen Gloy and so back to the main road at Glenfintaig Lodge. A short distance back along the road from here the railway line crosses the road and becomes passable again all the way to the B8004 near Gairlochy. On the far side of the B8004 it continues through Gairlochy Caravan park to the River Spean, where the towering remnants of the old bridge mark a dead-end – worthwhile though as it also passes the gaunt ruins of High Bridge (see p22).

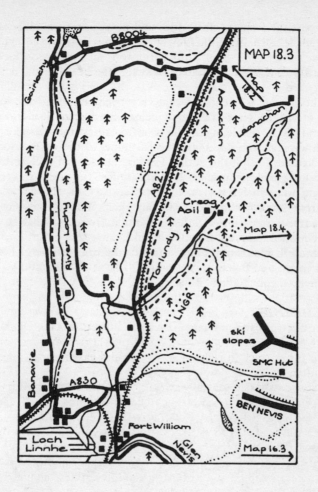

The west-side route along Loch Lochy begins at the south end of Loch Oich and follows the minor road to Kilfinnan beside the Caledonian Canal. Note that the canal towpath, normally an excellent walking and cycling route, is here no better than an overgrown and unpleasant path. At the road-end at Kilfinnan take the right-hand track to Kilfinnan holiday chalets and then fork left on a track that descends to the lochside. The remainder of the route is an excellent lochside forest track that goes all the way to Clunes to join the B8005 to Gairlochy (Loch Oich to

Kilfinnan: 2½ miles/ 4km; Kilfinnan to Clunes: 6½ miles/10km; 2½hr/mb:1hr + halts; Clunes to Gairlochy: 4 miles/6km).

SPEAN BRIDGE TO FORT WILLIAM

There are two easy routes between Loch Lochy and Fort William, each of which makes a lovely stroll or cycle, or can be combined with the other into a longer circuit. The most picturesque route, as elsewhere in the Great Glen, is that along the Caledonian Canal towpath, here a fine, flat track between the canal and the River Lochy. From Gairlochy at the south end of Loch Lochy it runs for 6½ miles (10km) to Neptune's Staircase at Banavie on the outskirts of Fort William and makes a very pleasant bicycle ride, which is best taken at the leisurely pace of the canal boats.

From Banavie the main road into Fort William has footpaths and cycle tracks on each side as far as Victoria Bridge, just before which you should turn right on the B8006 and cross the River Lochy by the walkway beside the rail bridge to reach the back streets of Fort William (Gairlochy to Banavie: 6½ miles/10km; 2½hr/mb:1hr + halts; Banavie to Fort William: 3 miles/5km).

The other route between Spean Bridge and Fort William is a forest track that runs close beside the West Highland Railway and in places coincides with Wade's Great Glen road. It begins on the Leanachan road

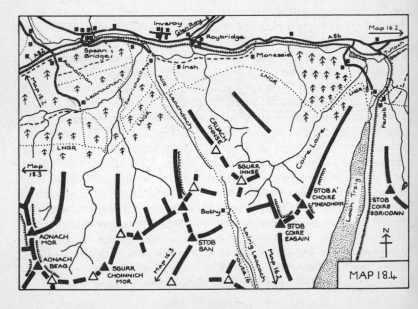

MAP 18.4

196

1 mile south of Spean Bridge and runs more or less level for 4½ miles (7km) to Torlundy, where it is necessary to rejoin the main road for the last 3½ miles (6km) to Fort William.

This route can be expanded into a fine cycling circuit through the Leanachan Forest. Tarmaced roads penetrate the forest from Torlundy to Creag Aoil quarry (GR 181777) in the south and from near Spean Bridge to Leanachan (GR 219785) in the north. The circuit is completed by a forest track (a right of way) that links Creag Aoil and Leanachan. The Creag Aoil road passes the Aonach Mor ski car park and at the time of writing is subject to redevelopment. Both it and the quarry can be avoided by another forestry track that at Torlundy branches right beside the railway to run past the car park; at its end join another track and then go right at the next crossroads to reach Leanachan.

GLEN SPEAN

Glen Spean is the main through route between the Great Glen and Spey-side. It carries the A86 and will be well used by those returning east from routes described elsewhere that end at Fort William or Fort Augustus. There is currently no practicable off-road route along the length of the glen, but large sections of the road can nevertheless be avoided by those prepared to seek out more interesting if longer alternatives.

Spean Bridge to Fersit
From Spean Bridge a pleasant minor road runs for 2 miles (3km) along the south side of the River Spean to a junction of tracks near Coirechoille farm. NB After about one mile (GR 232816) this road is joined by a forest track that comes in from the Leanachan road (GR 209800) to provide a connection with the Torlundy track described above. The right branch at Corriechoille is the Lairig Leacach track (see p175). The left branch continues beside the river past Insh farm and Monessie farm to join the A86 just east of Monessie gorge (GR 302810). The only route-finding problems are at Insh, where the track goes left and then right through a field, and beyond Monessie, where it is important to keep left at a junction to reach a footbridge over the Spean at the head of the gorge. (Spean Bridge to Monessie: 6 miles/10km). The gorge itself is worth exploring; note the pipelines that once formed part of a temporary hydro-electric scheme instigated in the 1920s to supply power for the building of the Fort William–Loch Treig tunnel (see below). From Monessie it is necessary to take to the main road for the next couple of miles, until a minor road branches right to the small cluster of houses at Fersit, from where a track continues eastwards (see below).

197

High up the hillside above Glen Spean the disused line of the Lochaber Narrow Gauge Railway (LNGR) offers a tempting alternative route from Fort William to Fersit. The line was constructed in the 1920s as part of an imaginative hydro-electric power scheme devised to supply electricity to the new aluminium factory at Fort William. Dams were built at Loch Treig, Loch Laggan and the upper Spey to carry water to the factory.

The railway was originally built as a temporary measure for the transportation of men and provisions during the excavation of the Fort William–Loch Treig tunnel, but once constructed it was kept in use for access purposes. The line was maintained regularly until 1971, after which forest tracks began to be used instead, and the last remnants of the line were finally abandoned in 1977.

From sea-level at Fort William the line climbs for 19 miles (30km) across the northern flanks of Ben Nevis, the Aonachs, the Grey Corries and the Easains, forming a high-level balcony above Glen Spean that reaches a height of 340m (1,120ft) before descending to Loch Treig. Unfortunately, its many bridge remnants are in too dangerous a state to be used, and therefore British Alcan do not encourage people to follow the route. The bridges can be avoided only by the negotiation of some awkward gorges, and the exploration of the line cannot be recommended unless you are fully aware of the difficulties to be encountered. Do not be tempted onto the bridges; heed the danger notices. In 1986 a mountain biker was killed by ignoring this advice.

The gorge of the Allt Leachdach (GR 257788) is especially difficult to negotiate, and as far as here it is wiser to use alternative approaches from Fort William. The line can be joined a short distance further along by a track that climbs from Insh on the Spean Bridge–Monessie track. Beyond this point it becomes ridable for a short distance before it crosses more dangerous bridges and degenerates into a boggy section. This is followed by the most scenic part of the route, where the line contours high above Glen Spean and gives good views. A shed is passed that used to garage locomotives but now serves as a shelter for cows.

Eventually, the line rounds a corner and veers away from Glen Spean into Coire Laire. It soon becomes ridable and eventually carries an excellent Land-Rover track that surmounts the almost imperceptible summit and descends to the Allt Laire. The line crosses the river and becomes very rough again as it descends around Creag Fhiaclach on the last leg of its journey to Fersit and Loch Treig. Mountain bikers can avoid this final section by descending the forest track from the Allt Laire to Inverlair, where the minor road to Fersit is joined.

Fersit to Lagganside
From the road-end at Fersit a track crosses the River Treig and the West
Highland Railway line and forks, both branches eventually reuniting to
enter the south Loch Laggan forest. The 3 mile (5km) section between
Fersit and Laggan Dam was originally a railway line built for access to
the Loch Treig–Loch Laggan tunnel during construction of the
Lochaber hydro-electric scheme. In those days Fersit was home to nearly
one thousand men and had it own halt on the West Highland Railway.

Ignore the left branch that descends to Laggan Dam (no access to
A86) and continue along the main track, which swings eastwards along
Glen Spean as a secret woodland route that provides a lovely gentle run.
There is only one short steep, rough section where mountain bikers may
prefer to walk. The track descends to meet the River Spean at Luiblea at
the west end of Loch Laggan, where a bridge gives access to the A86 (GR
432830; from Fersit: 7 miles/11km, 2½hr/mb:1hr + halts).

Just before the bridge a right branch continues the off-road route
eastwards along the south side of Loch Laggan or Lochan na h-Earba all
the way to Kinloch Laggan at the east end of the loch (see p164 for
description; from Luiblea to Kinloch Laggan via lochside: 9 miles/14km;
3½hr/mb:1½hr + halts).

GLEN ROY
On the north side of Glen Spean, Glen Roy pushes northwards into the
hills to provide a route to Melgarve at the foot of the Corrieyairack Pass.
The route is a right of way and is an attractive hill track in its own right,
whether you are walking or cycling. In its lower reaches the green and
charming glen is not like a Highland glen at all, but initial appearances
are deceptive, for, as it winds its way northwards, it becomes a deep
trough through the hills, and at its end lies a beautiful hidden valley
packed with scenic interest.

From Roy Bridge a picturesque road penetrates the glen for 8 miles
(13km). In its first 3 miles (5km) it rises 140m (450ft) to a high point of
230m (750ft) above the glen's narrowest point. Here a viewpoint offers
the best panorama of the renowned Parallel Roads, three level terraces,
10–30m wide, that cross the hillsides for 10 miles (16km) on each side of
the glen at heights of 350m (1,149ft), 326m (1,068ft) and 261m (875ft).
The road are more impressive at a distance than close up, but this need
not deter you from investigating.

For centuries the origin of the roads was a mystery. One eighteenth-
century writer, marvelling at their curious siting and precise contouring,
conjectured on whether the Romans could have built them. Locally they

were known as Fingal's Roads because Fingal and his acolytes were said to have used them for hunting. Their true origin is equally intriguing: they are the successive shorelines of an ancient lake formed during the last Ice Age when a glacier blocked the lower part of Glen Roy.

Beyond the Parallel Roads viewpoint the road descends to accompany the river to Brae Roy Lodge (cars may be taken to here), and then a Land-Rover track continues into the interior. A short distance beyond the lodge at the confluence of the River Roy and the River Turret is the picturesque single-arched Turret Bridge, said by some to have been built by General Wade. It does indeed look Wade-like, and some Wade enthusiasts believe that the route up Glen Roy and over the watershed to Melgarve was a former Wade road used to avoid the Corrieyairack in foul weather, but there is no historical evidence to support this.

The glen at Turret Bridge feels very shut in because of a high gravelly riverside terrace that was once the alluvial delta of a river that drained into the old glacial lake. On the far side of the bridge keep right at a fork and follow the continuing Land-Rover track along the north bank of the River Roy. Once past the riverside terrace the broad flatlands of upper Glen Roy form an attractive grassy bowl hidden deep in the mountains.

The track keeps close to the river, passing the Falls of Roy, where the river cuts a dog-leg through a rock band and forms a fine twin fall with deep pool. Just beyond the falls the Burn of Agie comes in from a wooded ravine on the south side of the river, and at the head of this extremely narrow and deep-cut ravine a natural bridge across the chasm is well worth (careful) investigation. You will have to ford the Roy to reach it, but note that you can also reach the south side of the river by a bridge just east of Turret Bridge from where a path follows the riverbank all the way to the natural bridge. Further up the Burn of Agie are numerous waterfalls, including the Dog Falls. The whole area makes a fine afternoon's excursion from the road-end.

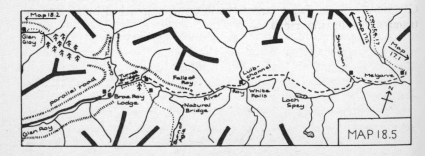

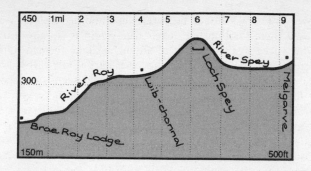

On the north side of the River Roy the track continues its way eastwards, rising out of the grassy bowl to end on the vast moors of the upper glen. Just before its end take a path that branches left to pursue an excellent course through the wild and featureless country. It passes Luibchonnal Bothy, situated in a superbly remote position near the picturesque White Falls, and then climbs gently across the watershed to descend past Loch Spey to the ruined cottage of Shesgnan. The going varies from rough to ridable, overall making an excellent walk and an intermittent ride. From Shesgnan a Land-Rover track continues to Melgarve (from Brae Roy Lodge: 9 miles/15km; 200m/650ft; 4hr/mb:3hr + halts).

A Note on Glen Gloy

Glen gloy is a long, narrow and steep-sided glen that runs between and parallel to the Great Glen and Glen Roy. There is a road and track all the way up the glen, and then a right of way crosses the watershed into Glen Roy, making the route an attractive proposition for those heading from Spean Bridge to upper Glen Roy and Melgarve. Unfortunately, the head of the glen is blocked by new forest, but by taking a forest track that climbs left from the main track at GR 306932 to the forest edge at GR 308934, Glen Turret and Glen Roy can be reached by a pathless tramp across the watershed.

19

ACROSS GLEN MORISTON

TRACK RECORD
One of the many lines of communication that centred on the historically important strategic position of Fort Augustus was Caulfeild's military road to Bernera Barracks at Glenelg. From Fort Augustus it crossed a barrier of low hills into Glen Moriston, continued through Glen Shiel and crossed the Mam Ratagan Pass to Glenelg. It was built in the 1750s but was abandoned a few decades later when the Jacobite threat had dissipated. Telford resurveyed the route in 1802, finding only 'vestiges' of the road, and his new road via Invermoriston finally consigned Caulfeild's road to history.

Much of Caulfeild's road has been obliterated by modern roads and for the most part only short sections remain (indicated on the OS map). Still intact is the first 7 mile (11km) section to Glen Moriston, and from there an old drove road crosses the hills towards Glen Affric, thus forming a useful cross-country link between the Great Glen and Glen Affric.

It has to be said that overall this route scores highly neither on scenery nor on terrain and is especially steep and tough for mountain bikers. The Glen Moriston side of Caulfeild's road has been shamefully eroded by vehicular access, and the scenic value of the whole route is undermined by electricity pylons. Nevertheless, the route merits inclusion in this book for its historical significance and its strategic position as a north–south link route.

ROUTEPLANNER
OS map: 34/25
Start point: Fort Augustus (GR 378093)
End point: Hilton Lodge (GR 285244)
Total distance: 16½ miles/26km + Hilton Lodge to Cannich: 6 miles (10km)

Total ascent: 830m (2,700ft); in reverse: 680m (2,250ft)
Total time: 8hr (mb:5½hr) + halts + Hilton Lodge to Cannich: 2hr
   (mb:1hr)
Fort Augustus: accommodation/provisions/campsite.
Hilton Lodge: no facilities; accommodation/provisions/youth hostel/
   campsite at Cannich.

The route is a right of way, except for the direct descent to Torgyle
Bridge, which has been approved for use by the Forestry Commission.
   There are tracks nearly all the way, but in places they are so rough
that they have the consistency of a stream bed, which after rain they may
well be.
   The route is described in a south-to-north direction so that it links
with the descriptions of the Corrieyairack Pass (Route 17) and Glen
Affric (Route 20) to form an extensive cross-country expedition. In this
direction also the worst going is tackled on descent; in reverse the section
from Glen Affric to Glen Moriston is easier, but from there to Fort
Augustus is harder. If a return route is required, there are several options
between Glen Affric and Glen Moriston (see below), but from there to
Fort Augustus the only alternative route is by road via Invermoriston.
Using Glen Moriston as a starting point, either half of the route can be
explored independently; on foot this perhaps has little to recommend it,
but by mountain bike some strenuous and exciting circuits can be made.

ROUTE DESCRIPTION
The route begins on the north side of Fort Augustus, following signposts
to Jenkins Park. Keep right at a fork beside a row of cottages to the road-
end at GR 371095. Go straight on along a forest track for a few hundred
metres, then turn right to follow Caulfeild's road up steep zigzags and
through Inchnacardoch Forest to the skyline. This first part of the route
is a lovely walk, with good views up and down the Great Glen; by bike it
is an unrelenting ascent that requires sustained effort.
   On descent into Glen Moriston the track deteriorates as it crosses a
boggy moor and reaches the Allt Phocaichain (*Foach*kachan, Pocket),
where a decision must be made. The easiest and most direct route down
into Glen Moriston goes right along a riverbank path to a line of pylons,
which lead down through a break in the trees to a forest track, which in
turn descends to the roadside near Torgyle Bridge (GR 307127; 7 miles/
11km; 370m/1,200ft; 3½hr/mb:2½hr + halts). Only military road
enthusiasts will wish to follow the main track across the Allt Phocaichain
and down through the forest to Achlain further up Glen Moriston. There

are a number of fine Caulfeild bridges, but the state of the track is disgraceful; in places it is little more than a quagmire.

The continuation to Glen Affric begins at Dundreggan a short distance down the road from Torgyle Bridge. From here take the left-most of two tracks that leave the roadside to climb steeply through a small wood and across moorland beside a line of pylons. By bike the ascent is relentlessly steep and tough, yet still easy compared to what is to come, for at 250m (800ft) the route to Glen Affric branches right on an incredibly rough track that in places is little more than a boulder ruckle. The track follows the line of pylons all the way to the distant skyline, and is far too steep and rough to ride for any distance.

Once across the skyline the track contours above Loch na Beinne Baine (*Bain*-ya *Ban*-ya, White Mountain) before beginning its descent across the moor and through Guisachan Forest to Hilton Lodge. On descent the track improves to merely rough and feels almost pleasant. Spectacular Plodda Falls, a short distance up the road from Hilton Lodge, is well worth a visit (see p218).

Other routes between Glen Moriston and Glen Affric
West of Dundreggan a track climbs from Bhlaraidh (GR 381165) to the south end of Loch ma Stac, and from the north end of the loch another track descends to the glen of the River Enrick, from where a path leads westwards towards Glen Affric (on OS map 26). Although rough, these tracks are generally in better condition than the Dundreggan track and pass beside pleasant loch scenery, but the route is much longer and

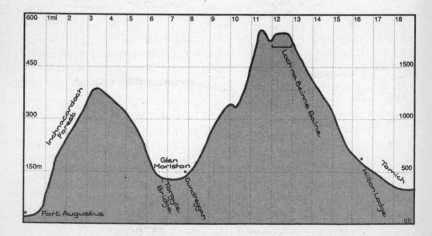

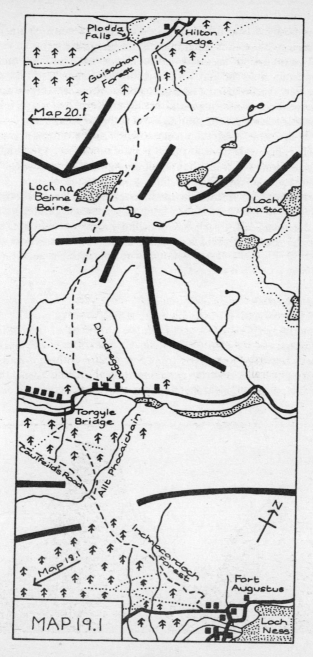

MAP 19.1

mountain bikers should note that bikes will have to be carried across the awkward peat hags beside Loch ma Stac. A circuit using the Dundreggan and Bhlaraidh tracks seems a reasonably straightforward mountain-biking expedition on the map, but in reality it is a long and testing route that is best left to enthusiasts and guidebook writers who know no better. Note also that the northern connection between the two tracks is complicated by new forestry roads that do not yet appear on the map.

East of Torgyle Bridge a viable though longer alternative route to Glen Affric for walkers takes the track that leaves the roadside at Ceannacroc Bridge (GR 226105) and becomes a path across the hills to Cougie, 4 miles (7km) above Hilton Lodge. Much further east near Cluanie Inn, and not viable as a continuation of Caulfeild's road without a lot of road work, a Land-Rover track climbs the defile of An Caorann Mor and descends as a path to Alltbeithe youth hostel in the heart of Glen Affric (see p217 for description). Both these routes are rights of way.

20
GLEN AFFRIC

TRACK RECORD

Glen Affric is a glen of exceptional length and beauty that strikes into the mountains west of Inverness. In this part of the Highlands the east–west watershed lies far to the east, and this gives the glen many miles of beautiful loch and forest scenery. The through-route to the west coast is a classic coast-to-coast trip across the breadth of Scotland, beginning amidst the green and pleasant farmlands of Strath Glass and lower Glen Affric and ending amidst the dramatic mountain landscapes of Kintail.

Travellers have used the route for centuries, and for a time drovers also came this way, en route from Skye to the trysts of the south. Most of the local population, however, was evicted during the clearances of the eighteenth and nineteenth centuries. In the upper glen Affric Lodge remains inhabited, and the remote cottage at Athnamulloch is also still used, but elsewhere little remains except ruins to testify to the glen's former importance. The arrival of hydro-electric and forestry operations in the twentieth century threatened to change the character of the glen completely, but fortunately they have been integrated into the natural environment with commendable foresight, and the glen survives as a showpiece for what can be achieved with good management.

Things could have been much worse. Early HEP schemes of 1928 and 1941 proposed the joining of Glen Affric's two major lochs, Loch Affric and Loch Beinn a' Mheadhoin (Benevan, Middle Mountain), into one huge dammed loch, whose low-water scars would have been irredeemable. The eventual scheme of the late 1940s sacrificed Loch Mullardoch further north instead, and its waters are now diverted into Loch Beinn a' Mheadhoin to reduce any unsightly fluctuations in water level. Loch Affric remains untouched.

Thanks should also be given for the survival of the remaining Caledonian pines for which the glen is famous. These were in danger of disappearing after centuries of felling, but since the Forestry Commission came to the glen in 1935 their management has saved the forest and healed the scars of the HEP scheme, allowing pine, birch, alder and other trees to reclothe the glen. Go there in autumn when it is a riot of colour and wonder at one of the great displays of nature. The building of the Loch Beinn a' Mheadhoin dam and the loss of woodland to the enlarged loch caused much bitterness at the time, but few will quarrel with the appearance of the glen today.

In its upper reaches, beyond the lochs, the trees and the day visitors, Glen Affric presents another face. Here it becomes a great green trench lined by imposing mountains that give some of the finest and remotest ridge walking in the north-west highlands. At the heart of this country stands the old cottage of Alltbeithe (Owlt *bay*, Birch Stream), now a youth hostel, which makes a fine base for exploration and a useful staging post on the route westwards. Further west still lies the watershed, and beyond steeply descending glens lead onward to Strath Croe and Loch Duich on the west coast. The scenery becomes increasingly dramatic, with pointed peaks cleaving the sky and gorges and fast-flowing rivers to be negotiated. There are few routes in Scotland that can compete with Glen Affric for the beauty, variety and excitement of its scenery, and a coast-to-coast crossing will live long in your memory.

ROUTEPLANNER

OS map: 26/25/33

Start point: East end of Loch Affric (GR 201234)

End Points: Dorusduain in Strath Croe (GR 981224)
        Morvich in Strath Croe (GR 967210)
        Loch Cluanie (GR 092121)

Total Distance: Dorusduain: 15½ miles (25km) Morvich: 17½ miles (28km) Loch Cluanie: 14 miles (23km) + Cannich to Loch Affric: 11 miles (17km)

Total ascent: Dorusduain: 400m (1,300ft); in reverse + 1800m (600ft) Morvich: 230m (750ft); in reverse + 230m (750ft) Loch Cluanie: 290m (950ft); in reverse + 20m (60ft)

Total time: Dorusduain: 7½hr (mb:6½hr) + halts Morvich: 7½hr (mb:5hr) + halts Loch Cluanie:6hr (mb:4hr) + halts + Cannich to Loch Affric: 4½hr (mb:2hr) + halts

Cannich: accommodation/provisions/campsite.

Strath Croe: campsite at Morvich; accommodation/provisions/campsite at Shiel Bridge

Loch Cluanie: hotel (1 mile).

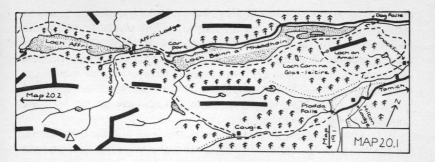

MAP 20.1

Accommodation en route: youth hostel at Alltbeithe (GR 079202); bothies at Camban (GR 053184), Gleann Lichd (GR 005173).
All variations of the route are rights of way.

An east-to-west crossing is recommended in order to leave the most dramatic scenery until last, but before setting out on the complete coast-to-coast route a good deal of pre-planning is required and some important logistical decisions have to be made. The starting point for walkers without private transport is the village of Cannich at the end of the bus route and at the foot of Glen Affric. Cyclists can reach here from Inverness by a pleasant 27 mile (43km) run along the Beauly Firth and Strath Glass.

From Cannich the road continues up Glen Affric for a further 11 miles (17km) to a car park at the east end of Loch Affric and here the route proper begins. Two routes lead onward: the old path along the north side of Loch Affric and a forest track along the south side. The track has better views and is better suited to cyclists, while the mostly excellent path will be better appreciated by walkers. The two routes join

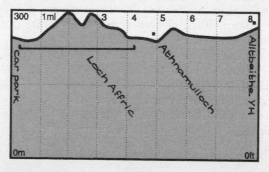

at the west end of Loch Affric and a rough Land-Rover track continues from here to Alltbeithe.

At Alltbeithe, 8½ miles (13km) from the road-end, important decisions have to be made as the way forward now becomes much rougher. There are three routes onward. The only easy one, especially with a bicycle, goes southwards through An Caorann Mor (An *Cœran* Moar, The Big Rowan) to reach the A87 beside Loch Cluanie, but this is something of an escape route as it does not lead to the west coast.

The other two routes continue westwards north and south of Beinn Fhada (Atta, Long) respectively. They both carry good paths that reach the roadside in Strath Croe a short distance from Loch Duich. Both pass through dramatic scenery and have their exciting moments, and walkers will have difficulty deciding which to take once they have read the descriptions below.

Mountain bikers have an even more difficult decision to make at Alltbeithe. The most tempting of the two routes westward is that around the south side of Beinn Fhada, because Land-Rover tracks run the entire length of the route except for a 3½ mile (6km) section between Camban Bothy and Glenlicht Hut. Unfortunately, this middle section is extremely rough and negotiates a deep gorge where a slip could be fatal; in places bikes have to be carried and extreme care is required – it is not a route for the inexperienced. The northern route is also very rough throughout its length and climbs appreciably higher; it is boggy in places and deeply rutted in others, but it is safer. The only easy way out for mountain bikers is An Caorann Mor; those continuing westwards should be in no doubt as to the task before them.

From Strath Croe it is only a short distance to Loch Duich and the A87. There are no easy off-road return routes to the east, but those with a sense of adventure and a taste for wilderness country will find more east–west cross-country routes to the north, notably via the sometimes pathless shores of Loch Mullardoch or Loch Monar. These are major backpacking routes, however, and should not be attempted by the inexperienced.

ROUTE DESCRIPTION

From Cannich the road up Glen Affric climbs steeply out of the lower glen through Chisholm's Pass and then hugs the beautifully wooded shores of Loch Beinn a' Mheadhoin. The cascading river below the loch forms some fine waterfalls, notably Badger Falls and Dog Falls, both about 10m (30ft) high. Just beyond Dog Falls a bridge over the river at GR 283283 gives access to an excellent forest track along the south side

210

of the loch, and although this involves an initial 110m (350ft) climb, it makes an attractive traffic-free alternative to the road along the north side.

From the car park at the end of the road, which in its latter stages is unsurfaced, the view westwards over the narrows of Loch Affric is very picturesque, especially in autumn, with the loch leading the eye along the glen to a distant Beinn Fhada. On the north side of the loch the craggy east face of Sgurr na Lapaich is prominent, and behind it ridge upon ridge rises to the as yet unseen peaks of the north Glen Affric hills.

The route along the north side of Loch Affric begins as a track to Affric Lodge, picturesquely situated on a wooded promontory. At the gates to the lodge keep right beside the fence and follow a path that winds through the upper limit of the pines along the foot of Sgurr na Lapaich. The peaks above are mostly hidden from view, but the path makes a fine walk and there are good views westward to the Glen Shiel peaks south of Alltbeithe. Beyond the end of the loch the path leaves the trees behind and stays high above the moraines that cradle Loch Coulavie before traversing back towards the River Affric to join the south-side track. The Loch Coulavie section can get very boggy in places.

The route along the south side of Loch Affric follows a dirt track. It is a more undulating route than the path along the north side and its surface is less pleasant to walk along, but mountain bikers will find it easier to ride. One undeniable advantage it has over the northern path is magnificent views of the north Glen Affric peaks mirrored in the surface of the loch. Under snow the castellated summit of An Tudair looks spectacular, and behind it towers the high bald dome of Mam Sodhail (Mam Soal, Breast(-shaped) Hill; 1,181m/3,874ft) which, together with its hidden neighbour Carn Eige (Carn Aika, Cairn of the Notch or, possibly, File; 1,183m/3,881ft), are the two highest peaks north of the Great Glen. The connecting ridges give wonderful ridge walking.

At the end of the loch the track passes some grassy promontories and forks. The left branch climbs into Gleann na Ciche to end beneath the fine peaks of Mullach Fraoch-choire (Mullach Frœch Chorra, Summit of the Heather Corrie; 1,102m/3,615ft) and A' Chralaig (A Chrahlik, The Creel; (1,120m/3,674ft) which can be seen ahead. The right branch is the continuing route along Glen Affric; it becomes a stony track beside the River Affric until it crosses the river near Athnamulloch cottage and joins the northern path.

Beyond the junction of the track and path the character of the route changes as Glen Affric becomes a broad flat bottomed valley. Loch and forest scenery are left behind for a long green corridor through the

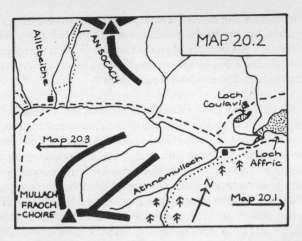

MAP 20.2

wilderness. Mountain after mountain is arrayed on each side like a guard of honour, lined up to usher you through the heart of Scotland; their great grassy hillsides dominate the glen.

The track traverses the foot of the hillside on the north side of the river, affording only occasional glimpses of the high peaks above, and it is now the peaks across the glen to the south that command attention, notably complex Mullach Fraoch-choire with its fine northern ridges. The track stays close to the river and is quite rough. There are occasional sections that look like a river bed and that is precisely what they are, for they have been constructed with stones dredged out of the river. Mountain bikers will nevertheless be able to ride most of the way, with the added spice of many water splashes after rain.

Eventually the red roof of Alltbeithe youth hostel comes into view and soon afterwards this oasis in the wilderness is reached (via either side of the loch: 8½ miles/13km; 140m/460ft; 3½hr/mb:2½hr + halts). The setting is magnificent. To the north a good path climbs to a bealach on the north Glen Affric ridge and from there ascents can be made westwards to the narrow summit arête of Sgurr nan Ceathramhnan or eastwards to An Socach and beyond. To the south rise the north ridges of Mullach Fraoch-choire and of Ciste Dhubh (*Keesh*-tya Ghoo, Black Chest or Coffin), two fine mountains usually climbed from Cluanie by their interesting south ridges. Westwards Beinn Fhada fills the glen; more a range of peaks than an individual mountain, it is perhaps the most magnificent of all the surrounding hills, and its many faces will enthrall you as you circumvent its flanks during the remainder of the journey.

Alltbeithe has a wonderfully remote setting, but the real heart of the wilderness and the key to the route onward lies a further ½ mile along, near the junction of a number of rivers that fan in from the amphitheatre of hills all around. The northern and southern routes around Beinn Fhada diverge here and are described separately.

Northern route: Gleann Gniomhaidh and Gleann Choinneachain
The northern path branches right from the continuing track on the far bank of the Allt Beithe Garbh (Garrav, Rough), the first stream beyond Alltbeithe. It continues beside the stream for a short distance but soon leaves it to rise across spongey ground into Gleann Gniomhaidh (*Gree-ava*, Active), a huge glaciated U-shaped trench that continues the corridor-like nature of the route. The glen gives a long but gentle tramp through the hills, with little to excite the eye until the cone-shaped summit of Beinn Fhada comes into view on the left. Ahead the long ridge that connects the summit to Meall a' Bhealaich further right seems to block the head of the glen.

There is nothing to suggest the variety of scener to come until you cross the insignificant bealach at the head of the glen and reach the remote upper reaches of Gleann Gaorsaic, where the large expanse of Loch a' Bhealaich laps against the foot of Meall a' Bhealaich (Myowl a

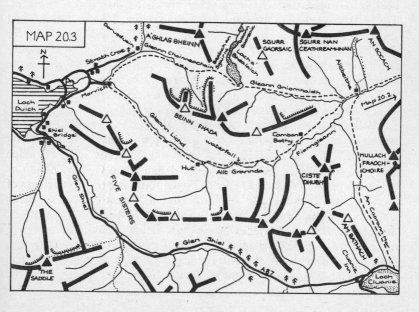

213

Vyalich, Hill of the Pass) and A' Ghlas-bheinn (A Ghlass Ven, The Grey Mountain; 918m/3,011ft). The route to Strath Croe crosses the high Bealach an Sgairne (Scarna, Noise of stones) between these two peaks. The path skirts the shore of the loch, negotiating peat bogs and moraines, climbs gently across the lower slopes of Meall a' Bhealaich to a viewpoint above the loch, then zigzags more steeply up to the narrow bealach.

Over the bealach another new and fascinating landscape awaits as you leave the gentle eastern glens and enter a rocky defile where the path picks out a meandering route through boulders that have fallen from the craggy slopes above. The place has an air of secrecy about it, with no surface stream to break the silence and only the sound of your own footsteps to accompany you. The mountain scenery becomes much more dramatic and there is a terrific prospect ahead as the rocky northern tops of Beinn Fhada come into view one by one as you descend into Gleann Choinneachain (*Choan*-yachin, Boggy).

Beyond the defile a fork is reached where a left branch climbs back up to Meall a' Bhealaich to make the easiest ascent route to the roof of Beinn Fhada. An ascent via this path and a return via the northern tops

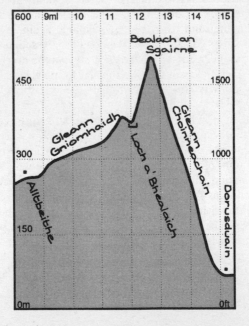

makes an excellent scramble from Strath Croe. The main path goes right at the fork to zigzag steeply down to the Allt Coire an Sgairne. Normally this stream is easily crossed on stepping-stones, but I recall one enervating and surreal night crossing when, swollen by torrential rain, it roared waist deep across our path and foamed menacingly in the beams from our head torches.

—All difficulties past, the path now descends the grassy glen without incident, the steep hillsides funnelling you down to the flats at the head of Strath Croe. Around the corner at the tail-end of Beinn Fhada, Loch Duich comes into view and the east–west traverse is nearly complete. A fork is reached where either branch takes you to a road. The right branch crosses the Abhainn Chonaig (bridge) to reach the road-end on the north side of Strath Croe at Dorusduain. The left branch continues for another mile or so down the strath to reach the road-end on the south side near Morvich outdoor centre.

Southern route: Fionngleann and Gleann Lichd

West of Alltbeithe the track continues up Fionngleann (White Glen) to Camban Bothy on the south side of the long eastern ridge of Beinn Fhada. The Allt Gleann Gniomhaidh is forded at its confluence with the River Affric or crossed using the bridge a short distance upstream if the water is high. The track is ridable for a while, deteriorates as it climbs the hillside above Fionngleann, then becomes ridable again as it contours across the hillside to its end at Camban. As you progress, pause to admire the view back down Glen Affric, where the peaks on the north side of the glen can now be seen to advantage. To the south fine views also open up of the narrow southern ridges of Mullach Fraoch-choire and Ciste Dhubh.

Beyond Camban a path continues with minimal gain in height to the low bealach at the head of Fionngleann, after which it becomes much rougher among glacial moraines. Those who have cycled thus far will now find a mountain bike a hindrance to progress and will need a great deal of determination and patience. The scenery, however, becomes increasingly riveting as the Five Sisters of Kintail rear ahead, with fine views up their little visited eastern corries to the cone-shaped summits that hover above. The walk along the narrow undulating ridge that connects the summits is a classic Kintail walk.

Even more exciting scenery is to come on the descent to Gleann Lichd (Licht, Slabby). The path contours across the hillside, undulating around the southern spurs Beinn Fhada above a lost green valley where the infant and grossly misnamed Allt Grannda (Ugly) begins its journey to

Loch Duich. Eventually, the river enters a gorge and plunges over a rock barrier in a prodigious 30m (100ft) leap.

The descent of the bowl into which the waterfall plunges is the most spectacular section of the route, with the immense peaks of the Five Sisters towering claustrophobically overhead and the path clinging to the mountainside in Alpine fashion. It is a very rough section with a real sense of exposure; mountain bikers especially need to take extreme care. It is easier to carry a bike than manhandle it along the path, but a slip would be fatal; only experienced mountain bikers should venture here. When the Kyle–Kyleakin crossing from Skye became fashionable for drovers after the railway reached Kyle in 1897, some drovers brought their cattle this way en route to Glen Affric and the east, and one wonders how they managed it. Falling rock is an additional feature of this part of the route. A boulder from on high almost brought this book to a premature end when it bounced across the path inches from your intrepid author.

Emerging from the gorge, the path remains extremely rough as it continues to descend steadily past more waterfalls to the head of Gleann Lichd. The bridges across the Allt Grannda and the Allt a' Choire Dhomdain marked on the 1974 OS map are now down, but a new bridge spans the Allt Grannda just above the old one and the Allt a' Choire Dhomdain is normally easily crossed dry-shod. Once you enter into the confines of Gleann Lichd, Edinburgh University Mountaineering Club hut is reached and immediately behind it is a Land-Rover track that will

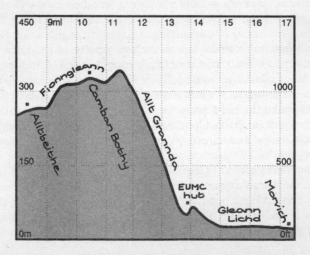

take you the remaining 3½ miles (6km) to Morvich in Strath Croe. The hut is locked but a lean-to is kept open for emergency shelter. The green pastures of Gleann Lichd, which once lured drovers eastwards, provide a gentle end to an exciting expedition. The track is rough, but is such an improvement on what has gone before that walkers will be glad to stroll along it and mountain bikers will simply be glad to get back in the saddle.

An Caorann Mor
From Alltbeithe the easiest and shortest route out to a road goes south-wards to Loch Cluanie. The path crosses the River Affric on a swaying wire bridge immediately below the youth hostel and crosses the hillside into the glen of the Allt a' Chomhlain between Ciste Dhubh and Mullach Fraoch-choire. It can become very boggy. Note that the path beside the River Affric marked on the 1974 OS map has now been superseded by this more direct path.

The path climbs the great grassy glen to the watershed and then descends the similar trench of An Caorann Mor to reach the A87 about 1 mile west of Cluanie Inn. The last 2½ mile (4km) section is now a Land-Rover track, making the route an attractive way out from Alltbeithe for mountain bikers. From An Caorann Mor Ciste Dhubh presents its finest angle, appearing as a pointed rock peak that is well suited by its mysterious Gaelic name.

OTHER ROUTES AROUND GLEN AFFRIC
There are enough mountains, lochs, waterfalls, paths and tracks in the Glen Affric area to keep walkers and mountain bikers happy for many a day. In the west the circumnavigation of Beinn Fhada using the two routes described above to the north and south of the mountain makes a fine expedition and introduction to the topography of the area. In the east roads, tracks and paths completely encircle Loch Affric and Loch Beinn a' Mheadhoin, the circuit of Loch Affric making a particularly fine trip. More adventurous walkers will find a number of excellent stalkers' paths climbing to the hill-tops on the north side of the glen. Easier walks leave the several car parks along the Glen Affric road and are well sign-posted with maps and directions; the Dog Falls walk is particularly attractive.

The glen to the south of Glen Affric, reached by a road from Cannich, also has some attractive routes. The tarmaced road ends just beyond the village of Tomich but a dirt road continues. Just beyond Tomich it forks. The right branch crosses the Abhainn Deabhag and ends at Knockfin (GR 299267), giving access to the low range of wooded hills that separate the glen from Glen Affric. From the road-end at Knockfin a track continues to a fork; the right branch cuts back at an angle and forks again. Both branches cross the hills from here into Glen Affric, the left branch reaching the south Loch Beinn a' Mheadhoin track and the right branch reaching the Dog Falls. Linked together they make a fine cycling circuit. Near its high point the left branch passes two signposted lochs that are worth visiting. Loch an Amair is a small lochan hidden in the trees, while the more interesting Loch Carn na Glas-leitire is a fine moorland loch at the upper limit of the trees, with a wooded island and spacious views.

By taking the left branch of the dirt road beyond Tomich, cars may be driven past Hilton Lodge to a car park above Plodda Falls at GR 280238. From the car park a path leads through the forest to these most spectacular falls, where a vertiginous bridge at the lip enables you to view the water take to the air in a single 30m (100ft) leap. The dirt track continues beyond the car park to pursue a westerly course past the remote house at Cougie, making an unexpectedly interesting route to Loch Affric.

At Cougie the track crosses the river and becomes rougher. It reaches an enlarged loch at the edge of the forest and then climbs steadily above a broad glen. It remains rough but mostly ridable all the way to its high point at the head of the glen, where it reaches 460m (1,500ft). The views all around are magnificent, especially westwards, where the north Glen Affric peaks hang like a frieze. At the high point (look for a cairn on a boulder on the right) Loch Affric becomes visible in the glen far below. The track bears left to a dead-end; to reach the track along the south side of Loch Affric, bear right down the pathless hillside and tramp through the heather.

BIBLIOGRAPHY

Aitken, Robert, *The West Highland Way* (Official Guide) (1988)

Ang, Tom and Pollock, Michael, *Walking the Scottish Highlands* (General Wade's Military Roads) (1984)

Baker, Joan and Arthur, *A Walker's Companion to the Wade Roads* (1982)

Gordon, Anne, *To Move With The Times* (The Story of Transport and Travel in Scotland) (1988)

Haldane, A. R. B., *Drove Roads of Scotland* (1952)
  New Ways Through the Glens (Highland Road, Bridge and Canal Makers of the Early 19th Century) (1973)

Howat, Patrick, *The Lochaber Narrow Gauge Railway* (1980)

Inglis, Harry, *Hill Path Contours of the Chief Mountain Passes in Scotland* (1963)

Kerr, John, *East by Tilt* (1987)
  Old Grampian Highways (1984)
  Old Roads to Strathardle (1984)
  Wade in Atholl (1986)

McNeish, Cameron, *Backpacker's Scotland* (1982)

Moir, D. G., *Scottish Hill Tracks* (Old Highways and Drove Roads) Vol 1, Southern Scotland (1975); Vol 2, Northern Scotland (1975)

Scottish Rights of Way Society, *The Cairngorm Passes*
  The Principal Rights of Way in the West Central Highlands
  Rights of Way (A Guide to the Law in Scotland)

Taylor, William, *The Military Roads in Scotland* (1976)

Thomas, John, *Forgotten Railways of Scotland* (1981)
  The West Highland Railway (1984)

Vallance, H. A., *The Highland Railway* (1985)

INDEX

Numbers in italics indicate contour plans and route maps

100 BEST ROUTES ON SCOTTISH MOUNTAINS

Ralph Storer

From gentle afternoon strolls to challenging scrambles to remote mountain sanctuaries – a major guide to walks in the magnificent Scottish Highlands.

* All walks are circular and accessible by road
* No rock climbing is involved
* Selected by an experienced Scottish walker
* Each route includes a peak over 2000 feet
* All Highland regions are included
* All walks can be completed in one day
* Each route has a detailed sketch map and ratings for technical difficulty, type of terrain and conditions in adverse weather

☐	100 Best Routes on Scottish Mountains	Ralph Storer	£5.99
☐	The Four Peaks	Rex Bellamy	£5.99
☐	Climb Every Mountain	Craig Caldwell	£4.99
☐	The Spirit of Whisky	Richard Grindal	£5.99
☐	A Dalesman's Diary	W R Mitchell	£3.50
☐	High Dale Country	W R Mitchell	£4.99
☐	It's a Long Way to Muckle Flugga	W R Mitchell	£4.50
☐	The Road to Mingulay	Derek Cooper	£4.50
☐	Finlay J MacDonald Omnibus	Finlay J Macdonald	£5.99

Warner Books now offers an exciting range of quality titles by both established and new authors. All of the books in this series are available from:

Little, Brown and Company (UK) Limited,
P.O. Box 11,
Falmouth,
Cornwall TR10 9EN.

Alternatively you may fax your order to the above address. Fax No. 0326 376423.

Payments can be made as follows: cheque, postal order (payable to Little, Brown and Company) or by credit cards, Visa/Access. Do not send cash or currency. UK customers and B.F.P.O. please allow £1.00 for postage and packing for the first book, plus 50p for the second book, plus 30p for each additional book up to a maximum charge of £3.00 (7 books plus).

Overseas customers including Ireland, please allow £2.00 for the first book plus £1.00 for the second book, plus 50p for each additional book.

NAME (Block Letters) ....

....

ADDRESS ....

....

....

☐ I enclose my remittance for _____

☐ I wish to pay by Access/Visa Card

Number ☐☐☐☐☐☐☐☐☐☐☐☐☐☐☐☐

Card Expiry Date ☐☐☐☐